SONGS IN THE KEY OF Z

Songs in the Key of Z

THE CURIOUS UNIVERSE OF OUTSIDER MUSIC

Irwin Chusid

CHICAGO
REVIEW
PRESS

An A Cappella Book

Library of Congress Cataloging-in-Publication Data
Chusid, Irwin.
    Songs in the key of Z : the curious world of outsider music / Irwin Chusid.
      p. cm.
    Includes bibliographical references, discography, and index.
    ISBN 1-55652-372-6
    1. Musicians—Biography. 2. Popular music—History and criticism. I. Title.
ML394.C56 2000
781.64'09—dc21   99-057640

Interior design: Lindgren/Fuller Design
Cover design: Greg Carter

© 2000 by Irwin Chusid
All rights reserved
First edition
Published by A Cappella Books,
an imprint of Chicago Review Press, Incorporated
814 North Franklin Street
Chicago, Illinois 60610
ISBN 978-1-55652-372-4
Printed in the United States

Dedicated to
Mencken, Mary,
and Mr. Mack

CONTENTS

Introduction • ix

Prologue: Transistor under My Pillow: A Memoir • xxiii

1 The Shaggs
Groove Is in the Heart • 1

2 Tiny Tim
I Get a Kick Out of Uke • 13

3 Jack Mudurian
Chatterbox Jukebox • 22

4 Joe Meek
Blast from the Past • 26

5 Song Poems
Bus Fare to the Grammys • 37

6 The Cherry Sisters
The Fruits of Clean Living • 46

7 Jandek
The Great Disconnect • 56

8 Daniel Johnston
Casper 1, Satan 0 • 67

9 Harry Partch
Hallelujah! He's a Bum • 79

10 Wesley Willis
Hell Ride • 93

11 Syd Barrett
Guitars and Dust • 101

12 Eilert Pilarm
The King of Sweden • 114

13 Lucia Pamela
Interstellar Overdrive • 119

14 Captain Beefheart
Inscrutable Dreamer • 129

15 Shooby Taylor, the Human Horn
Scat Man Do • 141

16 Florence Foster Jenkins
Widow's Peak • 147

17 The Legendary Stardust Cowboy
Wide Open Space Cadet • 154

18 Robert Graettinger
Sleep in the Grave • 166

19 B. J. Snowden
Mission to Venus • 178

20 Wild Man Fischer
Ritual of the Savage • 189

21 Snapshots in Sound
Elsewhere in the Curious Universe • 199

Afterword • 233   An Incomprehensive Discography • 237

An Incomprehensive Bibliography • 249   Permissions • 255

Acknowledgments • 257   Index • 259   About the Author • 271

INTRODUCTION

"Folklore is the arts of the people before they find out there is any such thing as art."

—ZORA NEALE HURSTON

genius? Forget it. *Talent?* Beside the point.

Welcome to the curious universe of "outsider music," a mutant strain of twisted sonic art that's so wrong—*it's right.*

Duke Ellington once said, "If it sounds good, it is good."

Well, sometimes if it sounds *bad,* it's even *better.*

Most people recognize "good" music when they hear it. Music that succeeds in the broader market—call it "popular"—adheres to commonly accepted standards of melody, harmony, and tonal logic. Rhythm is fairly consistent, and lyrics tend to address—profoundly or vapidly—our shared culture and experiences.

Occasionally popular music cleverly challenges or plays footloose with convention. But for the most part, basic formulas remain intact. There is *right,* and there is *wrong,* and producers, record execs, and radio programmers are paid obscene sums to determine what the market will accommodate. In an age of multitrack overdubbing and digital splicing, any performance miscue can be repaired. And though producers can work with serendipitous mistakes, even make them sound intentional, most studio professionals prefer to re-take a bum note or blown chord until done correctly.

Now, imagine a musical universe where such standards do not exist, where keys beyond G are explored with élan. This book is a pan-galactic map of crackpot and visionary music, where all trails lead essentially one place: over the edge. Picture a musical subclass glimpsed through the lens of Diane Arbus.

This book is about artists who are instinctively gifted with what might be termed "imperfect pitch."

Outsider music sometimes develops naturally. In other cases, it could be the product of damaged DNA, psychotic seizures, or alien abduction. Perhaps medical malpractice, incarceration, or simple drug-fry triggers its evolution. Maybe shrapnel in the head. Possession by the devil—or submission to Jesus. Chalk it up to communal upbringing or bad beer. There's no universal formula.

That's one characteristic that makes outsider music so refreshing: its *unpredictability*.

Adventuresome musicians have been known to deliberately—even maliciously—jettison traditional approaches to expand the boundaries of music. Way beyond the parameters of pop stood renegade composer-theorist John Cage (1912–1992), considered by many the most avant of all gardes. Cage studied under twelve-tone formulator Arnold Schoenberg, who insisted, "In order to write music, you must have a feeling for harmony." Cage lamented, "I had no feeling for harmony. [Schoenberg] then said that I would always encounter an obstacle, that it would be as though I came to a wall through which I could not pass. I said, 'In that case I will devote my life to beating my head against that wall.'" Cage proceeded to create a unique body of work that remains among the most influential of the twentieth century—and not everyone calls it "music." But no one doubted that he was in command of his mental faculties. Cage made a conscious choice to rebel, and regardless of the theoretical randomness of his aleatory (chance) music, he maintained control over his work.

But there are countless "unintentional renegades," performers who lack Cage's overt self-consciousness about their art. As far as they're concerned, what they're doing is "normal." And despite paltry incomes and dismal record sales, they're happy to be in the same line of work as Celine Dion and Andrew Lloyd Webber.

These artists populate the curious universe of outsider music. Lucrative careers in show biz are largely beyond their grasp, yet these quirky characters are compelled to create music, and public indifference is no deterrent. They orbit beyond the databanks of SoundScan and focus group surveys. They get little or no commercial radio exposure, their followings are limited, and they have roughly the same likelihood of attaining mainstream success that a possum has of skittering safely across a six-lane freeway.

The average person hearing outsider-type musicians for the first time might conclude that their performances are inept, or that these artists lack talent. Their vocals sound melodically adrift; their rhythms stumble. They seem harmonically without anchor. Their instrumental proficiency may come across as laughably incompetent.

A common first reaction to the Shaggs' landmark album *Philosophy of the World* is, "What were they thinking?" After witnessing a performance by the Legendary Stardust Cowboy, a club owner sneered, "That is the *worst shit* I've ever heard in my life." And a radio station director once remarked that Harry Partch would "be a really good composer if only he'd compose regular music."

Such reactions presuppose that these artists are attempting to meet conventional standards of musicianship, but are failing miserably.

To appreciate outsider music, however, an accommodation is required on the part of the listener. The rewards are ample: just when you think you've heard it all, outsider music reveals vistas you never imagined existed. Outsider music is created to entertain, and *does* entertain at levels that exceed the indifference it might engender if it displayed greater technical ability and self-awareness. The "wronger" it is, particularly with lesser degrees of self-conscious intent, the closer it approaches pure originality.

Millions of songs are written every decade, most of which flawlessly comply with the rudiments. The bulk of such work is bloodless, soulless, and academic. Obeying rules is hardly a benchmark of creativity, much less of that elusive quality we recognize as "genius." As some wag observed, "The angels love enthusiasm far more than perfection."

Long before the world knew him as the father of the *Simpsons*, Matt Groening was collecting weird sonics and writing about them as a critic. "I'm less interested in virtuosity than I am in the passion with which an album is performed," he explained. "That's why I love eccentrics like the Shaggs, Daniel Johnston, and Luie Luie."

It's undeniable that, on first listening, there's often a measure of comedic value to some of these artists. But inevitably there's a *je ne sais quoi* that transcends laughter. Each of these artists, regardless of accessibility, has a singular identity and a recognizable style.

New York saxophonist Ellery Eskelin, whose father Rodd Keith toiled in the conveyor-belt "your-lyrics-put-to-music" industry ("song poems"), declared, "I find that outsider music offers many of the same rewards in terms of satisfying the human spirit as does music traditionally regarded as being the best we humans have to offer. It's often inventive, certainly unique, and once you get past the humor factor, there's something there in terms of structure or melodic twist, issues that are purely musical, that I find very engaging."

The shadowy realm of outsider art has a long tradition, going back at least as far as studies of the psychotic creations of mental patients during the 19th century. It was championed in the 1920s by the French, who later called it *art brut*, raw art. Other labels include intuitive, folk, visionary, and self-taught art; fabuloserie; amateur vérité; and *art naïf*.

Over the century, figures have emerged in painting (Bill Traylor; Jim Shaw's *Thrift Store Paintings* anthology; Howard Finster, who also recorded songs); film (Ed Wood, Jr.); literature (Henry Darger; Adolf Wolfli, who also composed); landscaping (Leonard Knight's Salvation Mountain); sculpture (S. P. Dinsmoor's *Garden of Eden*); and architecture (Edward Leedskalnin; Simon Rodia; Edward James). By definition, there are untold numbers of these visionaries whose names we may never know.

"'Outsider art' was originally a technical term that referred almost exclusively to asylum and prison art—the creative works of the mentally ill and criminals," said Brooklyn multimedia performer Brian Dewan. "Then 'outsider' was expanded to include what people had previously termed 'naïve art,' made by those who lacked any formal training. I'd prefer if we just called these people 'artists,' and then we can call those active in the popular and avant-garde fields 'insider artists.'"

There are a number of books devoted to the broader field (e.g., Maurice Tuchman and Carol Eliel's *Parallel Visions*), as well as periodicals (*Raw Vision*), galleries, and preservation societies in many cities.

The phrase *outsider music* did not achieve currency until the 1990s, when interest began to grow thanks to books like *Incredibly Strange Music,* and a preponderance of CD releases by such previously unheard artists as B. J. Snowden, Wesley Willis, Lucia Pamela, and Eilert Pilarm.

"My personal musical passions go back a long way in the outsider realm," explained collector/archivist and small-label entrepreneur Paul Major. "But it's interesting to have that name applied, because people weren't applying that word to music. I've been into folks like Peter Grudzien since the early 1980s, but only recently does the concept of equating vanity and private pressings with outsider art come up in conversation. That's a totally fresh perspective, and it gives this music a framework."

Ron Moore, in his self-published discography *Underground Sounds,* describes outsider types as having a "realness" quotient. He defines *realness* as a "catchall description for artists that exhibit an alarming dearth of talent matched with a total lack of self-awareness or embarrassment." Moore also uses the term "to refer to artists with extremely idiosyncratic styles or outlooks. [Their] LPs are often unintentionally comic but emotionally quite moving."

Both for the sake of semantics and to clarify this book's definition of outsider music, a distinction must be drawn between what is commonly referred to as "folk art" and "folk music." The former is the catchbin of outsider practitioners, as defined above, working in various creative media. "Folk music," however, refers to an industry marketing category that encompasses everyone from Odetta and early Joni Mitchell to Pete Seeger, the Kingston Trio, and Dylan. This music is characterized by elemental, acoustic instrumentation, a country-derived sensibility, and a reverence for tradition. Despite relatively bustling sales by the above artists, folk music is a niche market with low to moderate record sales. For the purposes of this book, folk music is not considered a subgenre of folk art, and I don't categorize musicians commonly identified as folk singers as outsiders (though some certainly qualify).

Although the terms "outsider" and "avant-garde" are by no means interchangeable, they occasionally—in retrospect—overlap. Critical assignment to one category or the other lies in the ear of the beholder and in the eyes of history. There are countless examples of acclaimed pioneers who started on the "outside" and eventually came "in" when the listening public caught up with their radical ideas.

Charles Ives received a Pulitzer Prize after the debut performance of his *Third Symphony* in 1947—43 years after he'd completed the work, and a quarter-century after he'd stopped composing. Ives rarely consorted with other musicians, and composed largely in isolation. For most of his life his friends knew him primarily as a hardworking insurance executive, while his seemingly unplayable scores sat in a desk drawer, unknown and unperformed. ("Are my ears on wrong?" he once wrote in a moment of doubt.)

At the outset of Thelonious Monk's career, many considered this jazz colossus an atrocious pianist. To this day, a handful of moldy-fig traditionalists dismiss Monk as either a tin-eared primitive or a charlatan who conned critics and bandmates into proclaiming his genius by slamming the keyboard and striking notes at random. Monk no longer needs defending, but in the 1940s he was widely perceived of as, well, as an outsider.

Ornette Coleman violated jazz decorum by dispensing with chord structure and steady rhythm in favor of spontaneity based on an emotional response to a composition instead of the tune's basic framework. Today, Coleman's early recordings sound comparatively tame, but in the late 1950s and early 1960s his provocative notions were rejected by many, and he was viewed as a lunatic by some.

This is not to insist that the men and women profiled in this book will register comparable long-range artistic impact. But many have already influenced their musical descendants beyond measure. Syd Barrett, Captain Beefheart, the Shaggs, Harry Partch, Robert Graettinger, and even Daniel Johnston have significantly contributed—directly and indirectly—to contemporary popular music. (Various artistic family trees are addressed in specific chapters.)

Without outsiders, there might be no Tom Waits, no dub reggae (invented by an outsider, Lee "Scratch" Perry), no K Records or SubPop. The punk/new-wave/no-wave upheaval that undermined prog-rock and airbrush-pop in the mid- to late-1970s hyped itself with the defiant notion that anyone—regardless of technical proficiency or lack thereof—could make music as long as it represented genuine, naturalistic self-expression. "We're all outsiders."

From where do novel sound trends emerge? From the likely suspects, of course—the realms of the self-consciously experimental, the avant-garde, and popularizers of world music. They also trickle in from the outside.

Music critics often bemoan the death of innovation, hypothesizing that since the free-thinking experimentation of the 1960s and the radical negation of the late 1970s, too much contemporary music has simply recycled and reconfigured the creative alchemy of its forebears.

Outsider musicians introduce sounds so strange, so new, it could take centuries for the rest of us to catch up.

This book is not about "unpopular," "uncommercial," or "underground" artists. I have, for the most part, excluded well-known pop iconoclasts who are out-siders by attitude, but who are highly self-aware. Frank Zappa knew what he was doing; ditto the Velvet Underground and John(-ny Rotten) Lydon. I've dis-qualified just about anyone who could keep an orchestra or band together. Ditto *épater le bourgeoisie* upstarts like Gregg Turkington, John Trubee, Boyd Rice, Lisa (Suckdog) Carver, and Jello Biafra, who've earned reputations by uri-nating contemptuously on the welcome mat of conventional aesthetics. I can appreciate their audacity, but I see these miscreants as more influenced and inspired by outsider art than fitting the category.

Attitude alone cannot define outsiderness; in fact, categorical inclusion is rarely the product of rebelliousness. A lot of outsider music is very friendly. It *lacks* attitude, making few claims to self-importance. It's light-years from the music you hear in jukeboxes and at weddings, but doesn't call attention to its dis-tant standing. There's no posing. One finds more emphatic—and easily dis-missed—claims of originality ("sounds like nothing you've heard!") in the press kits of Marshall-stack headbangers and flavor-of-the-week indie rockers. One of outsider music's ironies is that when you're trying to make "conventional" music and instead creating something sui generis, it doesn't occur to you to brag about it.

The outsiders in this book, for the most part, lack self-awareness. They don't boldly break the rules, because they don't know there *are* rules. They sometimes lack any sense of the limitations of their technical skills; this, more than anything, can lead to inventive sonic breakthroughs.

Many outsiders are immune to the notion of defeat. They inhabit their own otherworldly cosmos, their simple goal being to share their music with anyone inclined to listen, even if that audience consists of their own family and neighbors, or a small devoted following.

Or, in the case of Jandek, virtually no one.

Outsider music is difficult to catalog. It's fragmented and lacking in common structural threads. It emerges from sprawling metropolitan hubs and from rural backwaters where three or four votes can swing an election. But there are qualities that define the music's progenitors and their outlook.

What these often self-taught artists lack in conventional tunefulness they compensate for with earnestness and heartfelt passion. Harbor no doubts about their sincerity—*they mean it.*

Terry Adams, longtime keyboardist with the New Rhythm and Blues Quartet (also known as NRBQ), is a connoisseur of dodgy styles. Adams admits, "When music gets too perfect, I don't want to hear it. When everybody's in tune and the rhythm is perfect and there's no mistakes, I find myself not really interested." Hence, his fascination with the Shaggs, a late 1960s sister trio from Fremont, New Hampshire, whose music sounds so uncoordinated it seems they're riffing off their common genetic code.

Outsider music offers an escape from designer trendiness rampant in the entertainment industry. Give me a genuine if misguided Gump to a megaplatinum cretin like Kenny G any day. For me, noncommercial simplicity trumps flashy consumer fetishism.

Some outsider types have achieved brief commercial success, such as acid casualties Syd Barrett (early Pink Floyd) and Arthur Lee (Love). Others have enjoyed respectable careers: the elusive desert rat Captain Beefheart, the mightily medicated Daniel Johnston, and Prince of Dorkness Jonathan Richman. A deranged songwriter named Charles Manson originally hoped to find fame clutching to loose threads on Beach Boy Dennis Wilson's surf blanket. Had Manson achieved even moderate success as a singer-songwriter, he might not have resorted to the unsavoriness that eventually brought him headlines and a life sentence.

Ironically, the biggest-selling outsider in music history could be the Beach Boys' mastermind Brian Wilson. Many of his 1970s and 1980s unreleased demos, long circulating among tape swappers, certify Brian's outsider status. Hell—dig some of the loopy post–*Pet Sounds* stuff that's been *released!* Wilson has much in common with everyone in this book: obsessions, delusions, and emotional volatility. He's tormented, drug-addled, and spent years under the "care" of Dr. Eugene Landy. Real damaged goods.

But Brian Wilson is not explored in this volume. He's way gone and a like-nobody musical genius, but considering the level on which he's been embraced by the public, it's difficult to make a case for him as an outsider. I've avoided other outré icons who have achieved wide public exposure, such as Frank Zappa, Sun Ra, Marilyn Manson, and the Butthole Surfers, to name a few. Many (if not most) major figures in the arts began their rise to stardom as nominal outsiders. Show business, more than most people realize, is the ultimate Revenge of the Nerds. Growing up, these misfits wouldn't or couldn't conform. They were loners who spent solitary hours honing their craft and battling the odds against success. Through perseverance and fortuitous confluence, they eventually hit the big time.

And every one of them has had a book or twelve written about them.

Songs in the Key of Z details those who lurk in the shadows. It's an overview of the gallery's less well-known and more bizarre exhibits, those who exist not simply *away* from the mainstream, but *disconnected* from it.

Many of these artists are very likable, if not commercially viable. The Shaggs, B. J. Snowden, and Lucia Pamela have a teddy-bearish innocence that goes over well with youngsters. Daniel Johnston's early recordings seem more suitable for babysitting obstreperous brats than anything released by that gutless blancmange, Raffi. Just a suggestion—they're your kids.

Some outsiders have money (Florence Foster Jenkins, Lucia Pamela); others struggle to cover the rent (B. J. Snowden, the Shaggs). Johnston and Wesley Willis are multitalented artists who earn sporadic income from their sketches and skewed pop. Eccentric rockers such as the Legendary Stardust Cowboy and Wild Man Fischer have achieved iconic novelty status, but their royalty income is a pittance. Equally iconic is the late Tiny Tim, who performed a monumental public service rescuing forgotten songs from antiquity, but whose financial status varied from pauper to high roller and back to pauper.

The book contains its share of pathos, chronicling some tragic figures who pulled into the parking lot of fame, only to inadvertently back over the treadle of misfortune, puncturing all their hopes and dreams. These include Syd Barrett, Tiny Tim, the Legendary Stardust Cowboy, Skip Spence, and Wild Man Fischer. Others, such as Lucia Pamela and Jandek, never got near the big time, and didn't seem to care.

Musicians categorized as outsiders, like folk artists in other media, typically lack formal training. However, this is not always the case. B. J. Snowden earned a degree from the Berklee College of Music; Lucia Pamela claimed to have attended the Beethoven Conservatory of Music and Voice in Berlin; and Florence Foster Jenkins was reportedly a graduate of the Philadelphia Musical [sic] Academy. Fortunately, as anyone who has marveled at these ladies will attest, higher education did not impede their raw talent.

Outsider musicians display a remarkable degree of resourcefulness. Their instruments can be acoustic, from Tiny Tim's ukulele to Harry Partch's instrumentarium built out of salvaged debris; or they could play sophisticated electronic gadgetry, like the synthesizers commandeered by B. J. Snowden and Wesley Willis. The Cherry Sisters ran their own farm. Lucia Pamela tried to raise funds to build an amusement park with a ride that would take visitors to another planet. Ray R. Myers got a driver's license.

Some artists are clearly mired in the past (Eilert Pilarm, the Cherry Sisters), while others dynamically embraced progress (Lucia Pamela, Robert Graettinger,

Captain Beefheart, Joe Meek). Tiny Tim, a sucker for nostalgia, nevertheless recorded interpretations of Pink Floyd and Led Zeppelin later in his career.

A few lucky outsider musicians, such as Daniel Johnston, Tiny Tim, Skip Spence, Syd Barrett, and Captain Beefheart, were signed by major record labels; whereas Shooby Taylor, Jandek, Peter Grudzien, and Eilert Pilarm can be heard only on homemade cassettes or on obscure discs, pressed in limited amounts, with spotty distribution. Many artists encapsulated in the book's final chapter have released records on vanity labels—the music business equivalent of publishing your novel through Kinko's. Many of these obscurities fetch astronomical prices among collectors. (When hunting for undiscovered gems, a good clue is a label catalog number that ends in "-001." Cheap, awkward cover design is another tipoff, although you could mistakenly end up with an early album by alt-rock pensioners Sonic Youth or the Fall.) A few figures in this book can't be heard at all. No recordings by the Cherry Sisters or Ray R. Myers exist, and print media provide our only impressions of their legacies.

Three of the artists profiled have played on Rowan and Martin's *Laugh-In*: Tiny Tim, Wild Man Fischer, and the Legendary Stardust Cowboy. Others would consider public access bookings a measure of success.

Some outsiders take medication to maintain their emotional stability (Daniel Johnston, Wesley Willis, Eilert Pilarm), while others sacrificed their psyches through overindulgence in mood-altering substances (Syd Barrett, Joe Meek, Skip Spence, Robert Graettinger). The Cherry Sisters boasted that their lips never tasted wine, though it's doubtful their performance would have improved either way.

Despite a preponderance of psychological disturbances reflected among this book's population, the vast majority of these artists have caused no physical harm to their fellow citizens. A few have exhibited violent episodes, and several committed assault. Yet the subjects in the book's main chapters account for just one murder and one suicide—and those by the same person, with both acts committed in the span of a few minutes.

Songs in the Key of Z does not include *all* outsiders. A comprehensive survey is impossible due to the elusive nature of the genre. You can research a book about acts who've hit the *Billboard* Top 200; their achievements have been quantified. But tracking outsider musicians involves equal measures of anthropology (visiting trailer parks), archaeology (digging under rocks), and spelunking (shining flashlights into damp caves). The category spans the planet. In the cases of interstellar voyagers like Lucia Pamela and Sri Darwin Gross, the diligent researcher may rack up frequent-flyer miles to far-off galaxies and parallel dimensions.

Before this book, there was no comprehensive study of the genre. Hence, the qualifications for inclusion are open to debate. I chose those who fit my admittedly broad definition, and who had stories worth telling. If your favorites escaped mention, I'd be glad to know about them. When reckoning this author's sins of omission, please consider the insightful words of Smithereens drummer, vinylologist, and music archivist Dennis Diken, who observed: "Everybody's compilation sucks but your own."

In attempting to codify and catalogue outsider music, I'm straddling a fence between two potential readerships. One is the existing outsider music audience, who know the genre and don't need to be convinced of its value. They might browse this book and feel I'm belaboring the obvious.

I am—because of that second group of potential readers: those who aren't aware of outsider music. I hope these curiosity seekers will buy and read this book, thereby gaining an appreciation of these artists and their work. With no elitist disdain intended, I recognize that the vast majority of my neighbors are unfamiliar with outsider music and would file it under "Difficult Listening." Such obvious nutjobs as Les Wilson, Wild Man Fischer, and Arcesia would leave them shaking their heads, wondering why anyone would waste their time on such lunacy. Why anyone would waste *a lot* of time on it.

Why anyone would *write a book* about it!

One reason is provided by Tony Philputt, who directed a film biography of the Legendary Stardust Cowboy (a.k.a. "the Ledge"). "I think the Ledge is important," observed Philputt. "If the history of music is only told from the viewpoint of people who were successful, it's like documenting an election by only interviewing the winners."

But the best reason for such a primer is the intrinsic value of this music to entertain and inspire.

This book will introduce many of these artists to a wider audience than they might otherwise attract through TV, radio, concerts, the Internet, even records. Perhaps B. J. Snowden and Jandek will sell a few more CDs, or one of their songs will end up in the soundtrack of a Julia Roberts film.

In selecting artists to profile, I've largely steered clear of musicians and composers in the idioms of jazz, classical, microtonal, and electronic, with three exceptions.

One is Harry Partch, with whom I've had a long-standing fascination. Partch is the subject of a book-length portrait (*Harry Partch: A Biography*, by Bob Gilmore), and has had several collections of his writings and memorabilia published. Nevertheless, he's a teensy blip on the cultural radar, and I relish any opportunity to expand Partch's audience by telling his story.

Another is Robert Graettinger, who composed and arranged for Stan Kenton's orchestra in the late 1940s and early 1950s. Graettinger became a fixation after I first heard—and was perplexed by—his monumental *City of Glass* suite, a challenging and controversial work. The more I learned about the composer, the more I felt Graettinger qualified for inclusion. He was a dark character, a loner, and his musical vision was very unsettling. In my estimation, he crossed the line between iconoclast and outsider.

Third, the delightfully daffy diva Florence Foster Jenkins, an operatic outsider about whom there seems to be too little available literature, merited a brief but amusing chapter.

Additionally, though Captain Beefheart and pop producer Joe Meek, like Graettinger, are not categorically outsiders as measured by the standards of naïve and folk art, they were outsiders vis-à-vis the music industry and, to some degree, society. Each was perceived by his contemporaries as operating on a solipsistic plane, and these insular misfits felt artistically distanced from their purported colleagues.

In other words, this book is not just about outsider music—it's also about *musical outsiders.*

Outsiderdom isn't just a curious universe—it's *big* as well.

Unlike some advocates of outsider art, I do not kick around the word *genius.* As with the term *classic* (e.g., -rock) its overuse has devalued its currency. G. C. Lichtenberg observed, "Sometimes men come by the name of genius in the same way that certain insects come by the name of centipede—not because they have 100 feet, but because most people can't count above 14."

Outsiderdom encompasses eccentrics, neurotics, and psychotics. It includes mutants, idiot savants, and postal workers, along with folks who can carve the Gospels on the head of a thumbtack. Some outsiders appear perfectly normal—until they open their mouths. The closest thing to a common syndrome could be RDD (Reality Deficit Disorder).

Jello Biafra describes outsiders as "differently sane." Some of this book's subjects, like Wild Man Fischer and Daniel Johnston, have been institutionalized; others, such as the Legendary Stardust Cowboy and Lucia Pamela, are just mild kinda crazy.

But psychoanalysis doesn't concern me. I have, for the most part, avoided digging into family dysfunctions that may have given rise to this music. I'm not a psychologist, and it would be presumptuous to delve into the aftereffects of childhood trauma or parental abuse suffered by any particular artist.

I've offered little in-depth musicological analysis of these artists' techniques, preferring simply to tell their stories. The readability of this book depends more on the colorful characters who populate it—peppered with the author's impertinent opinions—than on an academic dissection of their recordings.

This book is also not a buyer's guide to outsider records. I've avoided a disc-by-disc chronology of each artist's catalog, opting instead for overviews of their works and quirks.

As regards outsider art in general, there is a simmering moral debate that fingers the audience: Is this a freak circus? Are these guileless souls being exploited? Are they being ridiculed?

As a longtime follower of this music, my feelings are securely guilt-free about some artists and ambivalent toward others.

I'm a fan of director Todd Browning's macabre 1932 epic, *Freaks*. Browning employed authentic physical mutants: pinheads, midgets, an armless and legless human salami, a hand-walking human beachball with no lower torso. He portrayed these medical monstrosities sympathetically but without condescension. The director didn't make a case that these outcasts needed or wanted to be integrated into society at large, that some as-yet-unproposed Americans with Disabilities Act could make these people fire commissioners or flight attendants. They were neither worse, nor better than, the rest of us—just different, and existing apart. They had their own community and codes of conduct, and they were prey to the same petty jealousies, generosities, prejudices, and affections as all humans.

There are analogies to outsider music, except that outsider musicians have no musical communities other than their limited audiences. And this book.

I love many of the artists about whom I've written and feel dispassionate about a few. I have difficulty listening to Jandek and Wesley Willis, who for different reasons fail to capture and hold my attention. Nevertheless, I am fascinated by their hallucinatory perspectives and the processes by which they create their art. I also greatly admire each's perseverance and prodigious output.

When I began the Captain Beefheart chapter, I was not a fan but decided that he fit the rough subject profile and had great marquee value. While researching this notorious blues alchemist, I immersed myself in his LPs and CDs, got deep in Beef, and became enamored of the Captain's topsy-turvy take on fragmented pop.

I have met Lucia Pamela and B. J. Snowden several times and adore these delightful ladies. I've seen several Snowden showcases in the ultra-jaded precincts of Manhattan's Lower East Side, and her performances are always exhilarating. You can't help but be touched by her sincerity and intensity. B. J. puts ear-to-ear smiles on the faces of the most cynical spectators.

I leave it to readers to seek out available recordings by these artists and to judge for themselves. (A discography appears at the conclusion.) You won't be hearing 99 percent of these folks in the popular media. There's a reason why it's called outsider music, and neither pride nor snobbishness relegates it to the margins. This doesn't imply, however, that a pinch of outsider music can't be part of a well-rounded listening diet.

One appeal of outsider music is escapism. We all want to flee this earthly hell from time to time, to just *get away*. But short of suicide, our options are limited.

Outsider artists, however, have made it. They've escaped—if they were ever *here* to begin with. They're *somewhere else:* a Xanadu that appears more magical than where we reside. Cartoons depict a similarly altered state—a dimension where the laws of physics don't apply. Part of the radiance of outsider music is that it inhabits exotic and distorted levels of time, space, consciousness, linguistics, mathematics, perception, and self-awareness.

So, if you're still concerned about the freak-show aspect, but you honestly wish to enjoy listening to outsider music, the reassuring answer is:

Get over the guilt!

These people are *happy* making their music. They want to be heard.

A few are listening.

Are you?

Transistor under My Pillow: A Memoir

my penchant for outsider music developed gradually. However, my passion for *outréphonics* emerged serendipitously in 1966 when, at the tender age of 15, I discovered an enigmatic 45 rpm single.

It was to be my Epiphany Record.

Growing up in Newark, New Jersey, and later the Essex County suburb of Maplewood during the 1950s, my home was a rock-free zone. There were no musicians in my family, but the radio played constantly. My parents listened to WNEW 1130 AM (later WQEW 1430 AM, and at this writing a Disney children's channel), which cranked out the melodious fluffery of Perry Como, Frank Sinatra, Julius LaRosa, Patti Page, Rosemary Clooney, and Johnny Mathis. I barely knew about Elvis, but I sure loved "Mr. Sandman" by the Chordettes. I still enjoy most of this Cold War–era drivel. It's bland and safe—dollop upon dollop of musical mayonnaise, a metaphor for my upper-working-class childhood.

Around age five, I acquired the impression that singers and bands sat around in luncheonette basements, waiting for customers to punch up their hit records on the jukebox. When the dime dropped, the group stood up and played. When they were finished, they sat down again.

I bought my first transistor radio in 1961, and rock 'n' roll jolted my senses. Like an imaginary pal, that palm-sized plastic box with the rectangular nine-volt battery accompanied me everywhere, programming a daily sound-track of the Four Seasons, Del Shannon, the Orlons, Phil Spector's "symphonies for the kids," Roy Orbison, and "The Monster Mash." I went to bed with that ear-tingler resonating under my pillow. This led to a lifelong fascination with radio's overnight "graveyard shift" and a lifelong preference for musician's hours (stay up late, sleep late).

My father deplored this habit and claimed he could hear the tinny squawk two bedrooms away. He would poke his head in and order me to kill the radio, or he'd take it away. Guess he figured if I didn't get enough sleep, my school-work would suffer.

The following year, I discovered circular vinyl. My first 7-inch 45-rpm single was "Telstar" by the Tornadoes. A strange disc by 1962 standards, "Telstar" was one of the first hits to feature a keyboard synthesizer (a Clavioline; decades later, I discovered the man responsible for this remarkable recording, Joe Meek, who merited a chapter in this book). I bought stacks of singles by the Beach Boys, the Kingsmen, Paul Revere and the Raiders, Martha and the Vandellas, Stones, Beatles, Kinks, and Supremes. I stayed current with every Top 40 hit. When I bought my first drum kit in 1963, I played along with these records under headphones.

It was an exciting period in pop music, when radio was stylistically integrated. Soul, hillbilly, rock, and girl groups shared the airwaves and sales charts with schmaltzy ballads, novelties, and ethnic crossovers. Brenda Lee jockeyed for position alongside Clarence "Frogman" Henry; Ray Charles entered the Top 10 with Gene Pitney; Kyu Sakamoto's "Suki-yaki" descended the charts as Jan and Dean's "Surf City" ascended; and the only thing that prevented "Louie, Louie" from reaching number one was "Dominique" by the Singing Nun. This was an ear-opening education (and so unlike the consultant-reined narrowcasting of today). Segregation may have divided America, but you wouldn't know it from scanning the pop charts.

Thanks to a scientific quirk known as "skywave phenomenon," long-distance AM radio signals could bounce around the ionosphere and zoom hundreds of miles after nightfall when smaller, local stations signed off. In my New Jersey bedroom, I picked up Top 40 outlets in Nashville, Boston, Cincinnati, Ontario, and West Virginia. They programmed the same nationwide hits as New York stations, along with some regional surprises (and at night, fewer and lower-budget commercials).

One fateful occasion, my little transistorized chum reeled in a station from Cleveland. Around 2:00 A.M., I heard a strange garage-rock tune called "The Little Black Egg," by a group identified as the Nightcrawlers. It was a har-monious pop confection with slightly defiant overtones.

I was mesmerized. It was a *great* tune, catchy and as instantly memorable as "96 Tears." Radio-friendly; commanding attention.

Yet I had never heard this song on any New York station.

The following night, I tuned in Cleveland and again heard "The Little Black Egg." I was captivated by its jangly guitar and obsessive overtones:

[verse]
I don't care what they say
I'm gonna keep it anyway
I won't let them stretch their necks
To see my little black egg with the little white specks

[refrain]
I found it in a tree, just the other day
And now it's mine, all mine
They won't take it away.

The lyrics reflected my very discovery. I'd found this record. It was mine, all mine. My record-collecting high school classmates hadn't heard, nor heard of "The Little Black Egg." I found it in a tree. They doubted it was any good. They tried to stretch their necks. They couldn't take it away because ... *I didn't have it.*

I inquired about the record at a local grocery-cum-soda fountain that stocked the latest 45s and oldies. The shop owner had never heard of it either, and since it wasn't a hit in New York, he refused to order it. He didn't stretch his neck, though I did want to wring it.

I wrote to the Cleveland station, asking where I could buy "The Little Black Egg." If musicians could be cloistered in the basements of New Jersey diners, a major metropolitan radio station could personally answer a letter from a 15-year-old a thousand miles away.

A month passed. No reply. I despaired of finding that record before it faded from the Midwest charts and spiraled into obscurity. My anxiety fueled by too many episodes of *The Twilight Zone,* I began to doubt whether I'd ever actually heard the song. Perhaps I'd dreamt it.

One day, a package arrived in the mail—a flat, square cardboard envelope, postmarked "Cleveland."

It was "The Little Black Egg," on Kapp Records.

I tingled. Might've swooned.

I beamed with vindication. Rod Serling was stage left, brandishing a cigarette, leering knowingly at the camera and saying with a sly grin, "Submitted for your consideration . . ."

I held proof of the mysterious record whose existence was scoffed at by my peers. "The Little Black Egg" was accorded a place of honor in my collection. Owning that disc was like meeting someone you'd always admired but never expected to encounter. Others wanted to meet the Beatles; I was honored to make the acquaintance of the Nightcrawlers. (The Nightcrawlers were a quintet from Daytona Beach. "The Little Black Egg" was a Florida regional number one hit in 1965, though a remixed reissue on Kapp Records a year later—the version which tweaked my curiosity—barely cracked the national Top 100. It remains an enigmatic little treasure. Wanna hear it? Check out Rhino's boxed set, *Nuggets: Original Artifacts from the First Psychedelic Era 1965–1968*. It's on disc two.)

"The Little Black Egg" never became a hit in New York. I was the only one among my network of record collectors who owned it. Yeah, they stretched their necks, but they couldn't take it away. Fuck 'em.

For the first time in my life, I had something valuable that nobody else had. I was ... *cool*.

And I began to wonder....

What other music was fluttering around the ionosphere that the sinister New York radio overlords *didn't want me to hear*? This was a life-altering revelation. I'd been snatched by a UFO, briefed, and sent back to Earth on a mission.

I developed an obsession with the esoteric, the obscure, and the unknown. I sought the uncommercial, hidden treasures—and the failed effort. I wanted music others didn't have and didn't know about.

I started collecting strange little singles by overlooked garage bands and psychedelic upstarts. After FM radio switched from highbrow classical and jazz to album rock around 1966, I fetishized groups like Ultimate Spinach, the David, Spirit, and Group Image; post–British Invasion prog-rockers like the Nice and the Move; and poet-singers such as Hamilton Camp, Norma Tanega, and Leonard Cohen.

I became a snobbish little twit. A chart-climbing popular song was beneath contempt. There was no intrigue in knowing what everybody knew.

I played drums in a band that covered arcane songs by underground misfits like Clear Light, Love, and Moby Grape. We took the stage at a Newark YMHA dance—but nobody danced. The audience despised us for refusing to play the hits. Such ignorant riff-raff. In retrospect, I wasn't that sophisticated, but compared to the kids in the neighborhood, my tastes were creeping along the margins.

The pattern intensified when I entered the University of Bridgeport in 1969. I worked at WPKN, a hotbed of student radicalism and adventurous radio, where I discovered Harry Partch, John Cage, Terry Riley, Linda Perhacs, and a Canadian band called the Collectors. I opened up to jazz beyond Brubeck, dug the dirtier roots of rhythm and blues, and delighted in the "furniture music" of Erik Satie. My credo: if everybody else knew about it, it wasn't worth a fuck.

After quitting college in 1971, I tooled up and down the East Coast in my VW Beetle, rummaging through country barn sales and flea markets for 78-rpm platters. I discovered Ukulele Ike, the Duncan Sisters, and Sophie Tucker, along with New Orleans barfight raunch, nutjob drummer Sam Ulano, Hawaiian novelties from the 1920s, and jump-jazz cut-up Louis Jordan. Scattered amid these scuffed relics were one-of-a-kind demo discs, home recordings, and vanity pressings. I became attuned to the long-lost, and in some cases *unheard* history of recorded sound.

I was fortunate to begin and sustain a long-term broadcasting slot at WFMU, a New York–area free-form landmark where I've programmed a weekly show since 1975. WFMU is flypaper for misfits and malcontents, and the programs reflect an omnivorous staff appetite for cultural debris. (I'm grateful to WFMU for according me the opportunity to indulge my curiosities and share them with an adventurous listenership.) Working at WFMU brought me in touch with colleagues who shared my passions. I discovered an endless cavalcade of odd sonics in the station library and enjoyed exposure to a pan-galactic array of cultural crosscurrents.

Despite my early archeological forays, the true epiphany of outsider music didn't occur until 1980, when a friend gave me an album by "The Units," which turned out to be a solo work by an inscrutable loner who later called himself "Jandek." The chapter on this haunting recluse recounts one seeker's journey to the foggiest perimeter of the musical outside.

It took several decades of scouring tag sales and National Council of Jewish Women Thrift Shops to amass a collection of recordings that would later be termed "outsider," but which at the time were just considered freakish. This music was made by unknowns who seemed to have no clue how removed they were from conventional notions of competence. I recognized there was something unique about these artists, and as my jadedness with "normal" music heightened, it became refreshing to hear true visionary sounds.

Years later, I realized there should be a book about it.

IRWIN CHUSID
HOBOKEN, NJ, 1999

"I pick up the pen and God moves it."

HANK WILLIAMS

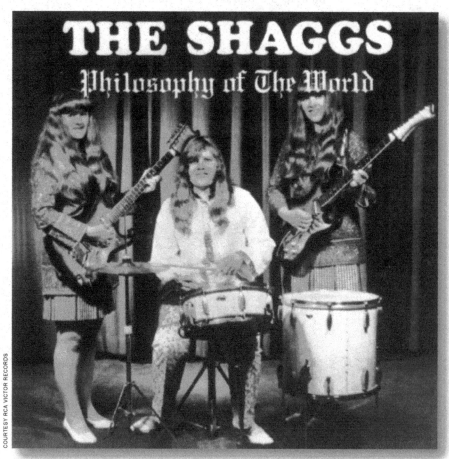

An aboriginal masterpiece

The Shaggs

GROOVE IS IN THE HEART

fremont, New Hampshire, in the late 1960s was a remote, culturally disconnected backwater. According to one visitor at the time, the town's citizens all looked vaguely related. The burg's main claim to fame was a colonial-era cooperage—that's where barrels are made.

Two centuries after the cooperage was built, a second local phenomenon emerged. Three sisterly hayseeds, Dorothy, Helen, and Betty Wiggin, encouraged by their father, formed a band featuring two guitars and drums. In 1969, these sibs entered a studio and recorded an album entitled *Philosophy of the World*. This monument of "aboriginal rock" was masterminded by proud papa Austin Wiggin, Jr., and released on the fly-by-night Third World label. Upon its release, the album barely made it beyond the town's borders.

One thousand copies were pressed; 900 disappeared.

Over the ensuing decades, *Philosophy* was declared by Frank Zappa as one of his all-time favorite records. *Rolling Stone's* 1996 *Alt-Rock-A-Rama* ranked it among "The 100 Most Influential Alternative Releases of All Time," "The Greatest Garage Recordings of the 20th Century," and "The 50 Most Significant Indie Records."

Yet many people hearing the Shaggs' legendary *Philosophy* album for the first time have a common, understandable reaction: this could be the "worst album ever recorded."

The Shaggs are a touchstone of unpretentiousness. Given half an ear, what they're playing sounds like ... *a mess*—as if the girls were recorded in separate chambers and had no idea what each other was playing. Hacked-at chords, missed downbeats, out-of-socket transitions, blown accents, and accidental convergences abound. Yet the Shaggs existed a decade before punk-inflected irony made DIY incompetence cute and fashionable. This wasn't an attempt at free jazz or expanding the boundaries of the avant-garde. As a major influence, the Shaggs cited cuddly 1960s Brit-rockers Herman's Hermits.

Despite its apparent qualification for federal disaster relief, *Philosophy* has great charm. It's 100 percent authentic and refreshingly guileless. Its backward innocence is not a product of major label fetishism, or self-conscious indie-rock trendiness. The Shaggs didn't hail from Athens, Seattle, or any MTV flashpoint. *Philosophy of the World* is outré classique, crowning these gals as the legendary—if unwitting—godmothers of outsider music.

A savage magic permeates the album's spastic grooves. Singer Dorothy's backwoods New England phrasing is endearing, as she earnestly waxes about young-girl-in-a-small-town concerns: parents, listening to the radio, a lost cat, spiritual salvation. The album's lost-chord wonderland transcends the traditional relationship between ability, technique, and originality.

And like most outsiders, the Wiggin sisters would have no idea what we're talking about.

When Zappa raved about *Philosophy* in a 1976 *Playboy* poll, practically no one outside the Wiggin clan and their neighborly circle had heard of it. As rare copies of the LP were discovered and cassettes began to circulate, other self-proclaimed fans came to include Bonnie Raitt ("They're like castaways on their own musical island"), Jonathan Richman ("They're the real thing"), and Carla Bley ("They bring my mind to a complete halt").

The band NRBQ reissued *Philosophy* on a Rounder Records LP in 1980. The 'Q's keyboardist, Terry Adams, compared the Shaggs to early Ornette Coleman; their music, he attested, "has its own structure, its own inner logic." Commemorating the reissue, *Rolling Stone* proclaimed the Shaggs "Comeback Band of the Year"—doubtless to the befuddlement of its Springsteen-geared readership. *Creem* magazine called *Philosophy* "uncivilized." Byron Coley, in *New York Rocker,* detected in the Shaggs "a new rock 'n' roll language, using the sophistication of Appalachian folk music and Dot Wiggin's brand of teen angst as ground zero." Bruce D. Rhodewalt in *LA Weekly* observed, "If we can judge music on the basis of its honesty, originality, and impact, then the Shaggs' *Philosophy of the World* is the greatest record ever recorded in the history of the universe." On a more picturesque note, Lester Bangs, in the *Village Voice,* asserted that Dorothy's guitar playing was "sorta like 14 pocket combs being run through a moose's dorsal," and that Helen's drumming sounded "like a peg-leg stumbling through a field of bald Uniroyals."

The group formed around 1967, originally with the three (of four) Wiggin sisters. (Rachel, the youngest, later played bass onstage. There are also two brothers, Robert and Austin III.) Dorothy (Dot) Wiggin, 21 when the album was recorded, wrote the group's songs, played lead guitar, and sang; drummer Helen was 22; rhythm guitarist and vocalist Betty was 18.

Dot now lives in Epping, New Hampshire, with her husband, Fred Semprini, and their two sons, William and Matthew. In a 1998 interview, Dot was asked a question that's doubtless occurred to many who have been flabbergasted and delighted by the mayhem on *Philosophy*—namely, "What were you thinking?"

"It's not what we were thinking," she replied, "so much as what our father was thinking. His big dream was to make the records, have us be popular, and eventually go on tour." At the time, Austin worked full-time at the Exeter Cotton Mill, a textile factory two towns from Fremont. The family was dirt-poor—except in the dream department. Austin bought the girls their instruments, and proceeded to play the part of Phil Spector—albeit in a John Waters casting call. Austin told them what to play, when to play it, and how to play it. "He was something of a disciplinarian," Dot concedes. "He was stubborn and he could be temperamental. He directed. We obeyed. Or did our best."

The name "Shaggs," devised by their father, referred to both shaggy dogs and the then-popular shag haircut. The girls' familiarity with pop music consisted entirely of what they heard on radio; they never attended an actual concert. "Our father didn't believe in them," Dot stressed. "Not for us to go to, anyway." Besides Herman's Hermits, their favorites included Ricky Nelson, the Monkees, and flash-in-the-pans Dino, Desi, and Billy.

Each of the sisters took music and voice lessons for two years prior to recording the album. To allow his daughters more rehearsal time, Austin pulled them out of the public education system and enrolled them in correspondence courses with Chicago's American Home School. "Fremont didn't have their own high school," Dot explained, "and my father didn't want us bused out. So he decided to have us do it at home. Then we could study our music at the same time."

Though the sisters could hardly play their instruments, Austin staged their public debut at an Exeter talent show in 1968. Susan Orlean, in a 1999 *New Yorker* feature on the group, reported: "When they opened with a cover of a loping country song called 'Wheels,' people in the audience threw soda cans at them and jeered. The girls were mortified; Austin told them they just had to go home and practice more."

A short while before they recorded *Philosophy*, the Shaggs—expanded with Rachel to a quartet—began a "residency" at the Fremont town hall, where they played a weekly Saturday night dance party in the second-floor auditorium. Local teens attended, sometimes 40- or 50-strong. And they *danced*. This continued for several years, until "a lot of trouble brewed up," recalled Dot. What kind of trouble? "Kids saying they were somewhere else when they were at the dance. Teenage fights—that good stuff. And smoking."

Smoking ... *what?*

"Cigarettes."

Austin, as quality-control chief, was on hand for every performance. He strutted the corridors of the town hall, and surveyed the musical proceedings from the dance floor, wearing a homemade pin that read: "Shagg [sic] Manager."

In March 1969, Austin booked time at Fleetwood Studios, in Revere, Massachusetts. The four sisters climbed in a van with mom, dad, and brother Robert, and drove a few hours south. Dot wasn't certain they were good enough to record. No matter. "Dad was paying for it," she shrugged. Austin later reportedly boasted to one of the recording engineers about his daughters, that he wanted to "get them while they're hot!"

Fleetwood did a brisk business recording school marching bands and local rock groups. Engineering for the Wiggin sessions was assigned to Russ Hamm. Another staff engineer named Charlie Dreyer probably spent time in the control room during the Shaggs' visit.

Musician/producer Bobby Herne was yet another Fleetwood staffer who witnessed the ensuing debacle. In an interview (conducted by Erik Lindgren shortly before Herne passed away in 1998), he said that Austin "came into Fleetwood and said he needed to cut some sides because he was the 'proprietor' of this band. The father—he called himself the 'proprietor.' He brought them in and they did this stuff. We shut the control room doors and rolled on the floor laughing. Just rolled! It was horrible. They did not know what they were doing, but they thought it was okay. They were just in another world. And they smelled like cows. Right off the farm. Not a dirty smell—just smelled like cows."

During the sessions, which were supervised by the "proprietor," the girls would occasionally interrupt recording halfway through a song. "Why'd they stop?" the engineers would ask. "Because they made a mistake," snorted Austin, in total seriousness.

The recordings included a song about sleek wheels ("That Little Sports Car") and Dot's gray-striped cat ("My Pal Foot Foot"). Dot didn't have a sports car ("That was like a dream"), and eventually she didn't have a cat ("Even though the song has a happy ending, in real life it went away and never came back"). A paean to mom and dad, "Who Are Parents," included the call-and-response chorus:

Who are parents?
Parents are the ones who really care
Who are parents?
Parents are the ones who are always there

Who Are Parents? Austin and
Annie Wiggin, mid-1960s.

The song that would become the album's title track addressed the Sisyphean
quest for contentment:

> Oh the rich people want what the poor peoples [sic] got
> And the poor people want what the rich peoples got
> And the skinny people want what the fat peoples got
> And the fat people want what the skinny peoples got
> You can never please any-bo-ho-dy
> In this world

When the hothouse phenoms had a dozen titles on tape, Austin, according to
one account, paid for the session with small bills, stashed in a coffee can. A
now-exceedingly-rare 45-rpm single was released on Fleetwood Records, featuring "My Pal Foot Foot" and "Things I Wonder."

Shortly thereafter, Dreyer and Herne parted ways with Fleetwood and
bought a studio called Third World Recording in Jamaica Plain, Massachusetts.
Third World was apparently hired to remix the Shaggs master tapes, and during
this phase Herne tried to "fix" the performances by having studio pros re-record
the rhythm parts. Terry Adams recalled hearing a studio outtake on which a session drummer tried to overdub a "real beat" over Helen's wobbly kit work—and
eventually gave up. "Can't do it, Bob," he huffed, throwing down the sticks.
Dot confirmed that she heard "real musicians" tried to "improve" the tapes.

Fortunately for history, they failed.

Dreyer, sensing a business opportunity, offered to press and distribute the Shaggs album—no doubt with Austin's money—on the studio's in-house Third World label. The gawky LP cover photo depicts guitarists Dot and Betty in paisley tunics over pleated, tablecloth-plaid, knee-length skirts; Helen, in a pantsuit that includes a Nehru-jacket knockoff, sits behind an unplayably arranged half drum kit. The trio poses unpresumptuously before a dusty green curtain on what could be an American Legion Hall stage.

The liner notes—whoever wrote them—were remarkably prescient. (The tone of quasi-defiance hints at the handiwork of the "proprietor.")

> The Shaggs are real, pure, unaffected by outside influences. Their music is different, it is theirs alone.... Of all contemporary acts in the world today, perhaps only the Shaggs do what others would like to do, and that is perform only what they believe in, what they feel, not what others think the Shaggs should feel.
>
> The Shaggs love you, and love to perform for you. You may love their music or you may not, but whatever you feel, at last you know you can listen to artists who are real. They will not change their music or style to meet the whims of a frustrated world.

Three names are conspicuously absent from the LP credits: Dreyer, Herne, and Hamm. Possibly they were so embarrassed by the record, they didn't want their names on it.

Dreyer was a strange character, an engineer and producer of considerable talent who may have felt justified in attempting to protect his reputation. Wayne Terminello, who worked as a shipper at Fleetwood late in Dreyer's tenure, recalled, "He was an oddball that no one knew much about. He wore a black suit every day—in fact, it was the same black suit. Remember, this was the hippie era—in those days, no one wore suits. He even slept in it. He kept a sleeping bag at the studio and crashed there for a while. He bought beer for me and my underage friends and we smoked grass together. He tried to turn on the sales act with folks like the Wiggins, but he was really as spaced-out as the rest of us. He was unstable and not very trustworthy. My boss, Ray Samora, finally got rid of him."

Veteran major-label executive Harry Palmer, while conceding Dreyer's eccentricities, admired his studio touch. "In those days," recalled Palmer, "engineers often were producers, in that they worked the board. Charlie could capture amazing layered recordings with a 4-track machine. He produced a lot of very good records at Fleetwood." Palmer's late-1960s Boston-based band,

Ford Theatre, recorded a live, album-length demo at Fleetwood with Dreyer at the controls. (That demo, with later overdubs, was released on ABC Records in summer 1968 as the band's debut LP, *Trilogy for the Masses*.) From that encounter, Palmer and Dreyer became friends and worked on subsequent projects together.

At this point in the tale, some historical correction is required. An often-repeated legend about *Philosophy of the World*'s fate is that a thousand copies were pressed, nine-tenths of which "disappeared"—along with Dreyer. Dot Wiggin herself attested, "He left the face of the earth. He took my father's money, gave us one box of albums, and ran. My father couldn't get in touch with him. He tried telephone calls, but no one knew where he was. I have no idea if he's even alive." This account of Dreyer's "theft" of 900 albums has been repeated in journalistic accounts of the Shaggs' history.

Dreyer's eventual fugitive status may be factual—Dot said she "heard that there were two or three other people looking for him"—but his absconding with the *Philosophy* LPs probably isn't.

Palmer and his then-girlfriend (now wife), Dawn Coffman, visited the engineer at Third World in late 1969 or early 1970. "I went to do some work with him," Palmer recollected, "and that's when we first saw and heard the Shaggs' record." Palmer and Coffman noticed several 25-count boxes of *Philosophy* stacked in a corner of the studio waiting room, and asked what they were. Dreyer described in macabre detail the now-fabled sessions, illustrating his story with random needle-drops on the vinyl.

"I heard 'My Pal Foot Foot' and fell off my chair," explained Palmer. "I was fascinated." Coffman said Dreyer beheld the tower of *Philosophy* LPs and muttered, "Austin refuses to sell these, because he's afraid someone will copy their music."

Dreyer gestured at the stack: "Take a box."

Palmer did.

Perhaps most of the copies "disappeared" this way. But for Dreyer to "steal" them makes no sense. Palmer noted that Dreyer went deeply in debt after borrowing tens of thousands of dollars for various recording projects, but there's no way hundreds of *Philosophy* LPs would've helped pay his creditors—the album was unknown and worthless. (It was also considered an artistic abomination.) The only reason Dreyer had possession was because Austin never bothered to claim the goods. The eventual disposition of those boxes remains a mystery. It's conceivable that at some point, since they were taking up valuable space, they were simply tossed in a dumpster.

Dot says that after *Philosophy* was pressed, there were "no reviews that I know of." Their shot at stardom having fizzled, the sisters continued entertaining at town hall dances, the Rockingham Nursing Home, local talent shows, and Fourth of July celebrations. Besides their originals, the girls covered such hits as "House of the Rising Sun," "Paper Roses," the Carpenters' "Yesterday Once More," and the Pipkins' "Gimme Dat Ding."

Meanwhile Palmer, back home with his carton of LPs, was on an evangelical jag. He collared friends, guitarists, record collectors—anyone with 10 minutes to spare—and made them listen to *Philosophy of the World*. "Everyone was blown away," he observed. He played it for Ron Eyre, head of United Artists's international division. Eyre laughed, but was intrigued. Palmer quoted Eyre as saying, "You know—it's aboriginal. It sounds like things I've heard in China and elsewhere around the world." Palmer had visions of developing something with the band—a production deal, a live concert. A friend with TV connections suggested that with one call he could possibly book them on the *Tonight Show.*

Palmer realized a pilgrimage to Fremont was in the cards.

After learning that the Shaggs played town hall every Saturday night, Palmer and Coffman drove up in 1970 or 1971 to attend a show. The isolated hamlet had a Norman Rockwell–meets–Rod Serling aura.

The Shaggs didn't disappoint. "They sounded exactly like the record," Palmer recalled. "It was unbelievable. The locals came out and danced in a clumsy, arrhythmic, *Night of the Living Dead* sort of way. It was cretin-like. I remember thinking, 'How can you dance to this music?' But they did!"

After the show, Palmer approached the Shagg Manager backstage, and discussed his ideas. But Palmer faced a serious dilemma. He said to Austin, with complete candor, "We could do something with the Shaggs. I think there are opportunities. It's a fascinating record. But you do realize, Mr. Wiggin, that there are people who laugh when they hear this music—laugh *at* the Shaggs. Is that a problem for you?"

Austin's exact response escapes Palmer's recollection, but it betrayed a certain resignation that what Palmer said was probably true.

"Whatever his answer," confessed Palmer, "suddenly the whole idea troubled me. On the drive back, I acknowledged that it had the aspect of a freak show. I couldn't bring myself to exploit these girls, who didn't realize they would be ridiculed." Palmer and Coffman drove to a hotel on the New Hampshire coast in the black of night, enveloped by a thick New England fog, with a state trooper on their tail over part of the trip.

"Dawn and I were spooked," he recalled. "It was a haunting experience. Witnessing the Shaggs, then groping our way blindly in this fog. It was like exploring a cold, dark planet, populated by alien creatures." It was his last contact with the Wiggin clan.

There was tragedy in the aftermath of *Philosophy of the World*. "Bob Herne mentioned Charlie Dreyer to me a few times in passing," remembered Jeff Landroche, who engineered at Fleetwood during the 1970s. "Bob—God bless him—talked a lot, but I filtered out a lot and now I feel guilty about not listening more carefully. I have a vague memory of his being screwed by Charlie, but don't really know how. Bob told me he had the publishing rights to the Shaggs, and the last I heard he was looking to find out where the publishing money was going. Then he died."

There was film footage and memorabilia of the band. "We had stuff stored in an army trunk in the attic of our house in Fremont," Dot recalled, "but it got stolen. There were tapes of the band that were taken. Not the master tapes from the recording studio, but I think that's probably what they were after."

Austin Wiggin died in 1975, after which the Shaggs disbanded. (Dot and Betty performed four songs at New York's Bowery Ballroom in November 1999 as part of a thirtieth anniversary concert by NRBQ.) After his death, anecdotal accounts emerged about Wiggin family dynamics, and according to some indications, there was paternal abuse that tragically scarred the sisters' lives.

Nowadays, three of the Wiggin sibs live in Epping; Robert and Helen reside in Exeter. Betty has two sons and a granddaughter; her husband of 15 years, Ricky Porter, was killed in a motorcycle accident in 1993. Helen is divorced from Henry Bickford; they have two sons. Rachel, her husband Lester Gould, and their son and daughter moved to Maine in 1999.

The original *Philosophy* LP was reissued in 1980 on Red Rooster/Rounder. Shortly before Austin passed away, he'd escorted the girls into the studio one more time. Landroche, who engineered that 1975 session, said, "I remember calling them in for a playback to see if they'd notice that the guitars were out of tune and the beat was all over the place. But they liked it." These later recordings, compiled on a Rounder LP entitled *Shaggs' Own Thing*, are slightly more proficient—and consequently, less interesting. A 1988 Rounder CD coupled both albums, although the *Philosophy* tracks were remixed and resequenced, and two previously unreleased demos were included; the Rounder CD did not depict the original album art. The original *Philosophy* sequence and cover art were restored for an RCA Victor 1999 CD reissue (which I co-produced with Terry Adams).

One of the Wiggins' Exeter neighbors, Ben Swiezynski, of Ben's Photo Shop, was hired to take some black-and-white snaps of the band back in the day. In retrospect, what did he think of their music?

"Have you played the record?" he replied, hesitantly. "They gave me one of the first pressings. It's different. As I listened to the music, I couldn't figure out if it's country music or what. But I'm not really musically minded. I'm a photographer." When informed that the record had been reissued, he inquired, with slight apprehension, "Are they coming back?"

The public might be a bit perplexed, but the Shaggs' modest legacy has impressed some pros. "Like many serious composers and arrangers, they make use of devices like odd meters, polyrhythms, altered tones, and modal interchanges," explained Peter Pickow, music editor-in-chief for Music Sales Corporation. "Even though the way they construct their melodies and harmonies seems completely naïve, the sincerity and self-confidence in the performances makes it clear that what you are hearing is the intended effect. I always hear something new when I listen to it—which I guess is *one* definition of good music."

After the reissues, how did the family react to the belated, and often comical, reviews—like Karrie Jacobs writing in Arizona's *New Times,* who said the Shaggs "sound like what garage sales look like late on Sunday afternoon"?

"I'm not offended," insisted Dot. "My sister Rachel doesn't want to hear or know anything about the band." Helen and Betty declined to be interviewed, deferring to Dot as their spokeswoman.

"Yeah, we weren't the greatest," Dot admits. "We could have done a lot more practicing and getting it together before we recorded. But I don't have a problem with those reviews."

The tributes didn't wane: the 1996 alternative rock compendium, *Rolling Stone's Alt-Rock-A-Rama,* compiled by Scott Schinder and the editors of Rolling Stone Press, contained three references to the Shaggs—each written by a different journalist, each of which assigned *Philosophy of the World* historical magnitude. It was third-listed (chronologically) among "The 100 Most Influential Alternative Releases of All Time," trailing the MC5's *Kick Out the Jams* and Captain Beefheart's *Trout Mask Replica,* while pre-dating the Stooges' *Fun House;* it was number three among "The Greatest Garage Recordings of the Twentieth Century," rating higher than albums by Pussy Galore and the Velvet Underground; and it was third-listed (again, chronologically) among "The Fifty Most Significant Indie Records." "Some have called [*Philosophy*] the tortured shrieks of sick minds sharing a lifetime of flogging and mutilation," Robot A. Hull wrote under the "Garage" listing. "Others define it as the poetry of virgins scrawled on their underwear beneath blankets after midnight.... The spirits of both Emily Dickinson and Melanie Safka hover in the background." The "Significant Indie" listing noted: "Nowadays, bands deliberately play incompetently or don't want to learn their instruments, but the Wiggins' enthusiastic amateurism wasn't deliberate.... As a result, this is the record that renders all future incompetency irrelevant."

How irrelevant? John DeAngelis, in the liner notes of the first Shaggs' CD reissue, theorized: "As mass media increasingly permeates our society with a sameness that is frightening, it seems unlikely that another band of this kind of quality and originality will ever come along again. Or maybe in some distant country, as you read this, a proud father is giving his daughters (or sons) instruments and is exhorting them—in whatever language—to 'do your own thing.'"

The Shaggs blazed a trail of precompetence for such artists as the Rain-coats, Beat Happening, Shonen Knife, the Mekons, and 1/2 Japanese. But with a big difference—good as those groups were, they lacked the Shaggs' self-unawareness. That quality is what differentiates "outsider" from "indie." As Andy Newman noted in the *Spin Alternative Record Guide*, "Because the essence of the Shaggs is utter unselfconsciousness and obliviousness to outside taste—qualities nonexistent in the modern musical marketplace and by defini-tion impossible to adopt consciously—their putative successors don't really have much to do with them. Like all true freaks, the Shaggs are genetically incapable of bearing progeny; the trail they blazed was a cul-de-sac."

Dan Forte, quoted in the original CD liner notes, commented, "I have yet to play a Shaggs cut for a professional musician who didn't roll his eyes and whisper, 'Where can I get this record?'"

Yet *Philosophy of the World* is not for everyone. Some listeners may feel uneasy and squirm in their seats when they find themselves entertained by the Shaggs. Others don't get it and never will, perhaps because they do not share the fear—if not the conviction—that those of us who love the Shaggs harbor: that we are *all* capable of combining scout's-honor sincerity with a near-total lack of conventional talent in a given area, producing similar results. And that we have doubtless done so on occasion. We just don't know about it.

The Wiggin sisters have very little money. They don't live the life of leg-ends. In fact, had Dot ever given an autograph?

"No," she sighed. "A bank where I have my checking account, a girl there recognized me from the dances, and she said she had the original album, which she'd bring in for me to sign. But I never saw her again when I was there. That was three years ago."

Tiny Tim on tip-toes

• 2 •

Tiny Tim
I GET A KICK OUT OF UKE

When Tiny Tim first began to appear regularly on *Laugh-In*, most viewers who snickered at his antics probably figured he was a joke, a scriptwriter's recurring one-liner. Little did those unsuspecting Nielsen couch-taters realize that the chalk-faced, corkscrew-coifed troubadour had a lengthy history—and would have an even longer future—on the fringes of showbiz. They were simply witnessing him at the peak of his popularity.

But as the world soon learned through his talk-show sittings and bizarre personal confessions, Tiny Tim was not comedic fiction. He was genuine. He was also a fluke: a guileless eccentric who suddenly attained heights of mega-stardom unprecedented in the annals of outsider art—then just as quickly spiraled back into the abyss of obscurity.

It was, after all, 1968. In the aftermath of LSD-sparked psychedelia, pop music was never weirder. Tiny had long hair. Maybe TV viewers thought he was a flower child. Actually, in his loathing of drugs and loose sex and his adoration for Nixon, Tiny was an anti-hippie.

Tiny Tim was a star for the 90s—the 1890s. He briefly tracked on the nation's cultural radar by doing what he'd been doing for almost two decades, and what he would continue doing for three decades thereafter: rescuing melodic relics from dusty cellars and practicing equally antiquated chivalry in the worship of womanhood.

A lovely lass and a great song—they were Tiny's recipe for contentment. He had three of the former in marriage, and thousands of the latter in performance. He was never less than a gentleman. He addressed all males as "Mr." and—Women's Lib be damned—all females as "Miss." His preferred age group for the opposite sex was 12 to 18, when, he insisted, "a woman is in her prime. That's when they're like ballplayers with a shot at winning the Most Valuable Player Award, or like Secretariat winning the Triple Crown."

Tiny Tim is an outsider object lesson in two ways:

1) He embodies the compulsion to create against astronomical odds. He could never quit. He had a destiny, which he would fulfill to the grave, regardless of public indifference, lack of money, or changing musical fashions.
2) He demonstrated how far a genuine outsider musician could go without a manufactured makeover. No one else in this book appeared on *The Tonight Show*. Tiny Tim made over 20 appearances. He also guested on the Andy Williams, Merv Griffin, and Red Skelton TV shows. He dueted with Bing Crosby. Played the Royal Albert Hall. Spent the night at Bob Dylan's house. Performed on a Beatles album. And in true outsider form, accomplished it all without modifying his style one iota—that is, without compromise.

Not that he had any choice in the matter. Like any for-real outsider, Tiny Tim couldn't be anything but himself.

Tiny Tim was born Herbert Khaury on April 12, 1932. His Lebanese father, Butros, and Jewish mother, Tillie, raised their only child in New York's Washington Heights district. They despaired of their son's propensity for failure: he dropped out of high school, was ridiculed as being "girlish" by kids in the neighborhood, and couldn't hold delivery-boy jobs. He had three abiding preoccupations:

1) 78-rpm records—particularly of *old* pop songs from bygone generations
2) Girls—only the most beautiful ("classics," he called them), though he rarely got—or wanted—his hands on them
3) The Brooklyn Dodgers (a loyalty later transferred to Los Angeles), though he was too much of a klutz to play the game

During his youth, rather than romp outdoors with other kids, Herbert sprawled on the floor of his bedroom for entire afternoons and evenings listening to his beloved 78-rpm discs on a wind-up Victrola. Transported by voices long departed, he daydreamed of a glamorous future based on an obsession with the past. Tillie wanted her misfit son to be an accountant or a lawyer; Butros cautioned her, "Leave the boy alone. When he's 13, 14 years old, he'll be a genius."

Instead of blossoming into genius, by age 20 Herbert had shocked his parents' conservative Jewish friends with his long hair, his ragged Goodwill-reject attire (Tillie: "He dressed like a bum"), and his obsession with face

creams and body lotions. He also expressed the unwavering conviction that
Jesus Christ was his savior. Though Butros defended him, his mother was not
so kind. "My mother never called me Herbie," Tiny told biographer Harry
Stein. "She always called me 'dope.'" Tillie tried several times to get her son
committed to Bellevue Psychiatric Hospital, but her husband forbade it.

The aching-hearted youth sought therapy by performing in squalid New
York clubs. As his preferred tool of accompaniment, the husky six-feet-one-
inch Meistersinger chose the weensy ukulele, an instrument that had gone out
of fashion in the first FDR administration and never regained vogue (Arthur
Godfrey notwithstanding). In Herbert's nimble hands, it was the perfect counterpoint. It don't mean a thing if it ain't got that 'pling.'

Tiny Tim began in the early Eisenhower years, strumming his uke and
crooning Vaudeville museum pieces at any talent show or smoke-filled gin
den that would let him onstage. Halloween arrived early: he quickly gained a
reputation for his stringy shoulder-length hair, mismatched carnival barker
duds, and powdered face. He was a lone bird, and eventually attracted a small
following. This cult included a succession of sleazoid agents and "business
advisors," who managed his money so deftly that young Khaury usually managed to not have any.

Harry Stein described one particular mise-en-scène that symbolized the
tawdriness of Tiny's predicament:

> Hubert's Museum and Live Flea Circus epitomized the underside of
> show business, the dream gone sour. Located in the basement of a
> penny arcade in ... Times Square, Hubert's was as low as a performer
> could sink. Customers ... showed up more to gawk than to be enter-
> tained, and they were rarely disappointed. The great pitcher Grover
> Cleveland Alexander, grown old and fat, was once reduced to putting
> himself on display.... So was Jack Johnson, the black former heavy-
> weight champ.... On the same bill as magicians, jugglers, and strong-
> men, there was invariably an assortment of human curiosities:
> Sealo ... had little seal flippers instead of arms; Jose de Leon, another
> regular, had no appendages whatsoever.... Albert-Alberta ... was billed
> as a living, breathing hermaphrodite.... In the back, Professor Roy
> Heckler [took] his trained fleas through their turns.

> Tiny Tim played Hubert's in 1959, when he was known as Larry
> Love. His stay in the basement was remarkable neither for its dura-
> tion nor for the attention he received. The fact is, he fit right in.

At Hubert's, "Larry" was marqueed as "The Human Canary," because
of his penchant for singing falsetto. He was also billed over the years as

Darry Dover, Rollie Dell, or whatever nom du jour sounded glamorous at the time.

In 1961, he acquired a manager, George King, who described to Stein his first meeting with the young singer: "He had long, scraggly hair, he was wearing an old raincoat, and he had this white gook all over his face.... [H]e was so emaciated from that goddam diet of his that he looked like he'd come from a concentration camp." King, who genuinely liked Tiny and appreciated his talent, got him gigs at such Greenwich Village hotspots as Café Bizarre, the Bitter End, and Café Wha. King also claims to have coined for his client the permanent moniker "Tiny Tim."

Tiny introduced his Victrola-vintage repertoire at the Little Theatre around 1962. Often following him on the program was the legendary blind street musician, Louis "Moondog" Hardin, by most accounts a sweet and gracious man. When he mounted the stage after Tiny, Moondog reportedly muttered curses about the travesty that had just preceded him.

Roy Silver, another ex-manager (there were many; Tiny was notorious for signing conflicting contracts), recalled, "When he performed, people were always yelling things like 'Get off, you fruit!' There was always the danger that some lug would run up and attack him. They simply didn't want to accept him as a performer."

Tiny was philosophical: "They're only laughing. People have been laughing at me my whole life."

While struggling on the Village circuit, he waxed a commercial 45 for the Blue Cat label in 1965. It fizzled. Meanwhile, at a midtown Manhattan storefront studio, Tiny cut countless one-off acetates written and recorded for—and given away to—a succession of darling damsels as tokens of admiration. "Hello, wonderful, lovely Miss Snooky," the opening groove would warble, "This is Tiny Tim. You are soooo beautiful. And that's why I composed this song for you." He hung with combative comedian Lenny Bruce. "We were both very romantic," he told *Goblin* magazine's Wesley Joost. "We liked to talk about girls a lot."

Besides the ladies, Tiny was obsessed with cleanliness—doubtless as an adjunct to godliness. His commitment to Jesus ran deep; he had a penchant for peppering his conversation with "ThankGodtoChrist."

Gigs at a lesbian club called Page Three and at Steve Paul's Scene sustained him, barely, while Tiny was mistaken for just another hapless freak strumming an acoustic stringed instrument. His big break came in August 1967, when Warner Bros. Records impresario Mo Ostin discovered the tousled apparition trilling away at the Scene, and offered him a contract.

Tiny Tim was just the act "Mr. Sinatra's Reprise Records" had been waiting for. They ushered Tiny, carrying his uke in a brown paper bag, into the

COURTESY WARNER BROS. RECORDS

studio; he stood before the mic, leaned back, opened wide, and released "the spirits of the singers who are living within me." Out flowed forgotten songs, sung in forgotten styles, in *anything* but a forgettable way. Tiny seemed to have memorized every Tin Pan Alley chestnut written between 1900 and 1945. If you're gonna preach, you gotta know the Bible.

God Bless Tiny Tim, the first album, was released in May 1968. Dogs liked Tiny's high notes; ships lost in the fog sought harbor in the low ones. The LP was produced by Richard Perry (who later worked with Carly Simon, Barbra Streisand, and Harry Nilsson, among countless others). *God Bless* is a bit like Harpo Marx's trenchcoat—you never knew what surprises lurked in all the hidden pockets. Spoken word narratives segued into rock 'n' roll, which jostled melodic cobwebs (the pre–World War I "On the Old Front Porch") and contemporary offerings ("Fill Your Heart," by then-upcoming writers Paul Williams and Biff Rose). Tiny could deliver both parts of dialogue in songs like "I Got You, Babe," alternating between his "sissy" falsetto and "macho" baritone. And, of course, the LP contained what would prove Tiny's trademark for life—"Tip-Toe Thru' the Tulips," a rusty 1929 pump that miraculously spewed a royalty stream through a culvert that had been dry for decades.

When Tiny became a regular on *Laugh-In* in 1968, he attracted the curiosity of reporters and gossip columnists, who found him good copy. He also became a "top 10 guest"—appearing with regularity every seven weeks or so—on the *Tonight Show,* where Johnny Carson was beguiled by Tiny's childlike candor. It was during this period that the nation discovered the depths of his weirdness: five showers a day; refusing to eat in the presence of others; a fortune spent on cosmetics; his sincere belief that aliens lived under the surface of the moon.

He awarded an annual trophy to the prettiest "classic" he'd met that year (these relationships were largely platonic). In conversation, he would spell, rather than utter, any word that was remotely risqué, including b-o-d-y and b-e-d. He volunteered to clean women's apartments—washed floors, vacuumed—just to be near them, content in the role of d-o-o-r-m-a-t.

But Tiny Tim was a history teacher masquerading as a buffoon. Predating by years the musical grave-robbing antics of Michael Feinstein, he reclaimed obscure relics from the songbooks of Bing Crosby, Rudy Vallee, and Irving Kaufman, and restored their vitality. He didn't just *know* these songs—he was familiar with encyclopedic details about them. Regarding "My Dreams Are Getting Better All the Time," from *Tiny Tim's Second Album*, he knew—who doesn't?—that it was a big hit for Johnny Long in 1945. But how many were aware, as Tiny told interviewer Ernie Clark in 1995, that "Long was the only left-handed violinist in popular music at the time"?

Speaking of hands, in 1969, crafty 17-year-old Victoria May Budinger offered Tiny hers in marriage. To assure everyone she was serious, "Miss Vicky" wed Tim on the *Tonight Show*, with 40 million witnesses. It was one of the highest-rated TV shows and biggest journalistic events of 1969—some fogies may recall we also landed on the moon that year.

Tiny was selling records (200,000 copies of *God Bless*), boosting network ad rates, and playing the most coveted showcases in the biz. He commanded 50 thousand a week in Vegas. For a guy who three years earlier had been bucking all musical trends in New York clubs at a plate-of-falafel pay scale, it must've seemed like a dream.

It was. And soon enough, it was over.

In short order, Tiny was divorced, remaindered, and bankrupt. Even the *Tonight Show* lost interest. Redefining "pathetic," Tiny was demoted back to carny culture, touring in a circus sideshow. And that was it.

Except for one thing: Nobody told him it was over.

Tiny continued to plug away, albeit on the fringes. He traveled alone and hired local, usually non-AFM players for backup. His bookings included urine-stenched clubs in Greyhound-circuit towns where a half-dozen drunken patrons would taunt him—but a few admiring fans (known as "Tinyheads") might also turn up to bask in what they considered his genius. County fairs, hotel lounges, riverboats—his compulsion to entertain was unquenchable. His perseverance earned him much respect from those who appreciate talented, neglected performers who circulate in the margins.

He was adventurous enough to work with younger artists in a variety of styles. These newcomers—musicians and producers—admired Tiny, and sought not to exploit him, but rather to help him exploit his talents. His appeal was cross-generational. Journalist Dawn Eden referred to Tiny's "eternal hipness." *Spin* noted that he "was post-rock when post-rock wasn't cool."

While he continued to retrieve pearls from the heyday of megaphone singers, Tiny indulged in modern genre-surfing, including heavy metal, rap, and disco. He explored Brave Combo's faux world music, Pink Floyd anthems, and Eugene Chadbourne's funhouse freakery. But through it all, he was unmistakably Tiny.

Brother Cleve (keyboardist of Combustible Edison) was hired in 1983 to back Tiny at the Rat, one of Boston's seediest punk dives. "He was traveling with a teenage girl—definitely jailbait—and a comic book–styled 'sleazy' manager, complete with pencil-thin mustache and greasy hair," recalled Cleve. "Tiny was the kindest, sweetest, most clueless idiot savant I've ever had the pleasure of working with. He played songs that none of us knew, in keys we couldn't deduce. He'd absorbed this incredible backlog of songs, but had no idea how to give directions to other musicians, except to say, 'When I spin my hand like this, play faster.' He had a peculiar concept of rhythm, and would change chords out of meter, without warning. I guess that's the result of decades of solo gigs. Yet he was unarguably one-of-a-kind, a performer whose faults became his charms."

His appeal to a new generation—and the devotion of his long-suffering loyalists—resuscitated Tiny from the career doldrums. He released more new albums from 1987 through 1997 than in all preceding decades combined. His audience may have been smaller than that of *Laugh-In*'s, but it was more faithful and more appreciative.

He still rendered the classics: *Tiptoe Through* [sic] *the Tulips/Resurrection* (Bear Family, 1987) and *Prisoner of Love: A Tribute to Russ Columbo* (Vinyl Retentive, 1995); but he also sustained his Tod Browning aura: *Songs of an Impotent Troubadour* (Durtro, 1995) featured a beer-besotted Tim raconteuring and wailing tunes he composed for Tuesday Weld, Elizabeth Taylor, and Jessica Hahn ("Jim Bakker came in your room / Who knows where or when / But when he left your lovin' arms / He sure was born again").

Ever ready for adventure, Tiny would hitch a ride on any musical bandwagon. Coming full circle from his 1968 *God Bless* debut, *I Love Me* (Ponk/Seeland, 1995) displayed an array of styles. It showcased Tiny's versatility with solo uke toss-offs, rockers, disco, cocktail jazz, and the obligatory "Tulips" song ("I Saw Mr. Presley Tip-toeing through the Tulips"). A 6:48-long "Depression Medley" featured Tiny's acoustic recordings hotwired into noise-art by Shockabilly sound skronker Eugene Chadbourne.

"Once [Tiny's] in a studio," explained album engineer Pink Bob, "if you shove the occasional food and fruit juice through the door, he'll never leave. He performs to the microphone as if it were a crowd of 100,000 fans."

Girl (Rounder, 1996), recorded with Brave Combo, gelled beautifully. The Combo had obvious respect for Tiny as a song stylist and never upstaged his vocals. The arrangements were tasteful, with horns galore, as Tiny tackled the Beatles ("Hey, Jude," "Girl"), antique songcraft ("Over the Rainbow," "Stardust"), and a new song ("Fourteen") written by his fan club president, James "Big Bucks" Burnett. "Stairway to Heaven" got a long overdue revamp: Tim and the Combo retooled the Led Zep leviathan as a jump-jazz finger-snapper for gimlet-eyed lounge lizards.

Also recommended for completists: the *Endless Discussion* fan club tapes, in which Tiny speculated on the possibilities of extraterrestrial life.

Despite his one-shot popularity pinnacle and long-loyal following, Tiny never inspired copycats. There was no uke revival; pancake makeup futures didn't register an uptick. His fans seemed content to sit back and enjoy the spectacle without any compulsion to emulate. The main reason, of course, is that Tiny Tim was *uncopyable*. "Originality" never had a more visible poster child.

One quality that distinguished Tiny Tim from legions of outsiders was his professionalism. He was smooth, poised. He could work an audience with great confidence. He was comfortable onstage, always in control of his performance. This didn't make him any less of an outsider; the element of the freak show was always part of the spectacle. Yet, Tiny once asserted, "I do not consider myself an entertainer. I consider myself more of a songplugger, trying to sell the song and the artist."

His death couldn't have been more poetic: performing on uke before the Women's Club of Minneapolis on November 30, 1996, Tiny suffered a heart attack. His third wife, Miss Sue (Susan Gardner Khaury), helped him back to their table, where the 64-year-old singer collapsed and expired. "I don't think he had time to feel pain," said Susan. "He died singing 'Tip-Toe Thru' the Tulips,' the last thing he heard was the applause, and the last thing he saw was me." Judging from her professions of love on her Web site, Sue *really* loved the guy—in all the right ways. Tiny was very lucky to have found her, and it's a tearjerker that he only lived long enough to enjoy 14 months of such wedded bliss.

After the troubadour's death, J. R. Taylor wrote the following haiku in the *New York Press:*

God, why Tiny Tim?
He could still hit the high notes
Unlike Robert Plant

Journalist Mykel Board observed, "Tiny Tim was a tragic figure. Both in his personal suffering—imagine living as a 'joke'—and untimely death, but more so as a loss to music history. He was a great repository of clever, slightly naughty songs from an innocent America. His death was like the burning of a great library."

He took that library with him. But he was looking forward to the afterlife. Tiny mused in 1975: "I dream that in the next world I'll be able to be with all the women I want. I don't want men around, except maybe my poor father, and Al Jolson. I will own them, all these beautiful creatures who never get old, and do whatever I want with them. There will be no body odor, and making *l-o-v-e* will be like it was in the Garden of Eden before the fall. I will never get tired, and my *s-e-e-d* will flow out for hours, like water out of a hose, in a stream of ecstasy."

ThankGodtoChrist.

• 3 •

Jack Mudurian

CHATTERBOX JUKEBOX

"**i** think I know as many songs as Sinatra," mused Jack Mudurian one day in 1981. At the time, he was a resident at Boston's Duplex Nursing Home. The mentally unstable Mudurian had been shuttling through various institutions for years.

His remark was overheard by David Greenberger, editor of the *Duplex Planet* magazine, and the home's activities director. Greenberger fetched a portable tape deck and cued up a C90. As the two men stood on the back porch, Greenberger asked if Mudurian would sing all the songs he knew.

"Sure," replied Jack.

David hit the "record" button. "Go," he said.

The ensuing 45-minute medley was eventually released—unedited—in 1996 on a CD entitled *Downloading the Repertoire* (Arf Arf Records). Though Mudurian's musical legacy consists of a single album, it contains 129 songs; Meatloaf, by comparison, is a strip of jerky. On *Downloading*, 99 Tin Pan Alley fragments pass the turnstile (30 are reprised). "Pistol Packin' Mama" careens into "Boola Boola," which abruptly segues into "Honeysuckle Rose." It's like a late-night TV ad for K-Tel's *100 Great Songs Sung By A Rambling Geezer*. Howard Stern is a fan—he occasionally cues up Jack's relentless jukeboxing on his coast-to-coast radio funfest.

"Jack was a real nice guy," recalled Greenberger, "though kind of high-strung. The medley reflects what he was about—jittery, with a nervous energy, filling the air with speech at all times."

Greenberger began working at the nursing home in early 1979 and stayed almost three years. Located at 12 Harris Avenue, the Duplex was stationed in a sprawling, century-old, wooden duplex house that had been converted into a privately owned nursing home in the 1950s. There were 45 residents—all male, aged 50 through 90. They reflected a wide range of decline, from old age to alcoholism to faulty wiring.

While employed at the facility, Greenberger recorded and transcribed countless surrealistic monologues and Q&A sessions with the residents. He has published these transcriptions in his long-running periodical, the *Duplex Planet,* as well as adapting them for theatrical performances, books, public radio programs, a comic magazine series, and CDs.

Mudurian entered the Duplex around 1980. He was U.S.-born, of Armenian ancestry, in his early to mid-50s. Extremely skinny, he was fond of wearing baseball caps and compulsively displayed exaggerated arm movements. "He almost had a Don Knotts look," said Greenberger. "He wore things that would accentuate that beanpole quality. He would cross and uncross his arms, but they would flail out to the sides, then cross. It all seemed informed by a lot of caffeine." Jack would talk incessantly—"to those around him, to himself," explained Greenberger.

Unlike many of his coresidents, whose connection to reality was tenuous at best, when Mudurian spoke, he didn't make things up. His mouth just went white-water rafting down his stream-of-consciousness. "I read that story, *Men Against the Sea,*" he once declared. "That's a true story, it's a pocket book I read. *Devil's Island* is another pocket book; it's an unfictitious story. I read it. I read the *Mutiny on the Bounty* trilogy; that's nonfictitious. I read about John Dillinger, the criminal. He has a mustache; I saw it in his picture. His mustache is the color white, or gray. I read Frank Buck, *Bring 'Em Back Alive.* I took it out of the library. I read it and then I returned it. Frank Buck, I read the whole thing. You know what he brought back? Elephants, monkeys, giraffes, and zebras. I know he brought back elephants and monkeys, and I think zebras and giraffes as well. The monkeys got wet, if I remember right. I would say that the monkeys were on the deck and got wet from the salt water, or from the water from the guy who was swabbin' the decks."

Another time, Mudurian blurted out, "I keep smoking, but what I really want is to drive around in a stick-shift car." Mudurian's brother often came to visit. "They were a couple of real characters," Greenberger recalled. "They looked similar, even dressed alike—his brother would occasionally show up wearing a goofy hat. But while Jack would retire to his room on the second floor of the nursing home, his brother would head back to South Boston and the family grocery store."

How did Mudurian come to memorize such a large catalog of songs? "He was a fan of music, whatever was on the radio," explained Greenberger, "one of those people who just let the popular culture wash over them." Before that fateful one-time session, Jack had never given any hint of the inventory stored in his memory banks. "He might sing, 'Toot-toot-tootsie, good-bye' one day, but there was no context," said Greenberger. "The previous Friday [before the taping], we'd held a talent show at a church one block from the Duplex. There were local youths and elderly performers. I took four residents from the Duplex, including Jack. He started singing, 'Chicago, Chicago, that toddlin' town, that toddlin' town.' Then he started singing it again. And again." Like a human skipping record. "They couldn't get him to stop," said David. "Finally someone came onstage, thanked him, and got everyone to clap—or else it was clear he was going to stay there and keep singing the same lines over and over." (*The Talent Show* was also released on CD by Arf Arf. It's a charming, naturalistic document of outsider performances.)

"Jack was always happy about music," Greenberger pointed out. "He thought he was good. He enjoyed singing." Mudurian's vocals were twice sampled by Shimmy Disc Records provocateur (Mark) Kramer—on "Bosom Friend," from his album *The Guilt Trip,* and on Captain Howdy's *Tattoo of Blood.* In both instances, Kramer failed to credit Mudurian, or to offer payment.

But perhaps Mudurian wouldn't have minded. "Money's not my best friend," he once insisted. "Money is the root of all evil. You go down to the depths of poverty when you go down into money, don't you? I don't want money, it's the root of all evil to me David, David Greenberger. Can you buy me a soda Dave? Root beer."

Greenberger once invited his friend Jad Fair's band, 1/2 Japanese, to play for the Duplex residents, on which occasion Fair met Mudurian. Later, Greenberger made a tape of Jack's medley for Jad, who copied Jack's convoluted a cappella arrangement of "Chicago (That Toddlin' Town)" for his own live shows.

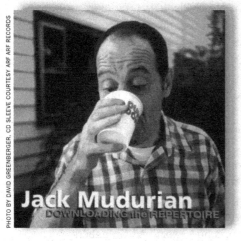

Jack refuels.

Downloading's cover photo shows Mudurian swigging a cup of Dunkin' Donuts coffee. The pic was taken while Jack was standing beside Fair, who'd bought the coffee. Mudurian gulped it down in one continuous chug, handed Jad the empty container, and exclaimed, "You buy one good cup of coffee!" Mudurian, in fact, was fueled by caffeine, as well as nicotine. "He'd stay tanked up on coffee constantly," noted Greenberger, "maybe a dozen cups a day." This explains the turbine-rev delivery and breathless recycling of every melodic scrap that ever entered Mudurian's hyperactive mind. "He also chain-smoked," explained Greenberger. "His fingers were completely nicotine-stained. He'd smoke 'em right down to the stub."

The CD's back cover photo (cropped on the album) is reproduced at right. "That's Jack standing alongside his buddy Bill Sears," noted Greenberger. "Jack would wear these striped shirts that would accentuate his skinniness. Then Bill would wear the identical shirt, and he was huge. They looked like Laurel and Hardy."

"It was heartening spending time with Jack," Greenberger mused. "You'd see these solitary figures hanging around the Dunkin' Donuts parking lot—semi-homeless and indigent, with too many layers of clothing, talking to themselves. It was amazing just getting to know someone like him. That's why I didn't want to know too much about the medical basis of his condition." Most residents at the Duplex were broadly diagnosed as "schizophrenic," or as having "deep neuroses"—vague words that Greenberger said "meant nothing to me. I knew this guy, and I had a better sense of who he was than that clinical definition."

Jack Mudurian (left) and Bill Sears standing outside the Duplex Nursing Home, May 1981

Perhaps Jack's real affliction was eternal youth. He would've been comfortable with that. "What's the trouble with kids today?" Greenberger once asked Mudurian. "Nothing," he replied. "I like the kids today."

"Well," Greenberger persisted. "What's *right* with kids today?"

Mudurian retorted, "They don't spit on ya."

The Duplex Nursing Home went bankrupt in 1987 and closed. Mudurian was transferred to another facility. A year later, he went to live with his brother, and Greenberger lost touch with the legendary medley-maker. "The trail just went cold at that point," he sighed.

Shortly thereafter, the former Duplex old age facility was replaced by a New Age center.

• 4 •

J o e   M e e k

british rock producer Joe Meek was a cross between Thomas Edison, Phil Spector, and Ed Wood, Jr., embodying the best and worst of all three. Like Edison, he was a largely self-taught inventor and a primitive, intuitive engineer. Like Spector, he was a recording studio maverick who produced transistor-friendly chart-climbers in the pre-Beatles era, developing a dense, atmospheric sound that influenced subsequent generations. And like film outsider Wood, he was dogged by failure, produced a vault full of dreadful work, was tormented by his sexual peccadilloes, and met a sordid end. (Tim Burton, take note.)

Whereas Wood drank himself into the hereafter, Meek's last glimpse of life was down the barrel of a hunting rifle. Joe had been undergoing a severe bout of depression, triggered by a debt-ridden ledger and a doomed career. After years of defiance against English music biz tradition with sporadic chart success, Meek was fed up, pilled up, and washed up.

Compounding his anxiety was an ongoing police investigation of homosexuals like himself following the gruesome dismemberment of a 17-year-old male acquaintance. The boy's butchered corpse had been stuffed in two suitcases that were discovered in a farmer's field.

On February 3, 1967, the short-fused Meek fatally drilled his landlady, Mrs. Violet Shenton, with buckshot, possibly in a dispute over unpaid back rent. A minute or so later, the 37-year-old Meek turned the gun around and launched his own face heavenward with volcanic dispatch.

His assistant, Patrick Pink, who rushed upstairs upon hearing the shots, said Joe's head looked "like a burnt candle."

.   .   .

Meek's U.S. claim to fame was the instrumental "Telstar," performed by the Tornadoes. It sold over five million singles worldwide from 1962 through 1963. A consummate control-room freak, Meek wrote, produced, and mixed the tune. He named it in honor of history's first orbiting global communications satellite, which was sent into space jointly by Bell Labs and NASA in 1962. The record had its own intercontinental significance, marking the first U.S. number one by an English beat group—a year before the fabled British Invasion that saw the Beatles and Stones recapturing what George III had lost.

Control-room freak Joe Meek, 1966

"Telstar" featured a catchy, spine-tingling melody played on a mysterious-sounding electronic keyboard—a Clavioline—underscored by otherworldly humming and propelled by a galloping rhythm. It sounded like nothing before, and nothing since. For all its majestic sonic trappings, the record sounded cheesy enough to have been recorded in someone's bedroom.

Which it was.

Meek worked out of his cluttered north London apartment, which he'd outfitted with three floors' worth of recording gear. He pioneered low-budget but sonically explosive studio techniques, his favorite being to overload the signal compressor to the point of willful distortion. Meek devised discount-store sound effects out of kitchenware, pocket combs, milk bottles, and flushing toilets. Occasionally he'd dispense with the bass drum and order a band to stomp on the floorboards in beat, as on "Have I the Right" by the Honeycombs. (This 1964 single was Meek's only other major U.S. chart entry, peaking at number five.)

Many of Meek's idiosyncratic productions reek of cheap echo and severe compression. His patented lo-fi crunch set the stage for the mid-60s Liverpool-to-London musical tidal wave that ironically rendered him anachronistic. The Dave Clark Five in particular used Meek's penchant for pinning VU-meters as a template for their 1964–67 string of hits. A decade later, Meek's ghost hovered over the U.K. Punk Class of 1976 and its onslaught of stripped-to-the-basics hooliganism. And as the first prominent U.K. independent producer, Meek cleared a path for the likes of Mickie Most, Robert Stigwood, Shel Talmy, and Andrew Loog Oldham, whose collective production resumes included The Who, The Animals, Donovan, Cream, and the Rolling Stones.

Even before Meek's death, many of his studio innovations had been copied to clichédom and surpassed. Sounds he captured using a thousand pounds of tape rigs, primitive processors, and household bric-a-brac can be reproduced today with a microchip.

But chips can't emulate Joe's reckless ambition, nor can they encode his near-homicidal belligerence. Meek was a world-rank outsider and a temperamental bully who inflicted much collateral damage on those who entered his orbit. A country bumpkin trying to make it in the big city, Joe didn't fit in anywhere and had difficulty getting along with just about everybody.

In an age when gays risked public disgrace in British society, Joe kept his homosexuality in the closet. Joe loved his mother dearly, and in his guilt-ridden London adult years always feared bringing shame to the family name. Tone-deaf and dyslexic, he also lacked hard business sense and was cursed with the family propensity for violent tantrums.

A 1989 U.K. bio, *The Legendary Joe Meek* by John Repsch, tells the story in all its luridness. The author calls his work "a murder-mystery." (Now out of print, this compelling book has been unable to attract a U.S. publisher.) Musician Dave Adams, who worked with Meek from 1958 until the producer's demise, observed, "Most of us who were close to Joe always felt he would suffer some kind of violent death."

ENA SHIPPAM

Left to right: father George Meek, Joe (age 4), and brother Arthur, 1933

Robert George Meek was born in 1929 to a simple farming family who lived in the Forest of Dean. From early childhood he was groomed for quirkiness. His mother Biddy nicknamed the lad "Joe" after a brother who had died during infancy. But Mrs. Meek really wanted a daughter, so she dressed her son in girly frocks for the first four years of his life. Joe's brothers, Eric and Arthur, were scuffling, tree-climbing "outdoor boys." Joe was a sensitive, radio-shacking "indoor boy."

While working as a staff engineer at IBC Studios in 1956, Meek was tapped to mix trad-jazz trumpeter Humphrey Lyttleton's recording of "Bad Penny Blues." Lyttleton, in a 1992 BBC documentary, *The Very Strange Story of Joe Meek*, recalled: "In jazz, the general idea was to stick a mic up and get as natural a sound as possible without mucking about. Joe over-recorded the drum brushes, and he also did something very peculiar by distorting the left hand of the piano. The [left hand] octave rolling up sounds very peculiar on the record, and it's very difficult to recapture that live, because that's not the actual sound that comes out of the piano. Had I not gone on holiday, had we all gathered 'round and listened to playback, I would have had a fit. I would have said, 'That's dreadful!' And I would have thrown Joe into one of his sulks. I would've said, 'You've over-recorded the drums, and I don't want that. And you've distorted the piano, and I don't want that either.' But in fact I wasn't there, and so it all came out like that, and became a [U.K.] hit—I think for those reasons." Lyttleton was stunned: "The idea of a sound engineer not doing what you tell him, but actually twiddling the knobs and distorting things—that was a totally new world for me."

It's little known that Meek first hit the U.S. charts in 1958, two years before he'd achieved any professional stature in the United Kingdom. "Put a Ring on Her Finger," a tune he'd written for English singer Eddie Silver, had flopped in the United Kingdom, but somehow caught the ear of American electric guitar pioneer Les Paul. The retitled single ("Put a Ring on My Finger") by Paul and his wife Mary Ford cracked the U.S. Top 40 in September of that year, generating a modest flow of royalties for the young composer-engineer.

By 1960, Meek, with his stubborn, argumentative demeanor, had disingratiated himself at several prestigious studios. Striking out on his own, he rented three floors above the A. H. Shenton Leather Goods shop at 304 Holloway Road, in a dumpy north London neighborhood. (Today a commemorative plaque on the brickwork notes this landmark address where Meek "lived, worked, and died.") His goal was to conquer the pop charts as an independent producer, working with his own chosen artists, in his studio, on his terms.

Meek's squalid quarters were crammed with jerryrigged equipment, tossed-together drum kits, and a rat's nest of wiring that resembled a "Danger: Don't Overload Circuit" fire prevention diagram. Mr. and Mrs. Shenton lived below and didn't appreciate round-the-clock feedback emanating from the upper floors. They would often signal their displeasure by banging a broomstick against the ceiling. Their ever-considerate tenant would respond by placing loudspeakers in the stairwell and cranking out pavement-rattling decibels.

Joe's first self-produced U.K. number one hit, "Johnny Remember Me" (1961), was recorded in his flat by TV actor John Leyton. "Johnny," an echo-drenched dead-girlfriend ditty, is in retrospect a mediocre song whose impact is best appreciated in historical context. At the time, the 45's success stunned Meek's rivals, who had him pegged as a bottom-feeder with a tin ear.

Leyton offered a snapshot of Meek's m.o.: "When I recorded 'Johnny Remember Me,' I was in the sitting room behind a little screen, and the rhythm section was in the room with me. The violin section was on the stairs, the backing singers were practically in the loo, and the brass section were underneath, on another floor altogether. And there was Joe next door, playing his machine like another musical instrument. It was quite bizarre."

"The record industry probably thought it was a prank," Mickie Most told the BBC. "At the time, record companies were very, very disciplined. Studio engineers used to wear white jackets, like doctors. I remember a sign at EMI Studios in Abbey Road, where it said, 'Sports trousers and jackets may be worn on Saturdays.' That's how disciplined recording was, and they took it all rather seriously. And here's this guy making these records and selling millions—*in his kitchen.*"

Meek released over 250 singles in the United Kingdom, scoring 45 Top 50 entries. (Hundreds more went unreleased.) His homemade platters defied prevailing standards of perfection, as he gleefully overloaded the sound gate and pushed drums to the top of the mix. In recordings like "Huskie Team" by the Saints, "Something I've Got to Tell You" by Glenda Collins, and Mike Berry's "Tribute to Buddy Holly," Meek created heavenly pop hits. Some of his best work can be heard on an 18-track U.S. collection called *It's Hard to Believe It* (Razor and Tie, 1995), compiled and annotated by Smithereens drummer Dennis Diken. Meek's brilliant production is evidenced throughout, though many tracks suffer from banal songwriting and clumsy lyrics.

Meek's instrumental sides with the Tornadoes are among his most enduring trademarks. The enigmatic "Telstar," Diken attested, "still sounds wonderful. Always will."

The Tornadoes, however, were less than proud of their "achievement." Having recorded some basic guitar and rhythm tracks, the band left in mid-session for a scheduled tour. In their absence, Joe directed his classically trained songwriting partner Geoff Goddard to overdub a heavily compressed Clavioline (a battery-powered, two-octave keyboard) and a few harplike piano-string flourishes. Meek topped the mix with some sinister humming on the final verse. Goddard recalled feeling cold shivers when he listened to a playback of the finished work.

And what did the Tornadoes think?

"When we heard it," recalled bassist Heinz Burt, "we couldn't believe it. Crap!" Drummer Clem Cattini was equally aghast: "Joe sent me a copy. I listened and thought, 'God, I can't tell anybody I played on that.'"

Their apprehension was premature. "Telstar" rocketed into the U.K. charts and remained there for 25 weeks. Forty years later, it remains the all-time best-selling British instrumental worldwide. Even Margaret Thatcher has expressed her admiration, calling it "a marvelous tune, full of life." It has been covered by the Ventures, the Ashley Hutchings Big Beat Combo with Richard Thompson, and Fairport Convention's Simon Nicol, among others. American twee pop progenitor Bobby Rydell crooned a regrettable vocal version on his 1963 cover-song fest, *All the Hits, Vol. 2* (Cameo). The lyricist remains at large, although Meek himself is the suspected culprit.

The creator of this classic tune was a combative browbeater with a volatile temper. Almost every musician interviewed in Repsch's bio explained that at Joe's studio, you played by Joe's rules. If not, the hotheaded Meek would throw things at human targets—a telephone or an electric razor, perhaps a tray of coffee, a typewriter, or tape reels.

Clem Cattini recalled an artistic disagreement with Meek: "Joe stormed out, which he normally did, and came storming back in with this stool—which he threw at me. I ducked. It hit the top of a tape recorder and shattered the tape holders. He hadn't even used the machine yet—it had only been delivered the day before. He was yelling away: 'How dare you criticize my work! Get out!' I said, 'All right, fair enough.' As I was walking down the stairs I heard Joe coming behind. I shot down the last flight. Suddenly I heard 'clatter, clatter, clatter' and looked 'round and this tape recorder's following me. I got out the door at the bottom just in time as it came crashing down against it."

Joe Meek (right) and secretary
Terry O'Neil, 1964

On another memorable occasion, the producer grew frustrated with a drummer who would not play a beat to his liking. Meek raged into the studio with a shotgun, cocked the pin, rammed it up the percussionist's nostrils and screamed: "*If you don't do it properly, I'll blow your fucking head off!*" The drummer, Mitch Mitchell—later one-third of the Jimi Hendrix Experience—obediently complied. Witnesses did not doubt Meek's intent. "We all knew that he was a little bit unstable," said organist Dave Watts.

"Unstable?" Meek was a tangled web of psychoses, compulsiveness, pettiness, and congenital nerdiness. "He most certainly had some kind of schizophrenic condition," said Dave Adams, interviewed by phone from his Rochester, New York, home. "At the time we were too raw to really know that. I don't think he ever admitted it. But he was definitely two people. You'd be

talking to him one moment then turn away and come back, and he was a completely different person. I always referred to his alter ego as 'Robert Meek.'
'Robert' was this bad person, and 'Joe' was this nice person."

Adams disagreed with the common perception that Joe was in constant
turmoil. "The [Repsch] book kind of bothers me," he lamented. "The general
feeling in the book is that Joe was this dark person, which wasn't true at all.
He had a separate group of people who were his personal friends. And when
those people were around him, he was this kind, caring, loving person. But
when he'd get into the music side of him, he started getting all that stress in
his head. Then he'd be a hard and violent person. He became 'Robert.'"

Ever mindful of the competition and the (real or imagined) laughter
behind his back, Meek struggled desperately to maintain a presence on the
pop charts. This happened with less frequency as the decade wore on. This is
no surprise—a substantial portion of his singles are the kind of banalities that
cause feverish bidding among collectors but aren't worth hearing.

Meek made pop stars out of tune-mangling actors (Leyton, Iain Gregory)
and groomed mediocrities for unattainable stardom (Heinz Burt, Tony Dangerfield). He made the first recordings of Tom Jones but couldn't get them
released. The producer auditioned a teenage David Bowie—and rejected him.
He once heard a young band and offered to hire them, provided they got rid of
their awful singer—a gravel-voiced 16-year-old named Rod Stewart.

Meek was an opinionated know-it-all, often to his detriment. In 1962, he
was wined and dined in London by a persistent young impresario, who
handed him a tape of an unknown quartet seeking a recording contract. Joe
listened but was not impressed. He dismissed the Beatles as "just another
noisy group covering other peoples' songs."

Meek was protective (read: *paranoid*) about his studio methods. He built
a mysterious "black box," wrapped in thick tape, which he used as a signal fil-
ter to create an eerie echo. After his death, the box was unwrapped to reveal
its contents: a garden gate spring. Joe swore that rival producers were parked
out on Holloway bugging his studios and monitoring his sessions via radio
transmission.

Meek may have had difficulty communicating with the living, but he was
certain he could develop a rapport with the dead. He was obsessed with the
supernatural, schlepping cumbersome tape decks into graveyards at midnight
to record voices from the hereafter. He was fixated with splattered rock icons
like Eddie Cochran and Buddy Holly—from whom he claimed to channel
musical ideas via Ouija board—and killed himself on the eighth anniversary
of Holly's unscheduled landing in an Iowa cornfield.

The stargazing Meek had recorded a 12-song "outer space fantasy," *I Hear
a New World*, in 1960. It could have been rock's first concept album—if any-

one had heard it at the time. "I wanted to create a picture in music of what could be up there in outer space," wrote the producer. Meek's cosmos, as evidenced by his song titles, was populated by Globbots, Dribcots, and Saroos who sang like Martian Chipmunks. The music featured ethereal Hawaiian guitar, a poorly tuned tack piano, and sound effects improvised with vibrating forks, clockwork toys, running water, and electrical short circuits. Except for a four-song EP of which Meek reportedly pressed (or perhaps *sold?*) 99 copies, *I Hear a New World* remained unreleased until 1991, when a semi-legit CD hit U.K. shops. Some goofy sped-up vocals aside, the album is a masterpiece, a work of visionary proportions. It foreshadows much of the genius tomfoolery Brian Wilson achieved several years later during his *Smile* period.

A few words about Joe's tone-deafness: a U.K. collection, *Work in Progress: The Triumph Sessions,* includes, along with 25 largely forgettable unreleased sides, two of the producer's personal demos. They reveal an adenoidal Meek grasping in vain for a melody over a slowed-down recording of Sandy Nelson's "Teen Beat." (There are reportedly hours of such cringe-inducing outtakes—and much more—in the attic of a noncooperative British gentleman. According to the Joe Meek Appreciation Society, this fellow possesses and refuses to release trunkloads of Meek audio artifacts.)

"I was there the night that 'Telstar' was written," explained Dave Adams. "It was the middle of the night. Instead of giving me a demo, he sang it in my ear—which he used to do quite often. I'd sit at the piano and transpose what he was singing—which was very difficult because he was tone-deaf. He couldn't play an instrument, and he couldn't read music. He could hear it in his head and knew exactly what it was. He just couldn't vocalize it. He would give you some vague melody, and you'd have to figure out what he was trying to get over. That would go on for maybe an hour or so, until I got the notes right."

Despite Adams's contention, there is a demo of "Telstar," and this author has a copy. Using the rhythm track of a song he later titled "My Baby Doll," Meek sings an approximate melody recognizable beyond doubt as what became "Telstar." It confirms all contentions about Meek's inherent lack of musical ability, as he meanders all over the musical map in search of a key.

"Telstar" should have made Meek a millionaire, but hundreds of thousands of pounds in royalties were withheld by a flimsy French copyright infringement suit. After six years, a French court ruled in Meek's favor—about a year after he'd painted the studio walls with the contents of his skull.

In England, where Meek has been near-deified in alt-rock circles, a number of compilations have attempted to provide an overview of his legacy. Qualitatively, these packages make for erratic listening. Castle Communications, owner of the Pye Records catalog, released on their Sequel label two volumes entitled, respectively, *The Joe Meek Story: The Pye Years* (two CDs, 48 tracks), and 304 *Holloway Road—Joe Meek: The Pye Years, Vol. 2* (26 tracks). Both are near-impossible to enjoy in their entirety. Along with such standout Meek confections as the Riot Squad's "I Take It That We're Through" and practically anything by the Honeycombs, the packages contain heavy doses of, well, crap. Many of Meek's original compositions are hampered by sub-song poem-grade lyrics. The man never met a *moon-June* cliché he couldn't recycle, and his song structures tended to be yawningly prosaic and formulaic.

Joy and David's "Doopy Darling" (composer-credited to "Robert Duke," one of Meek's tax-dodging pseudonyms) featured a boy and girl swapping nonsense syllables, each singing with repulsively overwrought cutesiness and sadomasochistic impute:

> Floop! Doop! Doo-be doo-be doo-be
> Floop! Doop! Doo-be doo-be doo-be
> Floop! Doop! Doo-be doo-be doo-be
> Floop!
> Be my doopy-doo pee-doopy darlin'
> I know that our love could be so charmin'
> Kiss me on my pimple
> Love me sweet and simple
> Be my doopy-doo pee-doopy darlin'
> When we walk in the park
> Listen to the birds sing, listen to the dogs bark
> They can see just like me
> That we're in love
> Be my doopy-doo pee-doopy darlin'
> When you look at me it's so alarmin'
> I don't care how you treat me,
> Love me, hate me, beat me
> But be my doopy-doo pee-doopy darlin'

Sequel's *Vol. 2* contains this author's nominations for two of the worst tracks Meek ever produced: Pat Reader's pathetically melodramatic "May Your Heart Stay Young Forever," and Iain Gregory's laughably wobbly "The Night You Told a Lie." There are countless other nominees, many unreleased, which have circulated over the years on tape among smirking Meek collectors.

John Repsch admitted that even he has difficulty enjoying a lot of Meek's work. In his book, he described Iain Gregory as "one of the most atrocious singing voices ever to be pressed into vinyl.... [He] sounded like he had taken lessons from a clapped-out alley cat and gone out and found an alley. For his recording of 'Time Will Tell' Joe had the inspired idea of putting Ian in headphones to help him keep a minimum of pitch singing along to the voice of Dave Adams. But that song [was] still painful and could only be recommended to penance-seeking sinners. Even though his voice had some of its inadequacies masked by echo and a bravely cheerful backing, the problem was that you could still hear it."

In England, the Meek Appreciation Society publishes a magazine called *Thunderbolt* and a periodic newsletter. These publications include where-are-they-now updates and interviews with former Meek sidemen who ducked flying debris.

The BBC documentary about Meek featured deadpan *Spinal Tap*–like interviews with Joe's farmer brothers, Eric and Arthur ("Joe was a great cook. He was very fond of sausages."). The mild-mannered Arthur lamented, "He was a sick man the last six months, there's no doubt about that. He needed a real good rest, that's what he needed."

Putting his troubles on hold for eternity with the pull of a trigger, Joe Meek at last settled into a very long rest.

Making records like they make sausages

• 5 •

Song Poems
BUS FARE TO THE GRAMMYS

"**S**ong Poems Wanted! Collaborate with successful writers, arrangers, and musicians! This could be your big chance! Send for free appraisal!"

Enticed by ads in the back pages of comic books and tabloids, such trailer park sonneteers as Mary Urrutia, Mrs. D. J. Scroggins, and Willie Justice III mailed lyrics to the Hollywood-based MSR Records during the 1960s and 1970s. In reply they received a flattering form letter proclaiming their song's hit potential. These swampland Sondheims were urged to remit a check (usually around $200), in exchange for which their lyrics would be given the "professional studio treatment."

Who could resist? Not Waskey Elwood Walls, Jr., composer of the patriotic anthem "Jimmy Carter Says 'Yes.'" Nor could Chester T. Finley, who authored the whimsical "Little Betsy and Her Goat." The topics ranged from TV stars to moon men and hippies. Scandals, fads, and social turmoil were common inspirations.

In what amounts to the music industry's counterpart to the vanity press, these homebrew lyrics would be recorded in song form by seasoned, if frustrated and rent-bent, session pros at the rate of dozens per day. These songs would roll off the conveyor belt, to be pressed on one of thousands of albums and singles released by hundreds of such labels nationwide. Copies would then be shipped to satisfied clients, who awaited fame and immortality when their songs became "hits."

As if.

The reality, of course, was that MSR tunes made it closer to Uranus than *Billboard*. Thanks to loophole-claused contracts that led mail-in lyricists to believe otherwise, these records weren't promoted or distributed much beyond the circle of songwriters whose works they contained. Nevertheless, fame and immortality have come belatedly (and probably unknowingly) to many song-poets: some of their more outlandish efforts have been lovingly reissued by collectors, many of whom appreciate them with a dose of irony. NRBQ drummer and vinylphile Tom Ardolino collected 16 tracks for the LP *Beat of the Traps* (Carnage Press); 12 of these were reissued on CD with 16 additional titles on *The Makers of Smooth Music*. Two subsequent 28-track collections, *I'm Just the Other Woman*, and *The Human Breakdown of Absurdity* (both on Carnage Press) expanded the available catalog. John Zorn's Tzadik Records launched their Lunatic Fringe series with 27 MSR tracks on a CD entitled *I Died Today*. It was compiled by New York saxophonist Ellery Eskelin, whose late father, Rodd Keith (Eskelin), was a featured vocalist and musician on countless MSR productions.

What characterizes a "song poem"? The man to ask is Phil Milstein, curator of the genre's on-line Smithsonian, the American Song/Poem Music Archives (AS/PMA). Milstein has devoted years to collecting, cataloging, and analyzing this hitherto neglected art form and is writing a book chronicling its century-long history. In the liner notes to *The Makers of Smooth Music*, he conceded that "a song poem is sort of the literary equivalent of the array of colors found in polyester leisure suits: ... it doesn't occur anywhere in nature, but you sure do know it when you see it." More to the point, Milstein's fascination with MSR-type recordings stems from his observation that "song poem songs are, by their very nature, bastardized ditties conceived in sin—the anonymous rendezvous between the innocent tabloid and comic book readers and the assembly-line recording studio Lotharios.... The music borne of this con rank among the most *mutated* sounds ever conceived."

Adding to the ad hoc nature of the arrangements was the financial factor: session hires—the usual complement of guitarists, drummers, saxists, and bassists, haggard from the previous night's wedding gig—were usually paid not by the hour, but per song. Most labels had a staff or freelance composer who would concoct melodies and draw up lead sheets. In some cases, ambitious customers submitted written music with their lyrics, or a melodic demo tape (which would be transcribed by a copyist). Considering a typical session workload, quick sight-reading skills were essential for singers and players to keep the factory humming smoothly.

"They'd get three or four musicians in a studio and do 30 songs in an afternoon," explained Eskelin. "The tape just kept rolling." The process generated such calamities as "John F. Kennedy Was Called Away," "Elmer 21 Century Hop," "Cities' Hospital Patients," and "Do the Pig." Not all recordings were fully original; some companies used—and re-used—pre-recorded backing tracks over which singers would improvise melodies. "They would some-

New Talent Needed All the Time!
Typical song-poem come-ons

times recycle certain instrumental beds," Eskelin revealed, "but not as often as you'd think. They had a lot of repeat clients they didn't want to offend."

The universe of song-poem singers is a shooting-star-studded cosmos, populated by names such as Dick Kent, Ralph Lowe, Bobbi Blake, Gene Marshall, Kay Weaver, and Norm Burns. Many vocalists used pseudonyms, for two reasons: 1) to avert union sanctions, since these were invariably nonfederation sessions and 2) to avoid professional embarrassment. "This was the bargain basement of the music industry," Milstein pointed out. He's particularly fond of their often-improvised vocal stylings, which he terms "odd cadences, bizarre inflections, and inscrutable deliveries." The musical arrangements are as varied as the lyrics: Nashville-style Countrypolitan, light piano pop, thumping marches, and every conceivable rock hybrid—although the performances at times get a bit sloppy.

These waxings were released on a variety of labels besides MSR (named after founder Maury S. Rosen), including Preview, Film City, Sunrise, Columbine (all L.A.-based), Sterling (Boston), Air (Miami), and Globe (Nashville). Ardolino describes these relics as "wild music with cheap electronic keyboards and out-of-control drum machines; drunk—or *something*—session musicians; and singers who sound like they never saw the words until the recording light was on. This kind of set-up can produce innocently beautiful works of art."

However, not all art is created equal. The vast majority (according to Milstein, at least 90 percent) of song poems are banal and cliché-ridden—the music biz equivalent of public-access TV. But the more extreme examples of hallucinatory lunacy are compelling in their preposterousness. Because these writers are amateurs, their lyrics tend to be—"naïve," said Milstein, finishing my sentence. "In this naïveté is the opportunity for them to be surprising, in a way you don't get with professional writers." In addition, these production houses employed talented musicians and singers with sharp sight-reading abilities, who could grind these things out. "The collision of the amateur lyrics and this professional music, recorded at a ridiculously quick pace, is part of the fun," explained Milstein. Quality would often be sacrificed to quantity. "It was a rush job, but they were doing the best they could," Eskelin asserted. "I find it far more charming and honest than a lot of legit pop music."

Song poets tend to be a serious-minded breed, often rife with evangelical fervor. "The Saddest Story" (comped on *I'm Just the Other Woman*) admonishes against interracial coupling. The male vocal is tinged with remorse in this moralistic ballad:

> When a white girl marries a Negro, her sun of light goes down
> Glaring spots of sin on her gown
> White and black men stand aghast, while viewing this strange role
> They'll wreck themselves, they'll damage other souls
> Days and nights she felt black lips, pressed against her own
> On the fourth night her troubled soul let out a frightful groan
> But they must meet face to face, so I stagger through my days
> Far from God's love and grace
> The saddest story ever told

"Saddest Story" lyricist John Kelly, though sincere and well intentioned, if not exactly brimming with sense ("black lips"?), presents a relatively clear theme. In other examples, lyrical ambition obscures focus, as in Carrie and Bonnie Postell's impenetrable "Virgin Child of the Universe," perhaps an elegiac protest against out-of-wedlock procreation:

> As the day comes to an end, the Virgin Child of the Universe
> Is swept up in her fierce drive of sexual encounters
> Orgasmic explosion of love, enhances the child
> While a floodgate of love circles throughout Saturnate

The missing link of oaths of allegiance, allegiance to love
Elucidates the child's destiny, elucidates the child's destiny
How can she escape this missing link, this missing link of destiny
When is the turning point, when is the turning point
I say, when is the turning point?

The singer's phrasing, as you'll have no trouble imagining, is awkward, with wordy phrases folded, crunched, and mangled to align with standard musical intervals. This is one of the common perils of adapting tone-deaf prose to music. "And when the composers couldn't find a way to shoe-horn the lyrics to any kind of metrical structure," Milstein observed, "they'd tell the singer: 'spoken word passage.'"

"The Ballad of MacLeod, Best, and Banting," written by W. R. Kerr and found on *Music of America* (Hollywood Artists Record Company) pays tribute to the researchers who learned to control diabetes through insulin. The lyrics, set against a stumbling waltz rhythm, explain that in the 1920s, Dr. Banting "heard diabetes might be here to stay," and he felt the disease "wasn't fair." The song recounts their difficulty attracting funding, the late nights in the lab, the ongoing struggle to find a cure—a lot of history in a song that's over and out in two minutes and forty seconds.

Only nine compositions by Thomas J. Guygax, Sr., have surfaced, but his literary alchemy deserves special attention. His "At the Time" (issued on *The Makers of Smooth Music*) was recorded by the MSR Singers in a mid-tempo, pedal steel-inflected country style, sung by a drawling female vocalist. The lyrics read like Guygax racked up words on a pool table and scattered them with a clean break shot:

Although by the also to have differed with yearly and all known
    dearly
Throughout and among, we use preferred
By the also of having choicefully
Three times a day, as the average, we use of thee among of our
    foods
Along by our knowledge of the well-kept adage by the more of all
    helpin' with the all of coulds
Towards being among our masters and the also by our intelligence
    while the passin' of time

Decides our manners by the also collectively to being with the
  tense
Throughout and among, we use preferred
By the also of having choicefully
Three times a day

Rodd Eskelin was the Elvis, the Phil Spector, the Berry Gordy, the Joe Meek of song-poemdom. He joined MSR in the mid-1960s, strictly for the money. For almost a decade, recording under the names Rodd Keith, Rod Rogers, and other aliases, his commitment to the art was exceptional, and his output prodigious. Sadly, Ellery Eskelin barely knew his dad; his parents had separated when he was very young. In reconstructing his father's career by talking with people who'd worked with him, Eskelin emerged with an impression of Rodd as a musical genius who considered MSR-style "song-sharking" a creative form of prostitution. "He's remembered as a guy who could pick up just about any instrument and quickly learn to play it," Eskelin discovered. "He had a great ear for harmony. He knew he was capable of much greater things in music, but for him it was an easy way to make money and pursue an 'avant-garde lifestyle' in Hollywood." Rodd, according to Ellery's mom, used to play "far-out" records in his son's room, "stuff that she thought would scare me or something," he wrote in the liner notes for *I Died Today*. Among the "scary" recordings was the Stan Kenton Orchestra LP of Robert Graettinger's *City of Glass* suite (see chapter on Graettinger in this book).

"When I compiled *I Died Today*," Eskelin admits, "I was aware that many people are into this music sheerly for laugh value alone. John [Zorn] wanted me to include just those tracks that were the most bizarre or funny, but I stuck to my guns—and I'm glad I did. I wanted to portray not only Rodd but song-poem music as something more than a joke. The Carnage Press releases are phenomenal, but I think *I Died Today* has more scope, even as it is less extreme. Rodd's musical legacy was indeed bizarre, and as such I see no reason to avoid that issue. However, I see this music as needing nothing in the way of exaggerated mock—or real—ridicule. It stands on its own, and indeed is more powerful and multifaceted when allowed to simply speak for itself."

The song-poem industry is quintessentially American in its underpinning that "anybody can be a star." It's not necessarily true that money is the root of all drivel. Pure creative expression is often without profit motive; if your work happens to attract a commercial following, you can quit your day job and pursue a career in the arts. But it's possible that most—or at least many—song-poem authors aspired to fame and fortune, in that order. These Carole King

DIONNE ESKELIN/ ACTIVATED ARTISTS

Rodd Keith Eskelin gets high.

wannabes may have gambled on songwriting as a highway out of rural drudgery;
but though it never worked out that way, having a song on a "real" record
might have commanded a modicum of respect from family and neighbors.
Others were in it strictly for art's sake. "Some of the customers verge more
towards vanity interest," Milstein stressed. "All they really wanted was to have
their words set to music and recorded. They were content just to get a few
copies for whatever their purposes."

Milstein has been tracking down and interviewing song-poem clients for
his book. One surprising discovery has been that when records arrived in the
mail, many writers were displeased with the production treatment accorded
their work. "Testimonials from satisfied customers were always included with
the promotional followup mailing," Milstein noted, "but from my experience,
most people were disappointed with the results. Some were downright angry."
Nonetheless, there was much repeat business, particularly from songwriters
who overflowed to the brim with lyrical compulsion. Chicago-based James
Wilson, Jr., was one of the more prolific—and often cryptic—song poets. His
offerings include "Isotopic Spatial Series," "Astrouniverse," "Joy Spoken in
Rhumba," "Psychic Cigarette," and "Liblanders Cahoot."

Milstein discovered a marvelous little Martin Denny-ish confection entitled "Song of the Burmese Land," sensually crooned by Cara Stewart, with lyrics
attributed to "L. Hazlewood," as follows:

> Burmese land is like monkeyland
> A bothersome, troublesome place
> Burmese land is like monkeyland
> Listen, I'll tell you so
> The AFPFL government told the people
> When 10 o'clock strikes night
> Don't make a noise, don't be a nuisance
> Let the people sleep
> If a permit you should get, you can make a noise
> If anyone asks, you can say
> A permit we have got
> Always at this feast, always at that feast
> Chinese, Burmese, Indian
> Doon doon doon dang dang dang
> Boom boom boom bang bang bang
> A permit we have got
> Burmese land is like monkeyland
> A bothersome, troublesome place
> Burmese land is like monkeyland
> To the lunatic asylum I'm going

Speculation swirled that the composer was legendary eccentric Lee Hazlewood, author of "These Boots Are Made for Walking," "Some Velvet Morning," and other hits for Nancy Sinatra. Sonic Youth drummer Steve Shelley
sent Hazlewood a tape of "Burmese Land," and inquired if he had composed
the song. Hazlewood's reply: "Maybe in the third grade. Not since the fourth
grade would I have written anything so bad." He denied authorship.

Milstein has traced the song-poem tradition back to 1901, when amateur
lyrics were juxtaposed with a tune and printed on sheet music. "I've even seen
references to the phrase *song poems* from as early as 1907," he noted. The first
such players-for-hire recordings seemed to emerge in the early 1950s, though
Milstein has heard anecdotally about 78-rpm discs from the 1940s.

In recent years, the cost of recording technology has declined to the point
where even food-stamp recipients can afford rudimentary home recording
gear. They no longer have to pay studio professionals to produce their
songs—they can do it themselves at home, or with friends. And although, to
these log cabin Lerners and Loewes, home recording might appear a less

assured route to national fame, it still holds the prospect of notoriety on a local level.

Meanwhile, the song-poem industry hasn't died, continuing to this day on such labels as Columbine, Rainbow, HillTop, Magic Key, Edlee, and the Ramsey Kearney Song Service. "It seems to be thriving, business-wise," Milstein remarked, "even if the results are not terribly interesting."

It's arguable, however, that the golden age of song poems ended on Dec. 15, 1974, when Rodd Keith died tragically at age 37. "He either jumped or fell off an overpass on the Hollywood Freeway into oncoming traffic," Eskelin explained. "It was possibly psychedelic-related." MSR folded a few years later.

• 5 •

The
Cherry Sisters

THE FRUITS OF CLEAN LIVING

not only do things occasionally get worse before they get better—some are best when they start bad and stay that way. Witness the Cherry Sisters—great-great-great-grandmothers of outsider music.

It's 1896: no radio, no TV. Motion pictures as popular entertainment are still a few years away. Berliner (discs) and Edison (cylinders) are laying the groundwork for the record industry. No cars, no planes. The epicenter of public amusement is the theater. Itinerant performers—singers, jugglers, dog acts, pianists, minstrels, and seltzer-siphon buffoons—work the circuit known as "vaudeville." There are stars like Lillian Russell, Anna Held, Lily Langtry—*and then there are the Cherry Sisters.*

Effie, Addie, Ella, Jessie, and Elizabeth Cherry of Marion, Iowa, were by contemporary accounts the worst act in showbiz. Their program, *Something Good, Something Sad,* was so atrocious it triggered a perverse public hysteria: it played to sold-out New York houses for 10 weeks. It put impresario Oscar Hammerstein's career in turnaround and rescued his floundering Olympia Music Hall from the brink of bankruptcy.

November 16, 1996, marked the 100th anniversary of the sisters' "heralded" opening on the Great White Way. But no one bothered sending a card. The whole family had long since gone to the one place even FedEx doesn't deliver. The last of the sisters—all childless spinsters—died in 1944. (Jessie's twin, Alfred, died less than a year after birth; a sixth sister, Inez, died in her teens around 1882. Their brother Nathan went to Chicago in 1885 and was never heard from again.)

In the half-century between their first appearances on the Iowa stage and the final obituary, countless stories were written about the now all-but-forgotten Cherrys. Many of these articles, particularly those in major metropolitan publications, contained misinformation, contradictions, and exaggerations. But even with a discounted measure of hyperbole, the story of the Cherry Sisters remains fascinating.

Their rise to the bottom began with an innocent ambition: earning enough money to visit the 1893 Chicago World's Fair (and perhaps to find Nathan). The prairie-bred farmgirls burned the gaslamps beyond bedtime hammering together an evening's worth of hokey, moralistic one-acts, derivative ballads, and awkward ethnic dialect routines. With no prior experience before the footlights, they trod the boards before uncritical friends in their home village. Encouraged by neighborly applause and a modest profit, the Cherrys took their cockeyed show on the road. They barnstormed through such 19th-century cultural citadels as Ottumwa, Muscatine, and Osage.

Slogging across the marshes and municipal auditoriums of the Midwest, the sisters were so awful that audience heckling seemed too polite. Patrons instead conveyed their critical consensus by flinging peach pits and overripe

Left to right: Effie, Jessie, and Addie Cherry, ca. late 1890s

COURTESY STATE HISTORICAL SOCIETY OF IOWA

tomatoes. At a Creston, Iowa, town hall performance, theatergoers threw eggs and chased the girls offstage. To protect her siblings from one overly rambunctious crowd, Addie brandished a shotgun. A regional reviewer described them as "wretchedly poor, homely, ignorant, and without a trace of taste." Another testified that "Jessie narrowly escaped being pretty; the others were never in any such danger."

In Cedar Rapids, where the backwater Bernhardts rented Greene's Opera House for 50 bucks, their gawky revue got a noisy reception: patrons blew tin horns left over from the 1892 presidential campaign. The sisters mistook the raucousness for approval, and considered the evening a huge success. Next day they were horrified by a nasty review in the *Cedar Rapids Gazette,* which stated:

> "If some indefinable instinct of modesty could not have warned them that they were acting the part of monkeys, it does seem like the overshoes thrown at them would convey the idea.... Cigars, cigarettes, rubbers—everything was thrown at them, yet they stood there, awkwardly bowing their acknowledgments and singing on."

Their honor at stake, the sisters sued the city editor for slander. Justice was uncommonly swift. A theatrical trial was held the following day at Greene's, with the Cherrys mounting the stage for the benefit of the magistrate, offering their performance as testimony. Despite being confronted with evidence of the plaintiffs' far graver crime, the jury found the editor guilty—and sentenced him to marry one of the sisters. (All parties declined to enforce the ruling.)

From Davenport to Vinton, month after month, the onslaught of rotten eggs and pension-aged fruit continued. At one show, patrons of the arts pitched slabs of fresh liver at the hapless troupe; in Dubuque, they were greeted by "a volley of turnips." Singing for your supper is one thing; having it hurled at you overhand is another. Finally, a compassionate promoter erected a wire-mesh screen between players and audience.

The sisters—virtuous ladies whose lips never tasted wine (they once refused to speak to their piano player for a week because he said "damn")—suspected that the unruly mob behavior had been instigated by stage managers whose (imagined) advances they'd rebuffed. Everywhere they went it rained cabbages, potatoes, rutabagas—any local crop surplus. One rowdy spectator heaved an old tin wash boiler onstage.

Then, things got ugly.

In February 1898, following a typical debacle in western Iowa, *Odebolt Chronicle* editor William Hamilton wrote:

When the curtain went up ... [t]he audience saw three creatures surpassing the witches in Macbeth in general hideousness ... Their long, skinny arms, equipped with talons at the extremities, swung mechanically, and anon were waved frantically at the suffering audience. The mouths of their rancid features opened like caverns, and sounds like the wailing of damned souls issued therefrom. They pranced around the stage ... strange creatures with painted features and hideous mien. Effie is spavined, Addie is knock-kneed and string-halt, and Jessie, the only one who showed her stockings, has legs without calves, as classic in their outlines as the curves of a broom handle.

Tomaters and warshbuckets they could deal with, but this—*this*—clearly crossed the line. Two weeks later, when the *Des Moines Leader* reprinted this passage, the Cherrys sued for libel.

In a precedent-setting 1899 decision (after what legal documents disclose was a very colorful trial), the suit was dismissed, the court affirming a newspaper's right to criticize public performers to the point of rhetorical overstatement. In 1901, the Iowa Supreme Court upheld *Cherry v. Des Moines Leader,* noting: "If there ever was a case justifying ridicule and sarcasm ... it is the one now before us.... [T]he performance given by the [sisters] was not only childish, but ridiculous in the extreme. A dramatic critic should be allowed considerable license in such a case."

Backtrack to 1896: While the Cherrys were quickening their reflexes dodging several of the major food groups, New York theater impresario Oscar Hammerstein had major migraines. His new "uptown" Olympia Music Hall at Broadway and 44th had staged a series of big-name showcases—which flopped. The venue, surrounded by smelly stables and a blacksmith forge, was inconveniently located; the theater district was then a half-mile away at Herald Square.

A story in the *Morning World* about the Cherrys, then touring the Midwest, caught Hammerstein's eye. They were described as "so grim and so serious that audiences were rolling in the aisles with laughter." Oscar mulled the possibilities. "I've been putting on the best talent, and it hasn't gone over," he acknowledged. "I'm going to try the worst." He dispatched stage manager Al Aarons to lasso the Cherrys (minus Ella, who wisely retired) and shepherd them east under contract.

Tomato futures skyrocketed.

On November 16, *Something Good, Something Sad* opened at the Olympia. According to one unattributed press account, "the four grim-faced [sisters] sidled out on the stage in hand-made red calico dresses and began their act."

Elizabeth played piano and Jessie slammed a huge bass drum while the sisters
sang to a purloined popular melody:

Cherries ripe, Boom-de-ay!
Cherries red, Boom-de-ay!
The Cherry sisters
Have come to stay!

Next, Jessie, draped in an American flag, sang an original, patriotic number
entitled "Fair Columbia." Lizzie followed with what must have been a jaw-
dropping version of a traditional Irish ballad—sung with a Midwestern twang.
In Effie's vocal centerpiece, "The Gipsy's Warning," Jessie portrayed a barefoot
flower maiden falling prey to a swashbuckling Lothario, played by Addie. Later
in the evening, a "living sculpture" tableau entitled "Clinging to the Cross"
featured Jessie suspended from a giant crucifix.

The first-night reviews were merciless. "It was awful," claimed the *World*.
The *New York Times* critic sneered, "All
too obviously they were products of the
barnyard and the kitchen. None of them
had showed a sign of nervousness, none
a trace of ability for their chosen work."
Another press witness, cited in a 1936
New York World–Telegram obit for Elizabeth, remarked, "A locksmith with a
strong, rasping file could earn ready
wages taking the kinks out of Lizzie's
voice."

According to a 1944 *World–Telegram*
article published upon Effie's death, the
Cherrys' Manhattan debut had been
greeted with "a stock of tomatoes, cabbages, and onions, [and] a great racket of
screeches, yowls, hoorahs, and catcalls."
Hammerstein assured his headliners
that the barrage was orchestrated by
jealous rival stars, "who hire people to
throw things at girls like you." (In fact,
the owner had allegedly recruited his
sons, Arthur and Will, to incite the
"truck-garden bouquets.") "Your talent is
so great," he explained, "that you can

[50]

expect fruit and vegetables to be thrown at every performance." Behind the now–de rigueur fishnet the Cherrys played to packed houses for two months, by some reports earning upward of a grand per week. It saved Hammerstein's hide—and his theater. Following their run at the Olympia, the gutsy quartet played an additional two weeks at Proctor's 23rd Street Theater, to continued standing-room-only houses.

Despite their celebrity, the schoolmarmish Cherrys rejected New York's glamorous nightlife. "We were invited to parties by Lillian Russell, Diamond Jim Brady, John L. Sullivan, and others," they told "Voice of Broadway" columnist Louis Sobol, "but we never accepted." On most evenings after the pulp-splattered curtain came down, the ladies took dinner at the Holland House, then went straight to bed. Occasionally they'd enjoy horse-drawn buggy rides through Central Park, but not after dusk. "We always wanted to see Coney Island," they told Sobol, "but we did not want to see women in bathing suits."

The triumphant Cherry Sisters embarked on a United States–Canada tour, allegedly drawing sell-out crowds at most engagements. Having achieved notoriety in New York, their reputation preceded them at every whistlestop. In Marshalltown, Iowa, a theater sign proclaimed:

IOWA'S FAMOUS SONGBIRDS
BAD EGGS, BLACK POWDER AND
TEN-GAUGE GUNS BARRED

Audiences hooted, howled, and heaved, but the gals persevered, chalking it up to jealous competitors.

When Jessie, the youngest, died in 1903 of typhoid fever, the sisters quit the circuit and retired to their Iowa farm. According to some claims, they'd amassed a fortune estimated at $200,000. The *American Weekly* observed that despite seven years of touring, "They began as the four worst professional actresses in the world and ended without improving one iota." Considering the barrage of organic shrapnel they'd endured, particularly before the netting went up, it was a miracle that none were seriously injured. One journalist attributed this to "nervous marksmanship on one side and amazing agility on the other."

The sisters never married. In fact, they boasted of never having been kissed. ("We are too devoted to each other to consider matrimony and we could never stand the shock of being dictated to by a man.")

A few years after their retirement, they were once again destitute. They eventually lost the farm and moved to Cedar Rapids, where they opened a bakery. Cherry pie, naturally, was a specialty. A local lad fondly recalled seeing a sign in the window: "Fresh Bread and Bull Pups for Sale."

Sadly, if understandably, the Cherrys were never invited to cut commercial recordings. However, Jessie cut a demo disc of her show-stopping "Fair Columbia." A few years after her death, a brief item appeared in an Iowa paper noting that the surviving sibs were trying to buy the disc from its new owner so they could hear their dear, dead sister's voice. Problem was, they couldn't afford the asking price of $100. (The record's current whereabouts are unknown. I will pay a four-digit bounty for the relic, in any condition.)

Effie ran for mayor of Cedar Rapids in 1924 and 1926, losing both times. Her William Jennings Bryanesque platform (anti-tobacco and no-liquor; longer skirts, longer hair, and longer consciences for women; and a seven o'clock curfew for minors) was decidedly out of step with the Roaring Twenties, even in the flat earth precincts of Iowa.

EFFIE CHERRY
Candidate for Mayor
I Stand For
Pure Drinking Water, Clean Alleys, Curfew, Economy in all Departments, Better Organized Police Force
CLEAN CITY·MAYOR

COURTESY STATE HISTORICAL SOCIETY OF IOWA

From time to time, the surviving Cherrys attempted comebacks, but even first-rank travesties lose their luster. At a Chicago theater in 1913, first-night receipts were seven dollars. Second-night gate figures improved—to 11 dollars. (The tally did not include the value of airborne produce.) The sisters blamed the dismal turnout on "lack of publicity." In 1935, the proprietor of a New York nostalgia venue called the Gay Nineties brought Addie and Effie back to town with much fanfare—but their compelling, negative charisma had evaporated. The *American Weekly* reported, "Some of the club's cash customers merely yawned and ordered the waiter to bring two more, quick. Others wanted to know if this was supposed to be funny, while many simply moaned and went out." The pathetic sight of two frumpy hags in high-button shoes trying to entertain jaded patrons in a New York nightclub was too embarrassing to endure.

Addie died in 1942, and Effie—the last of the line—two years later, forever sparing the world's gene pool. They never revealed their ages, but both were estimated octogenarians. Addie and Effie are buried in Linwood Cemetery, Cedar Rapids; the gravesites of Ella and Lizzie can be viewed at Oak Shade Cemetery, in Marion.

The *World–Telegram*'s Burton Rascoe, in an August 12, 1944, obituary, sensed an element of martyrdom in their Sisyphean saga. Rascoe lamented that the Cherry family "summed up in themselves, and took the blame for, all the bad acting in the world.... They were the targets for abuse that should have been more equitably distributed."

How could anyone—let alone an entire sibling clan—be so blind to such overwhelming public derision?

This question was addressed by journalist Jack El-Hai in "The Mystery of the Cherry Sisters," published in the Summer 1996 issue of *Tractor,* an Iowa arts and culture 'zine. El-Hai began dogging the Cherrys' legacy in 1993, and they sustained his fascination. He visited Cedar Rapids, scoured the archives in Iowa City, and made a pilgrimage to Marion. He read Effie's unpublished novel ("It's terrible," he said in a phone interview) and her unlikely-to-be-a-major-motion-picture memoirs ("Not exactly gripping"). He even poked around Chicago for traces of the elusive brother Nathan, to no avail.

HERALD TRIBUNE, TUESDAY, OCTO

Addie Cherry, of Cherry Sisters Famed for Ineptness, Dies at 83

Addie Cherry (right) with her sister Effie, the survivor, from a photograph taken during the height of their stage career

Was Member of Country-Girl Troupe That Swept to National Popularity on a Tide of Derisive Press Reviews and Audience Catcalls

CEDAR RAPIDS, Iowa, Oct. 26 (*A*)—Addie Cherry, of the Cherry Sisters theatrical troupe which won fame almost fifty years ago because their performances were so inept and Kansas. Whether they drew tears or over-aged vegetables depended on the primitiveness of their audience. The vegetables they always explained by blaming theater

The title of El-Hai's article was deliberately provocative. He admitted there were many mysteries about the sisters, but one superseded all others: "Were the Cherrys conscious of their own badness, and did they try to be bad in order to please their audiences?"

After a thorough study of the sisters' stern moral underpinnings, El-Hai grew convinced there was method to their badness. They were a "strange mixture of Puritanism and exhibitionism," he observed. Avery Hale, in a December 1944 remembrance in *Coronet* magazine, wrote that the Cherrys often attended cliché-ridden, off-circuit productions at Greene's Opera House in their formative years. They were "deeply impressed" by these programs, in which "virtue was usually melodramatically triumphant and retribution caught up with the silk-hatted villain just before the last-act curtain." If America was to overcome the forces of darkness, the Cherrys felt obliged to carry the lantern.

"They hated women performers who made the most of sex appeal," El-Hai explained, "especially Mae West, who included a disparaging line about the sisters in one of her films." When it came to morality, Effie, in particular, couldn't get off the soapbox. "Woman has been degraded by nudity on the stage today," she railed in 1934. "I'd clean up all the filthy literature and periodicals.... It is woman's place to wage war against sin which has infested us for so long." She thought ladies shouldn't smoke in public because "it loses their charm [sic] and makes them appear too masculine." (In the sisters' heyday, Jessie—pre-dating anti-tobacco hysteria by a century—had sung a cautionary tale of lost virtue entitled "My First Cigar.") Effie's mayoral platform advocated civic cleanliness, ankle-length skirts, and "more and bigger policemen." The Cherrys waged a lifelong campaign against decadence, and the stage gave them an opportunity, El-Hai said, "to become the theater's primary exponents of decency."

Make no mistake—the Cherrys were as talent-free as critics insisted, and oblivious to that fact at the dawn of their careers. "They couldn't have been good if they tried," El-Hai believes. But having captured the public's attention as "The World's Worst Sister Act" (as they were billed in St. Louis), they weren't about to forsake fame to protect the family name. The rewards—headlines, packed halls, and money—were too great to pass up, even at the cost of public humiliation. For the sisters, success was measured in numbers. A 1936 quote from Effie, then appearing with Addie at an Iowa radio station barn dance, bears scrutiny. Asked by a broadcaster if their act was any good, Effie retorted, "Good? There's 2,500 people out there, isn't there? Well, that's more than [comedienne] Ina Claire drew in this same theater a while back—and she's good, isn't she?" As for the relentless caricature in the press, the sisters gathered bad reviews like so many desiccated rose petals. "They viewed being bad as a means to an end," El-Hai figured, "as a way to keep themselves before audiences so they could uphold theatrical decency."

However, there's a curious paradox in all this. While the Cherrys were cultural throwbacks, embodying the notion of "old-fashioned," clinging steadfastly to fading 19th-century Victorian values—particularly about women—at the dawn of the 20th century, yet, in a mythic way, they were pioneering protofeminists.

The five sisters inherited the family farm following the deaths of their parents and the disappearance of their only brother. Rather than seek security in marriage or traditional ladylike pursuits, the girls chose to support themselves by maintaining a large farm, which was exhaustive work. They were roughhewn frontier women, with masculine attributes. They wore men's clothing, particularly overalls, while going about their farm chores and to market. Ella and Addie were handy with guns.

When the Cherrys took their show on the road, they oversaw their own business affairs (albeit badly). Effie and Addie were anything but demure; they never shied from getting in someone's face to save their own. The sisters engaged in combative behavior, and in one account (perhaps apocryphal), they punched out an editor.

The sisters had strong convictions. They were outspoken, rather than passive wallflowers. Effie ran for public office twice—in an age when few women entered the political arena. Fiercely self-reliant, none of the sisters married; they disdained the conventional family roles of wives and mothers. They didn't trust men, didn't need a man to tell them what to do. They looked after themselves and each other.

Were they more sophisticated than they let on? Did these hayseeds with pigslop under their fingernails parlay ineptitude into a long-term publicity stunt?

The sisters never blinked; they played greenhorns to the hilt, on stage and off. "I can't understand why we're persecuted as we are," remarked Addie. "Why, prominent men have raised their hats when passing our house in Cedar Rapids on the streetcar."

"Over the years," El-Hai came to realize, "a mythology grew up around them—about how bad they were, what was thrown at them, why they persevered. It's almost like they've become an urban legend."

A true verdict on their motivations may never be possible. "Either the Cherry Sisters are completely sincere and take themselves seriously," said the *Des Moines Register*, "or they are the most accomplished actresses the world has ever known."

• 7 •

Jandek

THE GREAT DISCONNECT

"Back when college radio was fun, there were two main camps:
those who thought that Jandek was a true genius on the level
of Monk or [Hasil] Adkins, and those who thought that we were
just looking for something so totally obscure, so unlistenable,
that we would just out-hip everybody.

"[Years later]...Jandek is still here...And his detractors,
well, they all work for Sony now, don't they?"

—C. KOON, *YET ANOTHER FANZINE*

how to describe the music of Jandek? Like most amateur rock critics,
start by comparing him to the Beatles. Then strip away melody, catchy
hooks, rhythm, and harmony. Next toss out vocal and instrumental ability,
along with any trace of human feeling other than dull, lingering pain.

Aside from these deficiencies, he's *exactly* like the Fab Four. Or maybe the
Velvet Underground after taxes.

Jandek, alone with a guitar and a microphone, sounds like a muttering
sleepwalker aimlessly plucking amplified bicycle spokes. His music is dark
and gloomy, but it won't make you sad—it will make you tense and uncomfortable. Here is the Ultimate Disconnect. You'll love it or hate it—and for
every one of the former, there are one *million* of the latter.

He accompanies himself on acoustic or electric guitar. But for the incoher-
ence of his zombielike strumming, Jandek's hands might as well be brushing
accidentally against the strings. His occasional wheezing harmonica approxi-

mates early Dylan having an asthma attack. Sometimes Jandek is backed by a drummer who seems unfamiliar with the kit, and who pounds away relentlessly with no ground beat. It's purgative.

OK—let's shuck the understatement. The above is a too-roseate portrait of Jandek's cave-dweller primitivism. Imagine a microphone cabled down to a month-old tomb capturing the subterranean munch of maggots nibbling a decaying corpse, counterpointed by the agonized howls of a departed soul desperate to escape tortuous decomposition and eternal boredom.

Cover of Jandek LP *Six and Six*

That's Burt Bacharach compared to Jandek. What Garth did for country, Jandek could do for suicide hotlines.

Jandek is a recluse named Sterling R. Smith, and he's holed up somewhere near Houston, Texas. (Please don't call the one in the Houston phone book—wrong guy.) Since 1978 Smith has issued 28 full-length albums, mostly on 12-inch vinyl. No 7- or 12-inch singles, no remixes, cassettes, MP3s, or videos. A few of his cryptic album titles: *Staring at the Cellophane, Telegraph Melts, Blue Corpse, Chair Beside a Window.* He didn't begin issuing CDs until the early 1990s.

A sampling of his song titles: "Painted My Teeth," "Twelve Minutes Since February 32'nd" [sic], and "Janitor's Dead."

His album covers reflect visual entropy: the front usually sports an out-of-focus, black-and-white snapshot of Jandek's expressionless face, or maybe a guitar or a piece of furniture; the text-only back covers list song titles, timings, and the label mailing address, but are otherwise devoid of liner notes, personnel, lyrics, or useful clues. Jandek has never issued a press kit and has never performed in public. He rejects all requests for interviews. They found the Unabomber, but Jandek remains at large.

Seth Tisue, curator of a Jandek Web site, noted, "His consistency in this regard far surpasses that of other legendary reclusives such as Thomas Pynchon and J. D. Salinger." Jandek's records rarely turn up in stores—even second-hand shops. Smith is pouring a lot of money into a deep dark hole. (If you'd like to pour in some of yours, write Corwood Industries, PO Box 15375, Houston, TX, 77220. Surprise!—he doesn't have a distributor.)

In 1978, Smith released his debut album, an LP entitled *Ready for the House,* recorded under the name "The Units." He adopted the "Jandek" moniker on his second album after discovering a band called the Units with whom he did not wish to be associated.

Richie Unterberger, in *Unknown Legends of Rock 'n' Roll*, quoted a paragraph of mine about Jandek. Let me return the favor. Unterberger wrote:

> When it comes to idiot savants with mystique, no one can beat Jandek ... who has self-released over two dozen albums featuring spooky, slightly demented stream-of-consciousness rambling and guitar playing which rarely strays from set notes and chords, none of which pick out anything close to a melody. His voice can range from a hushed whisper to a Janovian primal scream; unsettlingly, he hardly ever mines the wide territory between those extremes. Sometimes the guitar is acoustic, like a deathbed Neil Young; sometimes he sounds like the 13-year-old who's just gotten his first electric for his Bar Mitzvah.... The albums are issued in plain sleeves with no liner notes, and enigmatic cover photos with all the attention to framing and focus of the do-it-yourself stalls at Woolworth's.

On the positive side, Jandek is *not* pretentious. But he's not unpretentious. Neither adjective applies, although Kurt Cobain told *Spin* in 1993 that "only pretentious people like his music."

Jandek is an authentic human satellite orbiting in a chilly weightless dimension millions of miles from earth. And let's concede this: Jandek's music is *not derivative*. He seems to be a recording artist with *no* discernible influences.

Some would call this "genius." And have. Forced Exposure's on-line catalog refers to this musical question mark's "fractured, internalized song genius."

But such acclaim is rare. More common are assessments such the following post from a Guided by Voices Internet chat list. A correspondent we'll call "Glenn" ("I'd prefer that you not use my real name. I don't want him trying to get ahold of me!") wrote, "Jandek's music isn't the cool kind of lo-fi typical of GbV, the 'we-could-do-better-but-we-like-it-sloppy' school. It's just bad musicianship and bad recording. In my opinion, there's nothing cool about it. It's just pathetic."

The man understates the sheer horror of a Jandek record. 99.999997 percent of all sentient life on the planet could not listen to three Jandek tunes from start to finish.

Did someone say "rock and roll"? Jandek's neither "rock" nor "roll." He's not even "and."

.   .   .

In 1980, while working for a syndicated radio production studio called Thirsty Ear, I was given a copy of *Ready for the House* by coworker Keith Altomare. Knowing my predilection for odd sonics, Altomare winked, "I think you'll find this *very* unusual."

At home I dropped the needle on the first track, "Naked in the Afternoon." It was frightening. Accompanied by what sounded like stiff fingers strumming an out-of-tune tennis racket, a creepy, monotonous voice croaked:

> I got a vision, a teenage daughter
> Who's growin' up naked in the afternoon
> I know a brother close to his mother
> Who stays up late in the evening time
> I keep repeating, it takes a beating
> To grow up naked in the afternoon

The melody went nowhere. There was no rhythm or chord structure. No dynamics, no particular focus. The "song"—if that's what it was—just kinda meandered in low gear like a beat-up Ford without a driver.

I advanced to the second track, "First You Think Your Fortune's Lovely." Same non-story. Not just the same characteristics—except for the lyrics, it was the same, uh … *song*. Ditto track three. Ditto all the way to the end of the album, where quasi-relief arrived on the final track. "European Jewel (Incomplete)" featured *electric* guitar instead of acoustic, and a semblance of chordal tuning. Not much, granted, and the song still didn't make much sense or develop into an identifiable framework. Standout line: "There's bugs in my brain / I can't feel any pain." The parenthetical "Incomplete" refers to the track cutting off in mid-verse, as if the deck ran out of tape.

Ready for the House sounded like an album-length, real-time chronicle of a listless, beer-numbed, trailer-park teen picking scabs, mumbling to himself and accidentally stumbling over his guitar.

Who wouldn't be intrigued?

The LP wasn't just unlistenable—it was unashamedly repellent. And yet, unlike much of what passes for anti-music in some precincts of downtown New York, *Ready for the House* lacked attitude. It was devoid of artistic ambition; its repugnance was organic, naturalistic. The record jacket carried no liner notes, photos, or personnel; it disclosed nothing but song titles, track duration, and an address: Corwood Industries at a Houston post office box.

My antennae were atwitter. Who would release such a catastrophe? And why? What was "Corwood Industries"? A multinational run by a CEO with a retarded son who made home recordings? Did doting papa press this album without commercial intent as a simple gesture of paternal devotion?

I wrote to Corwood:

Oct 20, 1980
To Whom:
A friend passed along a copy of *Ready for the House*. I've listened to it three times [I lied], and I've concluded it is one of the most frightening albums I've ever heard. It is horribly grotesque. I've run out of adjectives to describe the shock of this record.

Can you give me any information? Who's on it? It could be the worst record ever released, but somebody went to a lot of trouble putting it together and I want to know why. I am mystified.

It could also be the greatest record ever released. I can't figure it out, but every time I place it on the turntable, it's like stepping into the Twilight Zone. Can you help?

I gave my address and phone number.

Two weeks later, Sterling Smith called. He rambled in a halting monotone, his speech punctuated by *aposiopesis* (the sudden breaking off in mid-sentence as if the speaker is unwilling or unable to continue). I asked questions; he gave oblique answers. He wouldn't explain what he did for a living. He'd pressed one thousand copies of *Ready for the House*—and sold two. He'd recorded enough material for ten albums and hoped to release them all. He'd written seven novels, but after they'd been rejected by New York publishers, he'd burned the manuscripts. He had no friends, but didn't seem concerned.

Great. A deranged loner had my phone number and home address.

I stressed how "unique" I found his music. "There's nothing like it—anywhere," I offered, truthfully.

"Do you know stores that will carry my records?" he inquired. "I need to move them." We chatted for about 15 minutes, and I chose my words carefully, mindful that New Jersey was a four-hour flight from Houston. The conversation was disjointed. Smith had an Etch-A-Sketch mind: one jostling distraction and his thoughts were wiped clean, the next sentence a non sequitur.

He was grateful for my interest and shipped me 25 copies of *Ready for the House*, which I distributed to my WFMU colleagues as Christmas gifts. One staffer, Jim Pansulla, used two sealed copies as a rump rest over the torn driver's seat in his VW Beetle for five years. (They eventually warped, but Jim never fell though.)

Smith and I exchanged a few letters, and he called occasionally. His confidence was bolstered by my "encouragement" and he promised more releases, which began to arrive in 25-count boxes. He once referred to me as his "mentor" for suggesting that he persevere despite public indifference.

One lengthy handwritten missive from December 1982 reveals more about Smith's modus operandi than perhaps any existing document. I had inquired about his switch on subsequent albums from acoustic guitar to electric, the occasional use of drums, and the mysterious emergence on several tracks of a mournful girl singer, presumably named Nancy (judging from such titles as "Nancy Sings"). A few excerpts:

> I was glad to receive your letter. I had been thinking of you just that morning and why I hadn't heard from you. You're my mainstay from the beginning.
>
> Nancy was Nancy [last name withheld], a southern Ohio cosmopolitan hillbilly type who ran across my path one day and I asked her to sing what I had written as I played the guitar. There were no notes or anything and she just picked up the paper with words and sang and I played guitar as simple as that! ... She's featured in many future cuts, mostly electric. The cut "No Break" on side 2 features her sister Pat [last name withheld] on vocals, myself on elec guitar and Nancy in a very unaggressive drum stint.
>
> [Other tracks feature] myself on 6 string elec guitar + vocals, John [name withheld] on base [sic] and John "Poe" on drums. They were around the house "Poe" lived there next door. I asked them to sit in. I don't believe "Poe" ever played drums before. I was so impressed. I couldn't think of another drummer so absolute except maybe Ginger Baker from Cream....
>
> There is a multitude of further electric composition. With a myriad (maybe 12) other performers. Also cuts on entire sides of myself overdubbing base, 6 string, vocals and drums all performed by myself. Thanks to your urgency prompting, you will be receiving them perhaps as early as february [sic]....

In follow-up correspondence, Smith's ingenuous marketing campaign persisted: "Send me some addresses of record stores ... that deal in my music," one of his notes implored, "and I'll ship them free boxes of my recordings. I need to move them." I received cartons of each new release up to the sixth or seventh.

Eventually we lost contact. I figured the mothership had returned to fetch the expedition.

New releases, however, arrived with admirable regularity at the radio station. In 1986, WFMU, WKCR, WFDU, and WSIA coordinated a late-night "Jandek Across America" conspiracy. From 1:15 A.M. to 2:00 A.M. the man's desolate murmuring seeped across the New York City noncommercial spectrum, programmed independently on each station.

COURTESY CORWOOD INDUSTRIES

Not playing with a full Jandek—typical LP covers: *Your Turn to Fall* (left) and *Staring at the Cellophane* (right). Sorry, no additional information available—*ever.*

He's been covered at least twice: by Charalambides, who recorded "Variant" (from the Corwood album *Blue Corpse*) on the compilation *Drilling the Curve* (Fleece Records); and by Dump, a one-man studio project of Yo La Tengo bassist James McNew, who released a 7-inch single of "License to Kill" (from *The Living End*) on 18 Wheeler Records. (On another CD, McNew covered the Shaggs.) At this writing, Jandek junkie Eric Schlittler of Pennsylvania is soliciting submissions for a tribute album.

By the early 1990s Jandek's recorded output rivaled Keith Jarrett's and John Zorn's in terms of petroleum-derivative disc manufacture. But only in those terms. The man has continued to release about an album a year, all of which escape critical notice. Each, to quote journalist and fan Byron Coley, "blows around the country like an old dead leaf painted purple."

Jandek's art has evolved. He's begun to display greater dynamics in the songs—although nothing yet approaches accessible pop music. His cadaverous crooning intones monotonously over guitar notes spattered Jackson Pollock–like on the musical canvas. Occasionally something approximating a chord miraculously resonates. The works seem meaningless in and of themselves, but like any form of expression can accommodate a sympathetic listener's own perceived significance.

Jandek uses no studio gimmickry—unless you consider occasionally bumping the mic stand an inspired technical gesture. He pops his "P's" and his "S's" sibilate. The voice-guitar mix often obscures the lyrics, even when he's playing softly.

The man has one undeniable quality: *identity*. If record stores would carry Jandek product, they could assign him his own bin-card: "Musica Incognita." But record stores *don't* carry his albums, so he offers ridiculous quantity discounts— $25 for a box of 25 LPs, or $80 for a carton of 20 CDs. He needs to move them.

Glenn (the GbV chat room correspondent) recounted: "My friend Max sent him a letter, and what does he get in return but a box of 50 Jandek albums. Max continued the correspondence and started getting more and more records shipped to him, Smith insisting that he not sell them but give them away. After a while, songs started to appear on the records about Max ('So Fly, Max') and his family members (the names of Max's sisters appeared in songs). We finally decided this guy was too weird, and Max wrote to tell him to please stop sending albums.

"I really don't know why anybody would want to listen to these," Glenn remarked. "They just make me feel unhappy and kind of creeped-out."

"One time," recalled McNew, "I bought three or four used CDs at a store in Boulder, and the clerk flipped through the titles I selected. When he saw the used copy of Jandek's *Glad to Get Away*, he shuddered, as though I'd slipped an autopsy photo in there." But McNew feels Jandek must be considered in relative terms. "If Jandek is horrible, miserable noise," he posits, "then what are Jewel or Dave Matthews?"

As evidenced by the ambitious nature of his Web site, Seth Tisue obviously registers deep devotion to Jandek. I requested comment from Tisue in February 1999. And in March. Again in April. And once more in late June. Seth finally replied.

Hi ... many apologies for not responding to your E-mails.
I have no good excuse.

His next paragraph provided one:

I'm sure I've listened to every [Jandek] LP at least a dozen times, and I've probably listened to my favorite, Blue Corpse, 100+ times easy.

At least I knew what Tisue had been doing for the past four-and-a-half months. In reply to my contention that I found Jandek's minimalist driftage "unlistenable," Tisue wrote:

I don't find Jandek unlistenable at all! I'm as susceptible to the non-musical aspects of the Jandek Mystique as anybody, but honestly, if I didn't really love the records themselves and not just the concept, I wouldn't do the site. I find Jandek especially suited for nighttime highway driving and for Walkman accompaniment to long walks through city or country.

When Richie Unterberger wrote Jandek in 1986 to request an interview, our mystery alien replied, "Questions etc. can't be arranged. Also, we think your article will be better without them. At least we hope so. Anything else, just ask."

Banking on my history with the guy, I requested an interview for this book via mail in 1998. A month later a package arrived from the familiar Houston POB. It contained two CDs—1994's *Glad to Get Away*, and his then-latest, *New Town*. No surprises in the packaging—artless, inelegant, uninformative. However, *Glad to Get Away* was ... uh ... wet. A brownish muck oozed within the shrink-wrap—not a drop escaped—as if the fluid had been injected at the manufacturing stage. I had to disassemble the jewel case and run the whole mess under a faucet. The parts felt slimy. The bubble-pack shipper included an envelope with a handwritten letter from Jandek—or rather, from his collective self:

You'll not be forgotten—ever...
The story must be crafted from what you have and know from the music. We cannot provide interviews or other exchanges of information outside of the releases at present. It's probable that your crafted story would be more interesting than any other. Intrigue goes a long way sometimes.
Please stay in touch.
Your friends at Corwood

The man continues to live with the curtains drawn and the phone off the hook. I gave the albums a spin. Same untethered spookiness. One song on *Glad to Get Away* began with the line: "Hey mister, can you tell me, is that a knife stuck in your face?"

Good night. At least he doesn't have my new home address.

Listeners aren't the only ones confounded by the Houston outsider. Jandek himself seems a bit unsure of his niche in the grander scheme of things, as evidenced by the lyrics of "Don't Know If I Care" (from *Later On*, 1981):

Oh Lord, help me to understand
What's going on in this world
I'll be (unintelligible) go different way
(unintelligible) to care
I don't know if I care

I don't know what's happening
Oh Lord help me to understand

(N.B. Indecipherability is common with Jandek lyrics.)

Seventeen years later, enlightenment remained every bit as elusive. From "Look at It" (*New Town*, 1998):

I just want to be real
And if this life ends soon
I'm done
Crash crash crash crash

Despite Jandek's reclusiveness and determination to avoid the press, he was stalked by journalist Katy Vine of *Texas Monthly*, who recounted her prowls around Houston in the August 1999 issue. Following various leads, Vine eventually found—and shared beers with—a gentleman who, she wrote, "looked like a late-thirties version of the youth on the record covers." She discovered him living "in one of the city's nicer neighborhoods," and described him as "neatly dressed in a long-sleeved white shirt with beautiful cufflinks, black pants, a black tie, and black shoes." But this fellow, who was obviously familiar with Jandek and Corwood, never outright admitted to being Jandek. He seemed extremely uncomfortable with Vine's inquiries, and spoke about the shadowy singer only in the third person. He insisted that *Texas Monthly* not publish his real name, occupation, or whereabouts; prohibited picture-taking and tape-recording; and extracted a promise, said Vine, that there wouldn't be "any physical evidence of our meeting." Over brews at an "upscale bar," they mostly talked about snap beans, milk allergies, and a North Texas town where all the residents have no cavities. His comments about the recordings were ... Jandekian. When Vine asked if he wanted people to "get" his music, he replied, "There's nothing to get."

After finishing their second round, he picked up the tab, and walked Vine to her car. She said he "stress[ed] that even though he had a nice time, he didn't want to be contacted in person by a fan or a journalist or anybody about Jandek ever again."

I received one more handwritten note from Corwood, explaining the seven incinerated novels [ellipses in original]:

Regarding the book burnings ... our experience living in lower Manhattan was ... necessary. Of course, we took the printed matter to the countryside for an unfettered, proper cremation. Stirred into ashes into the ground.

SONGS IN THE KEY OF Z

As for Random House ... they called me in ... twice ... I got tired of waiting two weeks and demanded the manuscripts. The countryside dirt was
hungry.

You have to admire the man's determination and his sincere intent. He's loyal
to his muse. You don't release over two dozen full-length albums—for almost
no audience—without a strong artistic commitment. Jandek is the musical
equivalent of a tree that's fallen in the forest—28 times.

Beyond any musical impact, his ultimate mission could be to test the mortal limits of patience, tolerance, and understanding. Perhaps he's the Messiah,
dispatched to Earth as an outsider musician, giving the human race one last
chance to accept the unacceptable, to embrace that which is infinitely difficult
to embrace.

If so, by failing to fully grasp his aesthetic, I may have forsaken salvation.
Come Armageddon, while Jandek ascends with his disciples to a place where
harps strum gently all day, I will descend to a region where mighty loudspeakers pipe in nothing but Jandek records for eternity.

Until then, maybe I can get a job at Sony.

·3·

Daniel Johnston

CASPER 1, SATAN 0

"**I**'ve been treated cruelly at times because people think I'm a dork," he declares without rancor.

Texas-based singer/songwriter Daniel Johnston is huggably pudgy, emotionally unstable, and disarmingly gnomelike. Within his oversized, adolescent frame, incongruously iced with gray hair, a history of unpredictable volatility coexists with prolific creativity in music and the visual arts.

PHOTO BY RON ENGLISH

No mere eccentric, Daniel has long been plagued by psychosis and beset with demons. He's been in and out of mental institutions since the mid-1980s. His prodigious daily intake of Coca-Cola and Kool 100s is augmented by copious quantities of mood-controlling chemicals.

Like the mayor of the straitjacket rock community, Syd Barrett, Johnston has an acute pop sensibility, and many of his songs have an immediate accessibility not commonly heard among outsiders. But unlike Pink Floyd's graduate zombie, citizen Daniel freely strolls the sunnier streets of Barrettville thanks to mind-leveling doses of Lithium and Elival (at least 15 pills a day).

On his early recordings, Daniel's vocals sounded like those of a helium-spiked adolescent. More recently, chain-smoking has sandpapered his vocal cords raw, and his speech is cracked and raspy. On his recordings, Daniel plays a child's plastic chord organ, approximately tuned piano, and off-brand acoustic guitars. A now-anonymous punk rocker was once criticized for using just three chords; "Yeah," the punk retorted, "but they're three *great* chords." Daniel's elementary strumming also features just a few chords, and they're not necessarily great, but they are serviceable. He can bash away at the drums, too.

Once in an act of frustration, Johnston bashed away at his guitar—"Got mad, did an old Who trick on it." He swung it down like a sledgehammer, shattering it beyond repair. "I kept asking people if they could fix it, but there wasn't much left to it."

Some of Daniel's songs sound like hymns; others evoke the fevered abandonment of good Southern gospel. It's no surprise that Daniel has a strong relationship with divine forces. He believes, prays, reads the Good Books. "I like *Proverbs* best," he burbled excitedly. "It has my favorite line: 'As a dog returns to its vomit, so does a fool return to his folly.'" Arty types otherwise repelled by Christian zeal allow a measure of tolerance for Daniel's spirituality. "Fuck Jimmy Swaggart. Fuck the Bakkers," wrote Art Black in *Psychotronic*. "The Lord's got Daniel Johnston on his side."

After Jesus, Daniel's backup savior is Casper, the Friendly Ghost, about whom he sings and whose marshmallowy figure he occasionally sketches. "I kinda identify with him," he laughed. "He's good-natured, and trying to do good when he's around a lot of bad people. Some of my friends turned out kinda bad, but I was, like, a real good little boy all through my youth. So I kept writing different songs about him, and drawing him a lot." Daniel, who admires comic artist Jack Kirby, also boasts a Captain America fixation, but does not expect to be asked to join the Superheroes Union. "I don't have a sponsor, or the suits or anything," he lamented. "But I draw a lot of them." He trades in his superhero sketches at an Austin shop, which gives him credit toward comic books.

Many of Daniel's songs reflect vulnerability born of a yearning for unattainable love, comingled with defiance in the face of rejection. His song "Ain't No Woman Gonna Make a George Jones Outta Me" was written, Daniel explained, "because Tammy Wynette left him, and I looked at his albums, and it looked like he really suffered. I'd just broke up with my girlfriend, and I said, 'I'm not gonna let that happen to me.'" Beyond exorcising demons and nursing his broken heart, Daniel is preoccupied with King Kong, cows, Frankenstein, and a prizefighter named Joe. They rock his world.

When Daniel first achieved national prominence, some fans latched onto his psychosis as a badge of hipness. Others deplored the shameless exploitation of a disturbed naïf. Richie Unterberger, in *Unknown Legends of Rock 'n' Roll*, called Johnston's output "cloying kiddie rock." Unterberger argued that Johnston "would have never even gained a recording contract had he not been marketed as a novelty of sorts—a mental incompetent who thinks he can sing and play."

In fact, Johnston *can* sing and play quite capably, albeit not by mainstream standards of radio-readiness. But as outsiders go, he's one of the prime examples of an electroshock poster-boy with an instinctive pop sensibility and soul galore. His voice is warm and his songs are drenched in passion, perhaps because the writer is an emotional wreck half the time. Eric Weisbard, in the *Spin Alternative Record Guide,* wrote that Johnston embodies "the Ramones principle applied to Beach Boy Brian Wilson: schizophrenically disjointed, given to desperate love tunes sung in an almost impossibly naked high quaver, but ultimately holding things together with pop genius."

Johnston's songs rarely follow conventional structures, but they are singable, and he can plant a hook in your subconscious. His piano technique, more virtuosic than his guitar flailing, is full of nuance and whimsy. As with many outsider musicians, Johnston is a taste you love at first listen, acquire after skeptical scrutiny, or forever detest. There's little room for indifference.

Fortunately for his career, some of alt-rock's finest have discovered musical compatibility with the boy with the rattled fusebox. Johnston has recorded with Jad Fair of 1/2 Japanese, members of Yo La Tengo, Poison 13, the Butthole Surfers, the Texas Instruments, and Sonic Youth. Testifying to the durability of his songs, Daniel's ex-girlfriend Kathy McCarty, formerly of Austin-based Glass Eye, recorded a CD of 19 Johnston compositions entitled *Dead Dog's Eyeball* (Bar/None). In addition, Johnston's songs have been recorded by Yo La Tengo ("Speeding Motorcycle"), Jad Fair and Kramer ("King Kong"), The Pastels ("Speeding Motorcycle"), 1/2 Japanese ("King Kong," "Casper"), the Dead Milkmen ("Rocket Ship"), and others. Sonic Youth, fIREHOSE, Pearl Jam, and others have played his songs live. But perhaps most momentously, the sainted Kurt Cobain was frequently photographed wearing Daniel's "Hi, How Are You" T-shirt.

Daniel Dale Johnston was born in Sacramento, California, on January 22, 1961. In a sort of reverse Manifest Destiny, his family later headed east to Utah, then to New Cumberland in West Virginia's northern panhandle. In the mid-1980s he emerged as a no-fi wunderkind thanks to several homemade cassette albums he'd recorded earlier in the decade; they were captured on one of those flat, hand-held monophonic decks with a built-in condenser mic that magnifies room noise. Daniel's simple keyboard-and-voice compositions summoned images of a hellhound-beset Appalachian Randy Newman. Forget the occasional signal dropouts and incessant tape hiss—that's part of the charm.

Johnston's early masterpieces, *Songs of Pain* and *More Songs of Pain*, chronicle his unrequited passion for a college bookstore clerk named Laurie, whom he met while attending a branch of Kent State University. (Laurie eventually married an undertaker.) The sound quality Daniel obtained from that rumble-prone deck is phenomenal; he also manipulated sound through chicken-enwire trickery. The result is a thickness, a density that occasionally expands to a Spectorian thunder. There are sheets of sound, sometimes achieved with just piano and voice (e.g., "I Save Cigarette Butts" from *Songs of Pain*).

Johnston's confessional elegies are not far removed from some of John Lennon's more desolate early 1970s recordings—reflecting that degree of anguish and extreme candor. Not surprisingly Daniel reveres the Beatles, Lennon in particular. Johnston's music echoes from a very private corner; but despite the privacy, it's a place where he can neither find comfort nor escape his hellish visions. Mike McGonigal in the *Village Voice* referred to Johnston's "painful sincerity that obliterates the distinction between performance and life." A review of his *Hi, How Are You* tape in *Your Flesh* conceded, "It's damned hard not to feel like a voyeur listening to this album. There's absolutely no attempt on Daniel's part to be discreet or embarrassed."

Johnston is an old-fashioned preacher, and his sermonlike songs reflect moralistic concerns. With a strong sense of right and wrong, he's preoccupied with sin, retribution, and passing judgment. Damnation looms for those who fail to control unholy impulses, as in "Never Relaxed" (from *Songs of Pain*):

There was this kid named Sid 'n' he was born
Maybe the doctor hit him a little too hard
He just seemed to have gotten off to a bad start
Never relaxed, never relaxed, never relaxed

Big brothers and big sisters gave him lots of attention
But Sid was a hyperactive kid
He just never seemed able to sit still
Never relaxed, never relaxed, never relaxed

He sat at school in detention
Drawing funny pictures on the wall
Not a moment of peace did Sid ever find
Never relaxed, never relaxed, never relaxed

Now when Sid discovered masturbation
He just couldn't keep a good thing down
But it didn't help much his condition
Never relaxed, never relaxed, never relaxed

Sid signed up for the army
Cause he got tired of working in the pottery
And they sent him over to a foreign country
Never relaxed, never relaxed, never relaxed

Sid met this girl in East Germany
And she invited him up to her room for some tea
Then she pulled out a gun and took his money
Never relaxed, never relaxed, never relaxed

She shot Sid though the head
And Sid died and went to hell
And he burned and he burned and he yelled
And never relaxed, never relaxed, never relaxed

Now the devil said this ain't fair
Most people who come have their share of comfort
So he sat Sid in a reclining chair
But it was an electrical chair
Never relaxed, never relaxed, never relaxed

After leaving KSU, Daniel returned to his folks' home in West Virginia, where he channeled his Laurie despair into songs about funeral parlors and librarians. He worked briefly at the Quaker State oil refinery in Newell, where his father was employed. But "for three or four years," he related, "I didn't have a job. I just lived at home, playing piano in the basement. My mom yelled at me all day." As she did, the tape deck rolled. Snippets of maternal harangue—"You're lazy! You have no shame!"—serve as between-song bridges on Daniel's early cassettes. Finally, the troubled lad split for Texas.

Yip/Jump Music and half of *Hi, How Are You (The Unfinished Album)* were recorded in a garage while Johnston stayed with his brother Richard in Houston. Dan's day job was operating the "River of No Return" ride at Astroworld. While working on *Hi...*, he accidentally dropped the tape deck. "It started slowin' down and makin' weird speed changes," he shrugged. "That's kinda noticeable in *Hi, How Are You*."

Next stop was San Marcos, where he moved in with sister Margy for a short-lived cohabitation. "My sister thought I was kinda crazy," he recalled, "and my parents wrote her a letter that maybe I should be committed to a mental hospital. So I did a disappearing act." He left town with a traveling carnival and spent five months on the road selling corn dogs.

When the carnival dead-ended in Austin, Johnston adopted that city as his new hometown. He rented an apartment, worked at Pizza Hut and McDonald's, and obsessively sketched cartoons in his free time. He walked the streets, he said, "handing out tapes of my songs to pretty girls." These normal-bias Radio Shack cassettes carried a disclaimer: "This album was recorded not under the influence of drugs." The cassette cases were adorned with Daniel's xeroxed sketches of one-eyed bats, macrocephalic mutants, and a disturbing number of people with lopped-off skulltops.

Artist and longtime friend Ron English, who met Daniel at this time, pointed out, "In his own guileless way, he actually did a remarkable job of distributing his songs." Johnston developed a strong following among local musicians, and became an integral part of the city's art community. "Daniel replaced Roky Erickson in the hearts and minds of Austin's music scenesters as the resident musical Forrest Gump," wrote journalist Gina Arnold. Bands scrambled to cover his tunes, and local critics shifted into overdrive with rave notices. His tapes were commercially released on the local Stress label, operated by Jeff Tartakov, who also became Daniel's manager. (Homestead later issued several Stress cassettes on LP and CD.)

These tapes reveal Daniel's instinctive sense of composition. He knows a few tricks of the pop trade and innocently makes up others as he goes along. His lyrics don't always wedge easily into available space. He's a clumsy poet, but so was Dylan on occasion, and Johnston is best accepted for what he is: a musician packaged with a special set of instructions. In "Cold Hard World" (from *Don't Be Scared*), rhythmic meter naps in the backseat while earnestness takes the wheel:

It's a cold hard world
It's a cold hard world
It's a cold hard world
Oh no!

It's hiking across the country looking for a bite to eat
You'd be surprised at the angles [sic] and the people you'd meet
Rolling down that highway with eyes fixed straight ahead
They had a caravan of cars to bury the dead
And Coke cans and pop bottles lined the streets like flowers instead

And this guy gave me a ride, I said, "This industrial waste sure
   stinks"
He said he likes that smell, 'cause that's the smell of money
I said, "Well, Mister, money stinks, too"

It's a cold hard world
It's a cold hard world
It's a cold hard world
Oh, no!

I met a fireman, he said you never forget burning flesh
And the librarian said, "Do you have a card here?"
I said, "I've been coming here for weeks
don't you recognize me by now?
I've checked out a million books just to get you to notice me"

It's a cold hard world
It's a cold hard world
It's a cold hard world
Oh, no!

Gretchen Phillips, formerly of Austin bands Meat Joy and Two Nice Girls,
witnessed the early stages of Daniel's rise to local prominence. "Glass Eye
invited him to open for them with a few songs," she recalled. "The audience
ate it up, but his obvious discomfort on stage made me squirm. I couldn't
tell if people were laughing at him, or if they were really enthusiastic and
encouraging."

When Johnston's profile reached phenom proportions, even journalists
seemed skeptical. "The Austin press could be rather mean to him," said
Phillips. "I remember one headline in particular: 'Daniel Johnston: Genius or
Gerbil?' I felt really bad for him. Why ridicule him publicly?" Cruelty aside,
the (former) "g-word" was invoked so frequently that Tartakov, fearing an ego-
imploding effect on Daniel's fragile psyche, issued a press release begging
journalists to avoid the term.

Johnston was launched to national renown after being featured on MTV
in a 1985 *Cutting Edge* profile of the Austin music scene. Thus began his
descent into a psychotic maelstrom. Convinced he was on the verge of mega-
stardom, he started dropping acid and turned into an emotional yo-yo. "I'd go
out walking around town for three days, until I'd be picked up by the police,"
he recounted. "I got in a fight with cops at a restaurant. I knocked them
around. It was a blast! But I ended up in jail for two weeks."

After Dan was admitted to Austin State Hospital around Christmas 1986, his father Bill brought him back to West Virginia, where he was diagnosed as manic-depressive. Medication was prescribed, and his moods stabilized in the presence of his family. But when Daniel embarked on a trip to New York City in 1988, the diabolical anti-Casper dogged him every step of the way. Johnston stumbled into one of the most disastrous escapades of his life.

His tape album, *Hi, How Are You*, was slated to be released on Sonic Youth's Blast First label. Figuring New York was his to conquer, Johnston arrived in Gotham with a few hundred dollars in his pocket—which he quickly blew on expensive Beatles bootlegs. Then he stopped taking his medication.

Daniel's few New York area performances were abysmal. He behaved irrationally, went on a Christian evangelical jag, and argued with his hosts. He borrowed money and racked up massive long distance bills, phoning Tartakov in Austin and firing him on a daily basis. One now-infamous day he physically assaulted Sonic Youth drummer Steve Shelley, who had graciously provided him with living accommodations. In a near-hallucinatory frenzy, Johnston believed—and told anyone who would listen—that meetings were imminent with David Byrne and Yoko Ono.

Friends attempted to have him recommitted, but Daniel wound up roaming the streets, camping in homeless shelters. On an afternoon excursion to the Statue of Liberty, he was arrested for scrawling anti-Satanist graffiti on the landmark with an indelible felt-tip.

By the time he left New York, Daniel had alienated most of those on the alternative arts scene who had tried to help further his career. According to Louis Black in *Spin*, Daniel "called Blast First so many times—often to tell them about deals he was making with other companies—that they told him they would only release his record on three conditions: that he rehire Tartakov, that he go home, and that he stop calling them." Eventually, the album project was shelved, as Daniel later ruefully acknowledged, "because they met me."

After a brief stay in New York's Bellevue Psychiatric Hospital, Johnston returned to West Virginia, where he was recommitted and his dosages were restored. He then headed off to Maryland, where recording a homemade album with buddy Jad Fair was uppermost in his mind. Lowermost was his medication, which he abandoned yet again.

After visiting some friends in West Virginia, another manic street-roaming episode ensued. He was causing a ruckus at 7 A.M., when a 68-year-old lady poked her head out the window and yelled at him to pipe down. Daniel suspected the woman was in the throes of satanic possession. He entered the building and began kicking down her security door, at which point the terrified victim leapt from her second-story window, breaking both legs in the process. Daniel later told Louis Black that he was attempting to "cast out this lady's demons." He told a different story when police arrived, insisting, "Hey, I'm Casper the Friendly Ghost." He recalled that "the cops were laughing. They just thought I was hilarious." And off he went to the house of mirth—the state's high-security Weston Mental Hospital. While there, he reportedly attacked another patient.

Under psychiatric care Daniel eventually got his marbles back in the box. His parents relocated to the small town of Waller, Texas, and Daniel lives with them, concentrating on music and art. His dad, Bill, a WWII fighter pilot with the Flying Tigers and a design engineer of Minuteman missiles, is very protective of his wayward son. Daniel reciprocates with a high measure of admiration for his pop, adding, "He's a real good friend." So is his mom, Mabel, even if she does keep after Dan to clean up his room.

Lately, Johnston has been relatively well behaved. His family serves as a firewall against his self-destructive potential. He no longer forgets to take his pills. He has a good reason to remember: "Captain America" (father Bill) instructs him to take the prescribed doses.

Perhaps in fulfillment of some obscure Biblical prophecy, in 1994 Johnston miraculously got signed to a major, Atlantic Records, making him Led Zeppelin's labelmate. The ensuing album, *Fun*, was produced by fellow Texan Paul Leary of the Butthole Surfers. Leary handled most of the guitar work, because at the time therapists were still regulating Daniel's medication. "I was so out of it, I couldn't even play," he shrugged. "I just showed Paul the parts." The vocals are unmistakably Daniel, but the album is sleekly produced, almost bloodless, lacking the naïve charm of the early tapes. It sounds like—well, like Daniel Johnston on a major label (a prodigious belch in the middle of "Catie" notwithstanding). Sellout? Nah—Daniel's incapable.

His followup, *Rejected Unknown*, took five years, and was recorded in his parents' home and released in a limited edition by Newimproved Music in 1999. It's easily the most sophisticated and ambitious studio project of Daniel's career, full of great songs and first-rate *understated* production. "The guy from Atlantic wanted to put me in the studio with Pearl Jam," Daniel revealed. "But I didn't know. I've made the mistake before about turning down major labels, including Elektra." He ended up recording in his spare time with Brian Beattie (ex–Glass Eye), who released the album independently. Daniel was assured he has not burned his bridges with Atlantic, despite album sales a mere whisper of Pearl Jam's.

Considering Daniel's psychiatric setbacks and his decidedly non-mainstream appeal, plucking a major label contract could seem evidence of a semi-charmed life. Faith in Jesus, Casper, and Captain America pays big dividends. At the same time, Daniel is learning from experience. He knows he's being watched—by those around him and by the Lord—and behaves accordingly, listening to those who love him, heeding their voices instead of the sinister

BEWARE THE MADDNESS!

VICTORY ON PARADE.

Daniel Johnston

noises inside his head. He's mindful of his mistakes; he's suffered because of his fuckups and knows he's caused pain to loved ones.

"I'm really very, very sorry [for what] happened," he told the *Voice*'s McGonigal. "I know it's gonna follow me for the rest of my life." Yet it's difficult to dislike Daniel. He's extremely vulnerable, and his friends and fans are very custodial toward him. Despite the occasional outbursts, he has a simple, loving soul. He's also very self-aware—what he says, he means. There is zero bullshit.

As moods permit, Daniel occasionally tours the United States or Europe, playing in clubs to a fanatically loyal following. He anticipates no repeat of his New York fiasco. He has professional representation for his art, and his tormented drawings have been widely exhibited, providing a sporadic income stream.

Gretchen Phillips remains skeptical about his audience. "I saw Daniel in New York in 1999 at the Knitting Factory," she said. "I was heartened by how many of his new songs were about the redemptive power of love. That's a very good place for him to be—a better topic than evil. But I still wonder if people go see him hoping to witness a nervous breakdown. Do they perceive him as their equal, or as someone they need to coax along and make feel safe? As much as the audience may genuinely love his songs, I sense a lot of condescension. That's always bugged me. I know the musicians who play with him and cover his songs are real fans, who worship his songwriting. But I'd rather listen to him on tape than in a crowd whose motives make me suspicious."

At home, Daniel is neither rock star nor art phenom. His father Bill isn't certain his son fulfills these roles outside the house either. "He's hardly making a living right now," said papa Bill. "When he has a one-day art show, he does real well. But he doesn't do that every day. He doesn't know how to properly market himself. And he gives his work away. He's very generous, always a soft touch for anybody who wants something." The elder Johnston accompanies his son to most of his gigs, explaining that "he needs a caretaker to keep him on the straight and narrow."

Despite making progress keeping the lid on his psychic pressure-cooker, Daniel was diagnosed as a diabetic in 1997. "His weight has been out of control," Bill pointed out, "and so is his smoking, which hurts his voice. We try to help him, but he won't always do what's best for him. We give him a lot of good advice he refuses to accept."

But having paid the price for past misdeeds, Daniel knows what's at stake. "I read about manic-depression to understand what I was going through," he explained. "I'd be depressed for months. Then there'd be this manic phase for the longest time, and I'd get lots of things done, as far as art goes. As long as you keep yourself busy, no matter what kind of illness you have, you can get stuff done."

He's also reached a reconciliation with Steve Shelley. "We made up on the telephone," sighed Daniel. "It's no big deal."

•9•

Harry Partch

HALLELUJAH! HE'S A BUM

harry Partch made a career move at age 29 that more smart young composers and songwriters might consider: he collected all the music manuscripts he'd written—14 years' worth of quartets, piano concertos, and symphonic poems—crammed everything in a pot-bellied stove, and torched the lot.

Then he started again from scratch.

Over the next 40 years, Partch would gain cult-level renown as the twentieth century's most eloquent musical primitive, carving a solitary niche in outsiderdom. The maverick philosopher-composer-carpenter devised his own 43-notes-to-the-octave scale. He sculpted percussion and string instruments out of artillery shell casings, Harvey's Bristol Cream bottles, and driftwood—and expected players to make music out of this debris. He camped in hobo jungles and abandoned shipyards, insulted well-heeled and well-connected patrons who offered help, and did just about anything an artist could do to ensure lack of widespread recognition.

The word *compromise* wasn't part of Harry's vocabulary.

The offspring of American parents who served as missionaries in China from 1888 to 1900, Harry Partch was born in Oakland, California, in 1901. He grew up in Benson, Arizona (pop. 300), a wild west town with 11 saloons and an endless influx of thirsty outlaws. The open-eared tyke was serenaded by a pancultural mix of "Christian hymns, Chinese lullabyes, Yaqui Indian ritual, Congo puberty ritual, Cantonese music hall, and Okies in California vineyards." He absorbed any and every sound, including train whistles echoing across the prairie and his parents' conversations in Mandarin. He fondly remembered a Hebrew chant for the dead played on an Edison cylinder by a local shopkeeper.

COURTESY PHILIP BLACKBURN

Harry Partch, 1943

You can hear traces of *all* these flavors in Partch's work. His biographer Bob Gilmore described one of the composer's instrumental passages as "suggesting the hollow moaning of wind rifling a deserted landscape."

The southwestern frontier cradle that aroused the boy's curiosity also nurtured a rebellious streak: "I recall watching through a telescope 'bad men' holed up in some nearby rocks," Partch later wrote, "and I fear that my five-year-old sympathies were all for the hunted."

As a teen, Partch played piano in silent movie theaters around Albuquerque and composed ambitious works in conventional western modes. Eventually, though, he felt handcuffed by "the tyranny of the piano scale." He resented the limitations imposed by 12 tempered tones and grew obsessed with the notes between the notes (microtones).

Partch's disaffection reached a decisive flash point in 1930 with that fateful bonfire. While stoking the ashes of his incinerated oeuvre in a New Orleans boarding house, he resolved never again to be anyone's pupil. Rather than contribute to what he considered a dead system, Partch—15 years short of a midlife crisis—opted out.

He sought not simply to reinvent the wheel, but to *disinvent* it.

Once upon a time
There was a little boy
And he went outside.
—ANONYMOUS INSCRIPTION DISCOVERED BY PARTCH

The reborn *enfante terrible* set about devising a microtonally extended system of "just intonation," carving an additional 31 notes out of Western music's conventional dozen. He also formulated a rather sneering philosophy to provide a context for his system and its applications.

In a century shellshocked by artistic jihads against tradition, Partch may have seemed a poster boy for the avant-garde. Yet he went forward by looking back: his "progressive" 43-note scale echoed ancient Eastern systems of tonality, as well as the musical crosswinds of his childhood in the Southwest. He was distrustful of modern technology, electronic music in particular, preferring organic sound sources. "What this age needs more than anything else," Partch harrumphed, "is an effective antidote."

To a great degree the complexity of his methodology—as well as his massive ego—alienated critics, academics, and audiences. He once admitted a compulsion "to ransack public libraries, doing suggested exercises and writing music free from the infantilisms and inanities of professors."

"Partch's crime," wrote journalist Ken Spiker, "[was] compounded by the fact that he dared to sin not only against God, but Bach himself." Just as vehemently, Partch rejected prevailing concert protocols. He detested the custom of musicians performing in tuxedos.

Venturing deeper into the artistic lost forest, Partch invented acoustic instruments to play his scale and composed a catalog of work that is largely percussive, plectral (plucked), and vocal, with a smattering of bent keyboards. As a frame of reference for Exotica enthusiasts, imagine Martin Denny with the pins and screws removed.

Partch's instruments were fashioned out of airplane fuel tanks, Buick bumpers, eucalyptus branches, and junk scavenged in the California desert. These sonic devices—all objects of stunning beauty—received intriguing names such as Crychord, Drone Devils, Zymo-Xyl, and Quadrangularis Reversum. The Mazda Marimba, named after the Persian god of light, displays banks of tuned light bulbs and sounds like a percolating coffeepot. The Cloud-Chamber

Bowls were derived from Pyrex carboys discarded by a Berkeley radiation lab. Onstage, it all looks like a Martian furniture showroom. Yet Partch once insisted, "I am not an instrument builder, only a philosophic music man seduced into carpentry." With these dumpster-reclamation sculptures, he created a kind of world music *avant la lettre*. His percussion-driven showpieces sound like a steel band after too much rum, or a clock shop gone haywire.

His compositions bear equally eccentric titles: "Eight Hitchhiker Inscriptions from a Highway Railing at Barstow, California"; "A Soul Tormented by Contemporary Music Finds a Humanizing Element"; and "The Cognoscenti Are Plunged into a Demonic Descent While at Cocktails." In the spirit of ancient Greek and Chinese theater, Partch insisted that his works be staged as grand spectacles, with narrators, costumes, masks, dancing, and elaborate sets.

The nomadic composer's theories and pointed opinions were put between covers in 1949. His manifesto, *Genesis of a Music,* was updated shortly before the composer's death and remains in print through Da Capo Press. *Genesis* is a dense treatise chronicling the history of musical intonation, spiked with Harry's dogmatic theories on pitch, acoustics, and corporeality. Before its original publication, Partch had had almost two decades to mull his apostasy. And Partch had *lots* of free time to think—his artistic auto-da-fé was anything

RICHARD A. MATTHEWS

Harry Partch and his Quadrangularis Reversum, 1966

but well timed. Being a musician during the Great Depression was difficult; launching a career as a microtonal visionary promised a hellbound odyssey.

Nonetheless, Partch accepted his destiny. Minus the wherewithal to turn a steady buck, he bundled his belongings on a stick and trekked off to the hobo camps. From 1935 to 1943, he hitchhiked through the American northwest, occasionally working as a proofreader, fruitpicker, and dishwasher. He turned this exile into an education, becoming the most prestigious graduate of Boxcar U. Riding the rails, huddled around campfires, Partch earned a Master's in Hobo Linguistics, studying the speech patterns of his dispossessed comrades. These conversations eventually formed the librettos of several works, earning him the sobriquet "the Operatic Kerouac" (or as writer David Hajdu cracked, "the Woody Guthrie of microtone theory").

"I kept my music in my hobo bundle wherever I went," Partch told Jonathan Cott of *Rolling Stone* in 1974. He also logged a now-lost migrant journal, the only existing eight-month excerpt of which is collected with other writings and librettos in *Bitter Music* (University of Illinois Press). The journal chronicles the observations of a refined gentleman who spent the better part of a decade begging food, hopping freight cars, and sleeping in transient camps beside bums and drunks.

One significant journal entry recounts Partch's rebuttal to an academic who lamented America's lack of musical sophistication:

[Beethoven] has only the feeblest roots in our culture, and those mostly among a class of people that thinks of concerts as social occasions.... [T]his music has almost no roots among [Americans].... It was the lowest of the social order—sailors, soldiers, criminals, and all their kin—who gave England one of the richest of musics [sic]. But whether given by the lowest, or by a higher class of people—it has to come from the people, just as Beethoven came from the people.... I'm trying to give myself, and others, a good basis for a new and great music of the people.... And that's why I work with words, because they are the commonest medium of creative expression. And words *are* music."

Speech—employed as drama and narrative—was the foundation of some of Harry's most idiosyncratic work. "If you went to high school in the Edwardian era, the Victorian times even," explained Partch chronicler Dr. Philip Blackburn, "there was always a class called 'Expression.' You'd memorize poems and stand up and recite. You'd also have this in your parlor at home as entertainment. The heightened recitation of highfalutin literature, or even doggerel, was much more a part of everyday life. Harry simply did it in a way no one else had quite done before."

The language and vignettes of Partch's dustbowl odyssey are captured vividly in his *U.S. Highball* (1943):

> One time I was in the [rail]yards in Pueblo, sitting with some other 'bos around a fire, waiting for the hotshot on the D & R G. Pretty soon, an old man with a long white beard come out of a piano box on the edge of the yards, and come over to warm his hands by our fire. He didn't say anything until some of the boys left to catch a drag that was just beginning to move out. Then the old man who'd just come out of the piano box, said, 'It's purty tough to be ridin' the drags on a night like this. I know. I was a bum once myself.'

Even in the midst of the worst protracted economic debacle in U.S. history, Partch embraced this nation's founding principles, which accorded him liberty, while rejecting the Philistinism that condemned him to the cultural fringe. Despite his Bryanesque platitude that music had to "come from the people," out behind the barn he was Nietzschean. "As between the political practices extant," he attested, "I would claim the American as my own without a second's hesitation—but I am for beginning the evolution of a superior race right here and now."

Not that Partch didn't crave some measure of popular acceptance. His early advocates included such patrons of the dispossessed as composer Henry Cowell, author/diarist Anaïs Nin, and composer/theorist John Cage. However, being worlds away from the mainstream, money was always problematic. "He was a pauper his whole life," observed later-Partch associate Dean Drummond. When he wasn't dodging creditors, Harry scuffled with the press, which tended to trivialize him. "He'd be a really good composer if only he'd compose regular music," said a Berkeley radio station director. In 1954, *L.A. Times* critic Albert Goldberg wrote, "one is inclined to doubt that there is much real creative force or originality to Partch's innovations." To which Partch shot back in a letter, "Obviously, you are a Euro-technique-inculcated hashbrain, which displaces a depth of water that a pollywog would die in."

"Harry was always going to pains to explain what he was about," observed Blackburn, "and somehow journalists always took a sensationalistic interpretation. He's always been lightly dismissed as a kook, or an amateur cabinetmaker, someone who was not educated—when in fact the truth is exactly the opposite. It just happened that he operated so far outside academia and institutional life, that no one could quite get a grip on him."

In the 1930s, Partch consorted with celebrated composers Cowell, Aaron Copland, Roger Sessions, and Ernst Bloch. "He knew all these bastions of the mostly East Coast culture," noted Blackburn. "And he kept on being driven away with his tail between his legs, because these people may or may not have liked his music, but they really didn't like his theories. And besides—who was this 30-year-old from nowhere—I mean, California was nowhere, it was a swamp in those days—coming to demonstrate this new thing he discovered?"

In 1933, while accepting a Carnegie Award to study abroad with poet W. B. Yeats and at the British Museum, Partch met John Cage. "Harry told Cage, 'It's too late,'" said Blackburn. "Now, this is a 33-year-old, from nowhere, saying that the world had already missed out on its opportunity to discover Harry Partch. He had some attitudes that wouldn't have endeared him to his supposed fellow colleagues."

Years after he had amassed a body of work that brought modest recognition, Partch would snare an occasional foundation grant or short-lived university residency. But his prima donna antics alienated patrons. A commission with dance trailblazer Martha Graham fell through in the 1950s. "Harry was cursing her left, right, and center," Blackburn recounted. "When another possibility of collaboration came along years later, Graham said, 'Oh, is he collaborating with a human? I can't imagine him collaborating with anyone but puppets!' He probably established a reputation early on as a whining young man, a precocious youngster. He pooh-poohed the New York establishment, and tried to go it on his own. When he came back for a Carnegie Hall debut, Aaron Copland blackballed that performance." Neglect haunted Partch as the greatest of defeats. "What sentence could be more dreaded by the murderer, or the rapist, or the defrauder of widows," he wrote in 1952, "than that he should be ignored? The musical malefactor, the pioneer, becomes one with idiots, criminals, and other deviates."

Ironically, Partch had one "deviate" tendency he probably preferred be ignored: his homosexuality. Being gay in a largely straight world no doubt reinforced the composer's lifelong sense of outsiderness. "Harry stayed in the closet. He was a queer when you could practically get hung for it, professionally and literally," recalled Francis Thumm, who played in Partch's ensemble during the early 1970s. "He was smart, he was a survivor. Why should he come out—so some fuckin' homophobe could beat the shit out of him? He had work to do. He was a hobo; he knew how to survive. He was that guy up in the rocks."

Like the greatest geniuses, Partch wasn't ahead of his time—he was a man without an era. "My own efforts to bring beauty into the world have come to aimless wandering," he wrote prophetically in 1935. This statement could have served as his epitaph when he died in 1974. He was apprehensive about posterity. "For decades," Partch wrote his friend Betty Freeman in 1969, "I've been reconciled to the very great probability that there will be no extension of my work beyond my death. If there is extension of spirit I'll be happy."

Though it's unlikely all Partch recordings will collectively go platinum before the U.S. Postal Service issues a Kurt Cobain stamp, it isn't for lack of inventory. Decades after the composer's death, there's a relative Ikea's worth of material to choose from in CDs, books, videos, and Web sites. And with Dean Drummond, current custodian of the Partch instrumentarium, transporting the fragile relics for mesmerizing concerts several times a year, the legacy is being maintained and extended.

The four-CD *Harry Partch Collection* (Composers Recordings, Inc.) consists of all material previously issued by CRI on vinyl or CD, along with out-of-print rarities originally released on Partch's cottage-level Gate 5 LP label. Initiates should start with *And on the 7th Day Petals Fell in Petaluma* (CRI *Vol. 2*). Scored for 22 instruments, *Petaluma* showcases the man's scales and textures; for jaded ears seeking an escape from American popular forms, there's no better vacation. Instrumental works such as *Windsong* are equally transportive. (*Windsong*, found on CRI *Vol. 3*, was recorded in 1958 by Partch on multiple instruments via overdubs and was the foundation of a later piece, *Daphne of the Dunes*.)

His choral works, such as *Water! Water!* (CRI *Vol. 3*) and the opera *King Oedipus*, can be tedious, particularly when instruments are subordinate to voices. The world premiere of his 1967 revision of *Oedipus* at the Metropolitan Museum in April 1998 disappointed many. Of the dozen-plus New York presentations of Partch this author has attended, *Oedipus* was the only one that was painful to endure. With the instruments reduced to a supporting role in the score and onstage, much of the magic was muted.

When voices are balanced with instruments, as in *U.S. Highball* (CRI *Vol. 2*), it's a great music-drama meld. Harry's own dry "intoning" vocals sound like your disreputable, gin-soaked uncle singing a ribald lullaby (CRI *Vol. 2*: "San Francisco: A Setting of the Cries of Two Newsboys on a Foggy Night in the Twenties"). CRI *Vol. 4* includes the complete recording of Partch's 75-minute 1955 dance-satire, *The Bewitched*. Authoritative liner notes for the CRI series were penned by Bob Gilmore, author of *Harry Partch: A Biography* (Yale University Press).

Perhaps the most ambitious exploration of the Partch legacy is Blackburn's *Enclosures* series (Innova), a six-installment labor of love developed over a decade and a half. *Enclosure One* is a VHS tape of *Four Historic Art Films by Madeline Tourtelot with Music by Harry Partch; Enclosure Two* is a four-CD package of unreleased recordings, Partch monologues, radio talks, and 46-plus minutes of comments from attendees at Harry's wake.

Enclosure Three is a lavish 524-page art book that "let[s] Harry speak for himself." You see what Partch must have witnessed just before he died on September 3, 1974—his life passing before his eyes: birth certificate, baby photos, and high school report card; newspaper tear sheets from as early as 1930; concert programs and reviews; personal correspondence and snapshots of the young composer skinny-dipping; handwritten scraps of paper; and a letter Partch wrote the day before dying of a heart attack at age 73. This breathtaking volume, gorgeously designed, is like a posthumous yard sale, containing no end of small, delightful treasures.

The *Enclosure Four* video features a 1971 film of *Delusion of the Fury* (1965–66), his 75-minute ritual drama, and a 1968 KPBS-TV documentary about the patriarchal iconoclast. *Enclosure Five* collects musical works inspired by the ancient cultures of Greece and Rome, including *Ulysses Departs from the Edge of the World, King Oedipus,* and *Revelation in the Courthouse Park,* based on *The Bacchae* of Euripides. Completing the series, *Enclosure Six* reissues the original 1972 Columbia Masterworks recording of *Delusion of the Fury.*

Despite Partch's apprehension about his posthumous legacy, more than a quarter-century after his demise, his music survives onstage. Not a prosperous existence, but a determined one. Danlee Mitchell, a longtime Partch aide-de-camp and devoted friend, had custodianship of the instrumentarium at San Diego State College for a decade and a half. In 1990, contemplating retirement, Mitchell turned over the collection to Dean Drummond, who'd worked with Partch since 1965. The instruments are currently housed at New Jersey's Montclair State University, about 30 minutes west of Manhattan. With his wife, flutist Stefani Starin, Drummond coordinates and conducts performances of Partch's works by their ensemble Newband. Their efforts to "extend" the legacy include composing and premiering new microtonal works played on Partch's musical furniture.

Drummond was 16 when he met Partch. The two worked together and maintained a friendship in the composer's final years. By that time, Drummond reflected, "Harry felt very underappreciated, and that the appreciation was coming too late. He was very moody, with periods of great depression." Cash flow, as ever, was disheartening. "He knew that John Cage was going all over the place lecturing and getting well paid," Drummond recalled. "But at the end of Harry's life, when a university would call him to give a lecture, he'd respond, 'I can't afford to come, I'm too feeble to come by myself. I need an assistant.' No one would go for that. And he would be outraged, because they were calling him 10, 20 years too late."

Because of their unique system-specific scoring, Partch's works were performed until recently only on his instruments. In 1996 the Kronos Quartet recorded his *Greek Studies* and *Barstow,* both arranged by Ben Johnston, a Partch protégé and longtime compatriot. David Harrington, Kronos's Artistic Director, feels Partch was a "major American composer whose music most

BETTY FREEMAN

Harry Partch ensemble and instrumentarium
at San Diego State University, 1972

concert-goers haven't had a chance to hear. I thought that was intolerable. That's why I wanted some pieces arranged for Kronos."

Not everyone was thrilled. "I see a problem in that Kronos does everything so beautifully and with such control," opined Blackburn. "Harry was kind of a messy guy. He wanted you to rape the instrument, or caress it, or fall on it, or miss the correct note as long as you did it with the right physicality and intent. But Kronos made it a pure-sounding kind of chamber piece. They took the teeth out of it a little bit, removed its bite."

After they recorded *Barstow*, recalled Harrington, "people were faxing me stuff off the [Partch] Web page. They were really pissed off. I know there's a lot of people who disagree with this, but I'm very pleased that there are some Partch pieces for Kronos to play. It doesn't sound like what it sounded like in the 1940s—it sounds like something else. But it's too important a body of work not to have it as music that can be played by musicians who are interested in exploring it."

Whether you prefer Partch black/no sugar or cappuccinoed, more virgin ears are likely to encounter the Kronos interpretations than Partch's original settings, particularly in concert halls. For all the man's creative ambition, almost as if by some grand unconscious design to remain marginal, Partch's arcane tuning system and fragile furniture cordon off his music from most of the world—then, now, maybe forever. "The instruments are big and cumbersome," laments Drummond. "They're priced out of what anyone could afford freight-wise. It prohibits much touring to Europe or even California.

"It's a weird contradiction," he continued, "but we live in a relatively free society. And even though Harry was poor, that freedom allowed him to do this. But what he created stands in the way of what he wanted to do. It's like building a bigger house than you can afford to upkeep. It's impractical to have three tons of musical equipment to do a chamber concert. It's a wonderful, glorious thing—and at the same time, a curse." Think of it as Partch's whammy. Following evictions, lease expirations, and such, Drummond had to pack up and relocate the entire collection five times during the 1990s. It's ironic that a vagrant who thumbed rides on blue highways with only a backpack of worldly goods left behind 6,000 pounds of hardware that his descendants have to lug around from place to place.

Partch was a quintessential American explorer whose trailblazing inspired generations in subtle and not-so-subtle ways. In one of the best examples of unattributed Partch discipleship, his words-as-music approach, theatricality, and microtonal tunings were flagrantly adopted in the early works of the Residents. Tom Waits recorded *Swordfishtrombones* under Harry's spell. "Hovering phantom-like over the whole album is the spirit of composer and hobo Harry Partch," wrote Waits biographer Patrick Humphries. "[Harry] dismantled and rebuilt his own version of the whole concept of music and its purpose," said Waits, "but I just like the sounds he makes." Waits also told *Playboy*, "Partch was an innovator. It's a little arrogant to say I see a relationship between his stuff and mine. I'm very crude, but I use things we hear around us all the time, built and found instruments."

More recently, mixologist/provocateur DJ Spooky offered a toast: "Harry Partch gave some sense of hope for American experimental music with his ability to absorb totally different styles and cultures without irony."

Others have put his creations to ingenious use. Producer Hal Willner's 1992 Charles Mingus tribute, *Weird Nightmare* (featuring Henry Rollins, Bill Frisell, Elvis Costello, and Robbie Robertson, among others), used the Partch collection to interpret works of the great jazz bassist/composer.

How reciprocal would the admiration have been? Partch had a mild curiosity about popular music, "a kind of condescending interest," Ben Johnston put it. "He didn't condemn it—far from it. He didn't like Gershwin or Tin Pan Alley. But he liked rock. He later knew Frank Zappa, who ate up what Harry did. I'm told they got along great." When Partch was rehearsing *Delusion of the Fury* at UCLA, Zappa took great interest in its progress.

Regardless of illustrious name-dropping, Partch will remain a teensy pinprick on the musical map. His original instruments are in need of constant repair, which doesn't augur well for long-term performance of his scores in their authentic context. The works themselves can be difficult to assimilate, and the broader public has neither the frames of reference nor the attention span necessary to appreciate such exotic sonics. This was Partch's destiny, and he knew it.

"Harry was a mixture of self-aggrandizement on one hand and self-deprecation on the other," observed Johnston. "He would go from the heights to the depths. In the depths, he would say, 'It's all shit—throw it away.' At the heights, he considered himself the savior of music. Well, he really did have something to contribute, but he felt at absolute loggerheads with ... *everything*. He was the last word in outsiders."

Despite this marginalization, much of it brought on by Partch's own stubbornness, he will be forever revered by his coterie of adherents.

"Maybe it's an American tenet or something," mulled Blackburn. "If you persist in your crankiness long enough, you become a guru or hero."

Wesley Willis: composer, artist, gourmand

Wesley Willis

HELL RIDE

Wesley Willis is a big teddy bear. A six-foot four-inch, 320-pound, schizophrenic teddy bear.

This musical Gargantua drools, spits indoors, and doesn't care much about hygiene. He gobbles heavy medication to control self-destructive impulses. He occasionally throws up onstage during club dates.

These qualities do not make Wes an outsider. In fact, he shares this behavior with many notable Grammy winners.

The Chicago-based Willis, who sings and plays electronic keyboards, records his original music prolifically—obsessively, you might say. In terms of repertoire, he doesn't offer a smorgasbord: if you've heard one Wesley Willis song, you've heard 6,000. He says he's written 35,000. That they sound remarkably alike hints at repetitive strain injury. To his fans, this is one of his more charming attributes.

Before he gained a following for his recordings and club appearances, Wes was widely known in Chicago as a street artist. One of his favorite illustrative subjects is public transport: he loves sightseeing on buses as much as he enjoys painting and sketching them. His regional renown was such that *ABC News* produced a profile.

But music eventually became his primary medium. Besides landing production/distribution deals with several established labels, Wesley presses and sells his own CDs. He's released over thirty albums—more than Culture Club, Boston, Fine Young Cannibals, Tone Loc, Nirvana, Men at Work, the Spin Doctors, and Blind Melon combined.

The general Willis compositional formula is a kicking dance-velocity synth beat over which he sings a chorus—generally consisting of the song title—in an off-key, adenoidal whine, followed by one or two verses delivered in a husky, commanding declamation. Beyond this simple pattern, there is rarely any variation. The pre-programmed, Devo-lite electrobeats mosey along for three minutes, even if Wes's vocals end one-third into the tune. There are no ballads. Some songs are uptempo. Some are slightly more uptempo. Others are—uptempo again. A typical Willis album sounds like one extended megamix with four-second, indexed pauses every few minutes.

Willis's lyric motifs include obsessions with junk food ("Rock n' Roll McDonald's") and power ("I Whupped Batman's Ass"). In fact, Wes kicks a lotta butt—Michael Jackson's, Saddam Hussein's, and Superman's, to name just three verbal victims of his extra-point tries. He's a bit gentler with his fans, with whom he shares playful head-butts—a gentle cranial collision that's his way of expressing affection.

Willis has a penchant for bellowing popular ad slogans as song codas (e.g., "Burger King—have it your way!" or "Pepsi—Generation Next!"). This serves the secondary purpose of signifying that one song has ended, and another is about to begin. Chris Prynoski, creator of *MTV Downtown,* is a big fan. "Wesley has tapped into the public's love for pop songs that all sound the same and go one step further," the animator proclaimed. "He's left a permanent bruise on the forehead of rock and roll. Budweiser! King of beers!"

Wes also cranks out songs about his favorite musicians. Greg Werckman, of the Alternative Tentacles label, which released some Willis recordings, said, "The thing Wes loves most in life is going to see bands. All the clubs let him in. He hangs with bands, then goes and records tributes." Willis has taped songs about Ted Nugent, Urge Overkill, Alice in Chains, Flaming Lips, Bon Jovi, and Liz Phair ("I will always love you like a milkshake"), among hundreds of others. They are essentially greeting cards with fill-in-the-blank names. It's not that Wes is lazy or content to follow formulas. It's part of the man's startup software. He sits down at the keyboard, triggers a beat, and launches into the band-of-the-moment, or today's ass-whup.

He orders food in a similarly robotic way: he'll have what you're having. Wes's diet is only as good as that of the support musicians driving him to his next booking. And by the time they arrive, they'll be the subjects of his latest song. "Who needs a Grammy or a Bammie," said Willis devotee Jello Biafra, "when you can win a Wesley?"

Demons are part of Willis lore. They haunt him. You and I can't see them, but to him they're *very, very real.* Allen Ginsberg once said—and being too lazy to research the original quote, I paraphrase—"I saw the best minds of my generation locked away in mental institutions." There's usually a good reason why, Al, and ordinary citizens are safer because of it. Fortunately, pharmaceutical mega-titans that Ginsberg's ilk would probably revile as profit-driven, corporate leeches have developed mood-stabilizing chemicals that allow psychological shipwrecks like Willis to function adequately in social settings, and even make a semi-living doing what they enjoy, without hurting anyone. As New York publicist/musician Heather Mount observed, "Wesley's not bored, and he's not unhappy. And that's good!"

Willis grew up in wretched poverty, his father having reputedly been a street hustler who sometimes fed his family, sometimes not. As a teen, Wes's escape routes from ghetto horrors were the CTA bus lines, which allowed him to explore the Chicago metropolitan area, including the suburbs. Willis's mental condition, damaged to begin with, took a turn for the worse in 1989 when his mom's boyfriend robbed him of his meager savings—while putting a gun to his head. The traumatized Willis has been hounded by diabolical inner voices ever since.

Rob Crow, musician-songwriter (Heavy Vegetable, Thingy, Optiganally Yours), reveres Willis. "Wesley has created some of the most passionate, honest, and soul-stirring music ever made," asserted Crow. "Unlike most musicians, whose muse might be money, a girl, or a good time, Wesley has to make music *or the demons will get him!*" In Willis-like fashion, Crow wrote "Song for Wesley," recorded by Heavy Vegetable on their CD *Frisbie* (Cargo, 1995). The honoree has not returned the compliment (yet), probably attributable less to his indifference than to the fact that HV hasn't toured enough for Wes to catch them live.

The Chicago trio Cats and Jammers toured the Eastern United States as an opening act for Willis in late 1998. Dates were sold out. Willis hit the road with 250 CDs to sell; five days later, at the New York club Coney Island High, he had 14 left.

How was it for the Cats, lugging around freight heavier than their guitars, amps, and drum kit combined? "Basically, he's no problem," observed C and J guitarist Scott Anthony Shell, "as long as he takes his medication and gets his shots. He attracts a lot of attention—especially in the more conservative towns. A very large black man—who's not very well groomed and somewhat smelly—traveling with three geeky white boys is bound to draw looks. We expected it. And we don't really care." Shell relished the camaraderie. "It's a blast," he explained. "Wesley is unique. He's very smart, a very unusual cat once you get used to him. He has this connection with audiences. It's not frat boys coming to his shows and making fun of him; it's punk rock kids who appreciate that he sings stuff people are thinking. Like, 'Michael Jackson sucks boys' dicks.' Wes writes a song about it. He has no inhibitions."

Part of road tripping with Willis, who can't drive, is being his caretaker: telling him when to eat, when to stop eating, when to wash down his pills, when to bathe. It's not unlike touring with a young child so large his head hits the roof of the van. At one motel, recalled Shell, "Our bass player Brad [Hunter] was taking a shower, and while he was drying off, Wesley walked in, sat down, and announced, 'I'm going to make a toilet stew.' Brad was a little embarrassed. And Wes just did his business. He'd do his business in public, if he could. We've had to remind him to use the bathroom. He doesn't seem to have a full grasp of social etiquette." Hunter elaborated: in five days on the road, he laughed, "Wesley's walked in on my shower three times. It's always me, and it's always right when I finish. I need to dry off, and he's sittin' there."

Willis is not completely oblivious to his conduct. He's something of a human trash compactor, and his song "I'm Sorry That I Got Fat" points to a growing self-awareness. "He seems to pick up on other peoples' conversations," noted Shell. "The band had been talking a lot about diet, and our drummer mentioned ordering a healthy salad. The next time we went out to eat, Wes picked a salad. This morning he said, 'Will you buckle up my fat ass?' I think he knows he needs to do something about his weight."

Thanks to some key fans in the business, Wesley isn't the only one putting his music on CD. Jello Biafra culled through Willis's self-released discs to compile *Wesley Willis' Greatest Hits Vols. 1* and *2* (Alternative Tentacles). Other releases include *Spookydisharmonious Conflicthellride* (Urban Legends); *Fabian Road Warrior* and *Feel the Power* (both on American, the latter recorded by the Dust Brothers); and albums on the Fuse, Oglio, and Typhoid Mary labels.

Success has been a mixed blessing. Mike Davis, a Chicago private investigator, has known Willis since 1992 and is working to become his legal guardian. "He's the sweetest guy in the world, and I cherish his friendship," said Davis, speaking very protectively about his ward. "I look out for him, keep him budgeted, talk to him. I can read Wes."

It's no easy task. Money is problematic for Willis—especially when he's got it. On the road, he regularly sells out clubs and does a brisk business with CDs. During a recent tour, he sold 350 discs at ten bucks a pop, netting $3,500 in walking-around money. Add in his gig fee, and he's pocketed a wad of banknotes, making him suckerbait for hustlers and con merchants. He's partly protected from physical assault by his Bunyanesque stature (Davis: "His size, color, and weight have saved him on numerous occasions"), but his oxlike brainpower betrays him.

"I've dealt with opportunists who've tried to steal from Wesley," Davis huffed. "And when I see that, I work my ass off trying to *fuck* that person. There's a music store in Chicago. If a

[96]

new keyboard comes out, they'll track Wesley down, pull him into the store and sell it to him. Wesley is 35 years old, and it's not illegal to take advantage of a handicapped person with money. They think he's loaded. They sell him a $2,500 keyboard, then a week later tell him to bring it back—they'll buy it back for half price—then charge him full price for another new keyboard. Fucking con artists. And there's nothing I can do."

Greg Werckman agreed: "Scumbags have been cashing in on him. I've warned Wes that not everyone has his best interests in mind. But part of being mentally disturbed is that he thinks he's going to be the biggest rock star in the world. Lots of people are feeding that delusion. He's a sweet guy, but it's disgusting the way some people are taking advantage of him."

Rob Crow echoed those sentiments: "It's a shame that, despite all his imaginary enemies, there seem to be real people who would take advantage and make fun of him. I would rather he gets better mentally and physically than be a misunderstood rock legend. I hope someday the demons stop, so he can just be an average person like the rest of us."

I had an opportunity to interview Willis before his set at Coney Island High, on New York's Lower East Side. The only semi-quiet spot in the congested club was two flights down, in a basement dressing room. Willis displayed a foul mood at having to trek down two long, narrow, rickety staircases, and he staggered with a visible limp while carrying a bulky travel case, a Walkman around his neck, and his own limitless girth. I descended first, and glanced back to note Willis having difficulty negotiating the stairs, grunting with each step. If he stumbled, I'd be smothered in the ensuing avalanche. The feeling when we reached the basement was akin to the sigh of relief when your plane touches down safely after an hour of turbulence.

Perhaps I didn't put Wes at ease, because at first the interview didn't go well. We were alone in a cramped, dimly lit cellar, amid mysterious fluids collecting in puddles on the cement floor. Split-level sets of three-chord monte reverberated from two upstairs stages. Wes gave mostly few-word answers, each preceded by a Richter-shock fist slam on the dressing room counter. Not knowing Willis personally—that is, never having had him walk in on me during a shower—I wasn't certain if this petulance was standard with prying journalists, or if he had a particular bug up his fat ass about me. Fifteen minutes of Q&A can be illustrated with a few brief excerpts:

Q: How many nights a year do you play live?
A: I'm just doin' my job to keep my ass busy!
Q: What do you think of Elvis?
A: I like him every day.

Q: Do you like all types of music?

A: I like swing, jazz, fusion, rock 'n' roll, heavy metal, death metal, glam metal, and all kinds of metal.

Q: Dizzy Gillespie? John Coltrane?

A: Yeah. I do.

Q: But you don't write songs about them

A: No. Because it doesn't fit my book.

Q: Do you think you belong in the Rock 'n' Roll Hall of Fame?

A: A lot of people think I do.

Q: What are you doing to get in?

A: I just keep busy and stay out of prison.

Q: Were you in prison?

A: No I wasn't. But I don't wanna go. I never will.

Q: Why do you keep beating your fist on the table?

A: I just wanna get up there and play.

Q: Why did you whup Batman's ass?

A: He was getting on my nerves. He called me a bum.

Q: What do you think of critics?

A: They suck.

Q: What else don't you like?

A: My demon! His name is . . . *Nerve Wrecker*!

Q: Why don't you whup his ass?

A: I will.

Q: You don't smoke. What do you think of cigarettes?

A: Cigarettes will kill your ass.

Q: If NASA wanted to put a real rock 'n' roller in outer space, would you go?

A: I'm not getting on a damn spaceship. Orbiting the earth is a waste of time. It's a waste of my life.

Q: Even if you had fans on the moon?

A: Is this interview a hell ride?

Q: That's for you to decide.

A: Are you writing a book about me?

Several answers were punctuated by Willis hawking up phlegm and dramatically spewing wads on the dressing room floor. At the chat's halfway point, tour publicist Heather Mount checked in to make sure artist and writer were bonding. Wes held her small hand and insisted, "Gimme a head-butt." They conked, and Wes laughed childishly. By the end of the interview, Willis gestured me for a head-butt, dispelling any apprehension of personal animus.

Despite his frightening mien, everyone I spoke with affirmed that Willis is a pussycat. "If he loses his temper," observed Mike Davis, "it's at himself, out of frustration. Then he hits himself." Biafra concurs. "People fear him because of his size," he wrote in the liner notes to *Greatest Hits Vol. 2*, "but I have never seen him act violently towards another person. He is gracious to strangers, to the point of introducing himself to other tables in restaurants when we go out to eat."

Back upstairs, I took in a bit of Willis's solo performance. The joint was packed, the congregation in a revivalist frenzy. Wes enjoys good-natured heckling from clubgoers who appreciate the antics of a genuine *primitive* rock 'n' roller. Between songs—which do sound pretty much the same, at similar tempos—he shares a communal call-and-response with the audience: they shout song titles, and he yells back things like *Shut the fuck up!* and *Suck my dick!* It's a one-ring circus, with the wild animal out of his cage. Everyone seems to be having a rollicking time.

I stayed for about 15 minutes—five minutes longer than one fan recommended to catch the full sweep of Wesley's repertoire. He whupped butt, tribbed a few bands, and spat venom at Michael Jackson and Saddam.

I walked out onto St. Mark's Place—which seemed oddly tranquil by comparison—and wandered into a used record outlet a few doors down where I found two stray Wesley Willis CDs. They were filed alongside Sam Kinison under "comedy." I bought them.

Willis deserves respect for his determination to live the rock 'n' roll life. Instead of being locked up in a padded playpen, he's on the road, earning a living as a one-man—and only slightly more psychotic—Butthole Surfers. Sure, he's a pathetic case, light years from reality, and not the most appetizing of human specimens. But he seems to burden few, while giving joy to many. No one would deny him his artistic ambitions. If pharmacological miracles would allow us to vacate mental institutions and steer every psychotic into careerist occupational therapy, then cranks like Ginsberg could spend more time on the street with the best minds of their generation.

Breakfast of champignons

• 11 •

Syd Barrett

GUITARS AND DUST

"Pink Floyd only made one album."

This was the opinion of a bloke named Angus, who'd worked for the band as a stage lighting technician in the late 1960s. Angus represented a handful—these days an ever-dwindling micropercentage—of Pink Floyd fans who didn't feel the group had released just one good album. They felt the group had only released one album *period*.

Angus was referring to the ancient quartet's 1967 debut, *The Piper at the Gates of Dawn*. This school of thought holds that from their second release, *A Saucerful of Secrets*, the band was Pink Floyd in name only. After the brash, beguiling *Piper*, the group's creative arc aimed toward *bigger, longer, slower,* and more *pompous* production, as they became the most expansive of arena schlockers, a lumbering motorcade of fuel-guzzling guitars, wide-load keys, tanker-grade vocals, and drums that don't accelerate beyond second gear. Rock's counterpart to the Chrysler Corporation.

(Yawn.)

The critical distinction between *Piper* and *Saucerful* was Syd Barrett. Syd was/is one of rock's great Lost Souls, a benchmark of drug-scarred lunacy. His self-destructive impulses helped pave the road to hell later trod by such demon-plagued washouts as Skip Spence (Jefferson Airplane, Moby Grape), Roky Erickson (13th Floor Elevators), Arthur Lee (Love), Johnny Thunders (NY Dolls, Heartbreakers), Ian Curtis (Joy Division), Andrew Wood (Mother Love Bone, which became Pearl Jam), Doug Hopkins (Gin Blossoms), and Kurt Cobain (Nirvana). Losers all, they launched auspicious careers with prominent, if not legendary bands, and burned out long before reaching their greatest potential. Some died. Others, like Syd, joined the walking dead.

Unlike most of this book's cast of characters, Syd wasn't always on the outside. During 1967, amidst Great Britain's counterpart of the U.S. psychedelic Summer of Love, Syd was definitely *in*. He was the glamorous face, guitarist, and songwriting genius behind one of the United Kingdom's most exciting and influential new bands.

But within a year, Barrett had migrated permanently to the outside. He was banished from Pink Floyd, as he tumbled into a psychological maelstrom and became pop music's premiere acid-fry.

But his recording career didn't end—hence, his inclusion in this gallery.

Although mind-altering chemicals were part of Syd's daily nutritional intake, some of his friends felt drugs merely aggravated a predisposition to psychic disturbance that would have overtaken Barrett sooner or later. His father's premature death when Syd was 12 had affected the lad greatly, and his mother seems to have overcompensated with relentless pampering. "We all felt he should have gone to a psychiatrist," said Pink Floyd replacement guitarist David Gilmour. "Someone in fact played an interview [with Syd] to [psychotherapist-author] R. D. Laing, and Laing claimed he was incurable."

Before his descent into the Gone Forever division of Rock's Where-Are-They-Now Club, Barrett wrote Pink Floyd's early hit singles, "Arnold Layne" and "See Emily Play"; composed most of the band's first album, on which he sang and played guitar; and recorded two rough-hewn solo collections. A third solo album of unreleased recordings was later packaged on CD, bringing his entire catalog to about four albums of material, not all of it entirely solid. Some downright dodgy.

Yet despite a sparse musical legacy, Barrett's influence on subsequent generations of rabbit-hole rockers is incalculable. It includes the British Canterbury movement, such as early Soft Machine with Robert Wyatt and Kevin Ayers, Caravan, and Mike Oldfield; Roy Harper; David Bowie; Fairport Convention and its numerous offshoots; the Nice; Marc Bolan; Nick Drake; TV Personalities—and really any U.K. band that ventured into the realm of psychedelic rock from 1967 to the present. Daevid Allen of Gong performed with a snapshot of Barrett perched on his amp. Robyn Hitchcock's entire career has been one endless—and not unsuccessful—attempt to fill the void left by Syd's premature vaporization. And in making it cool to withdraw, Syd became a patron saint to countless shoegazers and mope rockers of the 1980s and 1990s.

Barrett's songs have been covered by Bowie ("See Emily Play"), The Jesus and Mary Chain ("Vegetable Man"), The Lightning Seeds ("Lucifer Sam"), R.E.M. ("Dark Globe"), Slowdive ("Golden Hair"), Smashing Pumpkins ("Terrapin"), Love and Rockets ("Lucifer Sam"), Hitchcock's former band the Soft Boys ("Gigolo Aunt"), Teenage Fan Club ("Interstellar Overdrive"), This Mortal Coil ("Late Night"), and the Walking Seeds ("Astronomy Domine"), among others.

But Barrett isn't particularly moved by any of this adulation. Syd isn't moved by much of anything, having remained creatively catatonic since around 1972.

Roger Keith "Syd" Barrett was born in Cambridge on January 6, 1946. His mother ran a boarding house that was frequented by students and scruffy young bohemians, many of whom drifted to swinging London in the 1960s to indulge their artistic fantasies.

A local named Storm, of the British album-sleeve design firm Hipgnosis, told *New Musical Express (NME)* that Syd was a "bright, extrovert kid. Smoked dope, pulled chicks—the usual thing. He had no problems on the surface. He was no introvert as far as I could see."

In the early 1960s, Syd learned guitar and banjo, then switched to bass, playing in now-forgotten groups specializing in blues-based rock or Shadows covers. While attending London's Camberwell Art School, he crossed paths with a band called the Abdabs, which consisted of Regent Street Polytechnic architecture students Roger Waters, Rick Wright, and Nick Mason. Syd had known Waters and Wright in Cambridge, though they were several years older. All shared a penchant for American R&B. The Abdabs, with Syd on guitar, became the Tea Set in 1965.

Wright welcomed Barrett's entry into the band. He told *Mojo* magazine in 1994, "Before [Syd] we'd play the R&B classics, because that's what all groups were supposed to do then. But I never liked R&B much. I was actually more of a jazz fan. With Syd the direction changed, it became more improvised around the guitar and keyboards. Roger started playing the bass as a lead instrument, and I started to introduce more of my classical feel." Shortly after joining, Syd rechristened the band by compounding the first names of two Georgia blues patriarchs, Pink Anderson and Floyd Council.

Syd and his mates fashioned themselves after the prevailing British pop styles that had evolved out of the 1963–64 Beatles explosion. By 1966, the era of flower power blossoming in San Francisco and sprouting across the United States began wafting spores across the Atlantic, causing revolutions in music, clothing, and inner consciousness. Syd allegedly wore out a copy of the Stones album *Between the Buttons* and the first album by Love. (The riff for the Floyd instrumental "Interstellar Overdrive" was nicked from Love's version of the Bacharach-David tune "My Little Red Book.") The quartet's approach became more surreal, science fiction–oriented, and drug-tinged.

The *only* Pink Floyd album that matters.
(Barrett is in the upper right.)

Pink Floyd charted with their first two Barrett-penned singles, "See Emily Play," about the fantasies of a romantic little girl, and the creepy "Arnold Layne," about a jailed sex pervert. The recordings, which featured lots of fractured guitar, electronic keyboards, and studio gimmickry, landed the foursome gigs on TV's *Top of the Pops*.

Piper at the Gates of Dawn, recorded in 1967, was considered one of the stellar releases of the year. Though its impact in the United States was marginal, in the United Kingdom it was considered by many second only to the Beatles' *Sgt. Pepper's Lonely Hearts Club Band* in galvanizing British youth culture.

Songwriter and lead singer Barrett, undeniably the group's focal point, was an adorable, noodle-coifed moppet with the androgynous aura of an 18th-century dandy. In snapshots and publicity pix, he appears slightly spent, always with a semi-deranged look in his dark eyes.

Barrett songs such as "Flaming," "Bike," and "Matilda Mother" were playful and fairytale-ish. With references to dollhouses, unicorns, and gingerbread men, his dream imagery reflected the English tea-party whimsy of Lewis Carroll, Edward Lear, and *The Wind in the Willows*. "The Gnome" described a curious forest dweller named Grimble Grumble, who wore a scarlet tunic with a blue-green hood. Grumble spent most of his time "wining, dining, [and] biding his time," until one day "he had a big adventure" (further details were not available then, or at press time).

The title character of "Lucifer Sam" was an inscrutable feline:

At night prowling sifting sand
Padding around on the ground
He'll be found when you're around
That cat's something I can't explain

"Bike" is a Prince Valiant attempt at chivalry that includes the chorus:

You're the kind of girl that fits in with my world.
I'll give you anything, everything if you want things

though it veers off into a typical Barrett non-sequitur:

> I know a mouse, and he hasn't got a house
> I don't know why, I call him Gerald
> He's getting rather old, but he's a good mouse

The Floyd quickly became Day-Glo poster boys for the nascent British psychedelic scene, playing all-night spectacles at London's UFO club. Their musical performances, tabbed "avant-garde" because of their extended instrumental forays, were augmented by elaborate light shows. The live Floyd experience was, in fact, quite different from the hit single–geared studio band. As Barrett told *Melody Maker* in 1967, "The sort of records we make today are impossible to reproduce on stage, so there is no point in trying." Early Floyd studio productions were notable for such idiosyncrasies as incomprehensible speech submerged beneath layers of rhythmic cacophony, unidentifiable sound effects, and queer signal-processing embellishments (many descended from pioneering British producer Joe Meek, who committed suicide in 1967).

Barrett's electric lead work—shards of sound that vacillated between jaggedness and melody—was hailed for its originality and intuitiveness. Syd's thunderous low notes bristled with malevolence, and in mid-song he could fire off bursts of feedback like ballistic missiles. His playing inspired guitar-noise pioneer Fred Frith, who called Barrett's aggressive attack "a revolutionary source of electronic racket."

Syd's instrumental savagery posed an interesting counterpoint to his storybook lyric motifs. In retrospect, it probably echoed his propensity for psychological disengagement and impending madness. "Whether he was entirely conscious or in control of his art is impossible to determine," speculated Kris DiLorenzo in *Trouser Press* magazine. "Perhaps it's enough to say that he was indeed effective."

But hallucinogens became a deeper preoccupation. Syd was surrounded by the typical rock-star entourage of groupies, sycophants, and drug-buddies. Coupled with his own lack of self-discipline, he careened into a vortex of mental and professional chaos. Photographer Mick Rock described Syd's flat as "a burnt-out place, the biggest hovel, the biggest shit-heap; a total acid-shell. There were so many people, it was like a railway station." The population included two cats, Pink and Floyd, who were routinely slipped LSD. "You know what heavy dope scenes were like," said Rock.

These brain shampoos sapped Barrett's will and triggered erratic behavior. He'd arrive late for gigs. Onstage, tripping ferociously, he'd play two chords all night, or none. He might de-tune his guitar, then bash the strings a bit. Or he wouldn't take the stage at all, preferring to remain on the tour bus.

Barrett gained renown for "The Stare," a glassy, vacant gaze he'd lapse into for no apparent reason, at no particular time. "The head would tilt back slightly, the eyes would get misty and bloated," wrote Nick Kent of *NME* in 1974, "then they would stare right at you and right through you at the same time."

One oft-told incident was emblematic of Barrett's sanity-scrub. The band was onstage preparing for a set, but Syd was MIA. The wack guitarist was still in the dressing room, trying desperately to contend with his tousled tresses. He emptied a jar of Mandrax (a methaqualone sedative), crushed the pills, and mixed the granules with a jar of Brylcreem hair lotion. He then poured this gelatinous muck on his head and worked it in, before joining his cohorts. As the set progressed, the hot stage lighting made the gluey compound liquefy and dribble downward, causing Syd's face to resemble molten wax.

Around this period, Barrett allegedly beat up his girlfriend and locked her in a room for a week, pushing crackers under the door to fend off starvation.

Trying to capitalize on their U.K. singles success, in November 1967 the Floyd arranged a U.S. tour, including several prime TV spots. They faced the cameras on Dick Clark's *American Bandstand* to mime a recording of their new Barrett-penned single, "Apples and Oranges." But as band manager Peter Jenner noted, "Syd wasn't into moving his lips that day." An appearance on the *Pat Boone Show* had the preppy host asking Barrett typically innocuous questions and in reply getting mute, paralytic stares.

Upon their return to England, disgusted and distressed, the band hired David Gilmour as second guitarist. Gilmour, an old Cambridge mate, was a gifted stylistic impersonator who'd been slinging Hendrix pyrotechnics with various bands in France. He was told: "Play like Syd." For a month or so they tried working as a quintet, but to no avail. Barrett continued his solipsistic stage ways, riffing a single chord of an evening.

In April 1968, Syd became Pink Floyd's ex-guitarist. As Roger Waters told *Melody Maker* in 1971, "We got to the point where any one of us was likely to tear his throat out at any minute because he was so impossible." There was hope that Syd could remain a nonperforming, songwriting member of the band, like Brian Wilson and the Beach Boys. But Syd's continuing psychotic behavior quickly put that biscuit back in the tin.

The last recorded Barrett composition on a Floyd album was "Jugband Blues," from *A Saucerful of Secrets*. It was Syd's only identifiable presence on the record, and considering the swan-song circumstances under which the lyrics were written, "Jugband" is fittingly *Saucerful*'s closing track:

It's awfully considerate of you to think of me here
And I'm most obliged to you for making it clear
That I'm not here

And I never knew the moon could be so big
And I never knew the moon could be so blue
And I'm grateful that you threw away my old shoes
And brought me here instead dressed in red
And I'm wondering who could be writing this song

Peter Jenner called "Jugband Blues" the "ultimate self-diagnosis on a state of schizophrenia." The arrangement included a non-sequitur, mid-song passage by a Salvation Army sextet, to whom Syd instructed, "Play what you like."

Equally self-referential was "Vegetable Man," one of the last songs Barrett wrote while in the band. The chorus, "Vegetable Man—where are you?," climaxes verses in which Barrett itemizes what he was wearing when he wrote the lyrics. He dispels any doubt that the title is autobiographical: "It's what you see / It must be me / It's what I am." "Vegetable Man" was recorded at the same session as "Jugband," and although it's never been commercially released, bootlegs have proliferated. The song has even been covered twice, by the Soft Boys and the Jesus and Mary Chain.

Saucerful was a transitional record, a departure from *Piper*. The mood is more ethereal, less song-oriented, less playful, and more space-jam infused. The album lacks Barrett's elfin spirit, and lends credence to the naysayers who assert that the Floyd only made one album, and it was *Piper*. By comparison, parts of *Saucerful* are downright tedious. (The album arguably represents the cornerstone of the temple of prog-rock pretentiousness.) With the exception of "Jugband Blues," the track that most harkens back to *Piper* was Roger Waters's snotty, antimilitary send-up "Corporal Clegg," though Barrett does not play on the piece. Syd reportedly contributed slide guitar to Rick Wright's Bo Diddley-goes-to-art-school "Remember a Day."

Syd spent his immediate post-Floyd days locked in his London room, in a flat he shared with artist pal Duggie Fields. Barrett avoided the public and his former bandmates. He'd lay in bed, apprehensive about getting up, wondering if it was worth it ... and if he did get up, what would he do? Fields told *Trouser Press*, "He had great problems committing himself to any action.... He'd set off, lose his motivation, and start questioning what he was doing—which might just be walking down the street." Barrett also spent a lot of time mesmerized by TV.

In March 1969, Syd briefly snapped out of his embryonic seclusion. He wrote a letter to EMI Records, expressing interest in re-entering the studio. Production for the sessions was assigned to Malcolm Jones, a young executive who was busy setting up EMI's new affiliate label, Harvest. Jones produced a number of Barrett tracks before Waters and Gilmour offered to finish the project. (They would possibly have gotten involved earlier, but they were working on the next Floyd album, the two-LP *Ummagumma*.) The title of the resultant 1970 release, *The Madcap Laughs,* while undoubtedly artist-descriptive, in fact came from a playful line in the song "Octopus."

Madcap included solo tracks featuring a woebegone Barrett mechanically strumming an acoustic guitar, interspersed with after-the-fact ensemble arrangements. Waters and Gilmour played on the album, as did uncredited Soft Machine members Robert Wyatt (drums), Mike Ratledge (keyboards), and Hugh Hopper (bass). Later in 1970 a second album, *Barrett,* was recorded and released; it was produced by Wright and Gilmour. Though darker and flakier than *Madcap, Barrett* like its predecessor featured solo acoustic numbers alongside small ensemble settings, which included organ, piano, and harmonium by Wright.

Syd Barrett, ca. 1970, surrounded by the trappings of
stardom in his London apartment

The pair of albums sounded like they were recorded in a padded wood-shed. The songs are inconsistent, as befits a fractal personality. Some are rambling manifestations of dementia, while others reflected the haunted pop craftsman who still inhabited Barrett's body at least part of the time. They tacked from the brilliant ("Terrapin," "Baby Lemonade," and "Gigolo Aunt") to the crackpot-indulgent ("Love You," "It Is Obvious," and "Rats"). Oblique autobiography abounds. On "Dominoes" Syd sighs, "You and I and dominoes / the day goes by," an apt description of a routine post-Floyd Barrett afternoon.

Syd's gentle, brooding baritone occasionally breaks, or seems hesitant. He strains for high notes without confidence and mutters to himself, confronted with a seeming disconnect between what's swirling around his brain and what emerges from his mouth. He strums arrhythmically, grappling with the rudiments, flubbing notes, then unexpectedly careening into a surge of brilliance. Shaggs-like moments occur, as rhythmic transitions stumble, and Barrett drifts off mic or strays off-key.

The standard practice for multitrack recording is to first tape bass and drum tracks—to lay a foundation—before overdubbing vocals and lead instruments. Barrett's producers reversed this process. They first captured Syd's vocals and guitar parts, then added the rhythm section. They probably feared that the Madcap would waste valuable studio time trying to synchronize with a live band. Barrett had difficulty staying in beat, resulting in all manner of odd, haphazard meters. "If [the song] 'Love You' was a little irregular—Syd went into the next verse, occasionally, after six-and-a-half or seven bars instead of eight," observed Jones—"then 'It's No Good Trying' was positively impossible! ... [It's] very hard for a musician other than the composer to follow."

The desolate, claustrophobic atmosphere of Syd's solo work is all the more striking when contrasted with the adrenaline-rich, paisley-bedecked majesty of *Piper*. On *Madcap* and *Barrett*, Syd is emotionally dissipated, occasionally just going through the motions. The talent is still evident, the voice is as distinctive and disarming as ever, but he's basically a human crater. "There's no way to avoid feeling," wrote Kris DiLorenzo, "that the two albums are the portrait of a breakdown." The party was over, but no one was left to clean up the mess. Nick Kent said the songs "exist completely inside their own zone, like weird insects and exotic fish, the listener looking inside the tank at the activity."

If the above descriptions sound rather negative, it should be stressed that many of these qualities are what make Barrett's solo work so compelling and rewarding. As with outsiders in general, perfection is never the point, and the abundant flaws make Barrett's vulnerable performances charming and endearing, like a torn teddy bear with one eye-button dangling by a thread.

Barrett's press interviews during this period were disjointed exercises in grasping at smoke-rings. Michael Watts of *Melody Maker* tried to address the drug issue with Syd in a 1971 chat, but Barrett couldn't focus on the question.

Michael Watts: There were stories you had left [Pink Floyd] because you had been freaked out by acid trips.

Syd Barrett: Well, I dunno, it don't seem to have much to do with the job. I only know the thing of playing, of being a musician, was very exciting. Obviously, one was better off with a silver guitar with mirrors and things all over it than people who ended up on the floor or anywhere else in London. The general concept, I didn't feel so conscious of it as perhaps I should. I mean, one's position as a member of London's young people's—I dunno what you'd call it, underground wasn't it—wasn't necessarily realised and felt, I don't think, especially from the point of view of groups....

MW: Were you not at all involved in acid, then, during its heyday among rock bands?

SB: No. It was all, I suppose, related to living in London. I was lucky enough.... I've always thought of going back to a place where you can drink tea and sit on the carpet. I've been fortunate enough to do that. All that time ... you've just reminded me of it. I thought it was good fun. I thought the Soft Machine were good fun. They were playing on *Madcap*, except for Kevin Ayers.

Trying to get Barrett to address the conflicts that led to his expulsion from the Floyd were just as frustrating:

MW: Would you say, therefore, you were a difficult person to get on with?

SB: No. Probably my own impatience is the only thing, because it has to be very easy. You can play guitar in your canteen, you know, your hair might be longer, but there's a lot more to playing than traveling around universities and things.

Although the albums did not sell well—touring to support the releases was out of the question—they did further the cult of Syd.

Barrett continued writings songs and behaving in an unpredictable manner. He gravitated further from the sphere of reality, often lapsing into zombielike trance states. Conversations with friends were as muddled as the interviews.

Barrett finally left London and moved back to his mother's Cambridge cellar. He'd transcended this worldly consciousness. He shaved his head to a layer of fuzz, a style known as a "Borstal crop" (after the shearing administered in a boys' prison). He saw very few people and generally stayed home. "I'm disappearing, avoiding most things," he told Mick Rock of *Rolling Stone* in December 1971. "Mostly I just waste my time. I'm full of dust and guitars." Rock described the 25-year-old Barrett as "hollow-cheeked and pale, his eyes reflect[ing] a permanent state of shock. He has a ghostly beauty which one normally associates with poets of old." The *Rolling Stone* interview was a forlorn encounter, full of reflections and regrets, bereft of hope. "I think young people should have a lot of fun," observed Barrett, "but I never seem to have any." He wistfully noted, "I'd like to be rich. I'd like a lot of money to put into my physicals and to buy food for all my friends."

In 1972 Barrett returned to the studio to record. "It was an abortion," Syd's friend Peter Barnes told *NME*. "He just kept overdubbing guitar part on guitar part until it was just a total chaotic mess. He also wouldn't show anyone his lyrics—I fear because he hadn't written any." The sessions were scrapped.

Later that year he was asked by Cambridge friend and drummer Twink to form a local band, called Stars. Several historical accounts assert that Barrett was hired for his marquee value, and that the band was a mediocre, forgettable outfit. Stars played a couple of local shows but got bad reviews, which further demoralized Barrett. At a January 1973 gig, after about an hour of technical glitches and uninspired hackery, Syd unplugged his guitar, walked offstage, and it was all over. He went back to his mother's cellar, and the group went into the dustbin. It was Barrett's last public appearance on stage.

Syd occasionally dropped by his London publisher, Lupus Music. During one such visit in 1974, the company's manager, ever hopeful, asked Barrett if he'd written any new songs. "No," replied Barrett, who turned and departed without further comment.

Shortly thereafter, in a fit of self-exasperation, Barrett smashed his head through his mother's basement ceiling.

In 1974 Harvest Records repackaged Syd's solo albums in a gatefold two-LP sleeve, whose inner panels were cluttered with snapshots of a beautiful but doomed young artist who never smiled for the camera. Rick Wright was quoted in the press as saying he found Syd's songs "appalling ... musically, they're atrocious." Yet Roger Waters told Q magazine in 1987, "I could never aspire to Syd's crazed insights and perceptions.... I'll always credit Syd with the connection he made between his personal unconscious and the collective group unconscious. It's taken me 15 years to get anywhere near there. Even though he was clearly out of control when making his two solo albums, some of the work is staggeringly evocative. It's the humanity of it all that's so impressive."

Barrett remained lost in the wildwood, disoriented, wrestling with his inner demons. He reportedly sat around watching the telly and gaining weight, as his once-curly tresses receded into male pattern baldness. Old friends like Kevin Ayers and old fans like Brian Eno and Jimmy Page tried to talk Barrett into returning to music. But Syd preferred to remain cloistered with his family.

Pink Floyd, feeling sentimental, wrote and recorded a Barrett tribute, "Shine on You Crazy Diamond," for their 1975 album *Wish You Were Here*. In one of his few social outings, Barrett attended the final mixdown session for "Shine on." When asked by Waters what he thought of the song, Barrett dead-panned, "Sounds a bit old."

Since his retreat, Barrett has rarely been seen in public. Yet his legend grows. In England, Syd sightings are almost as common as Elvis spottings in the United States. Such reports are only slightly more reliable than those involving the King. The reclusive Barrett has been seen, but he won't—or can't—perform music or give interviews, isn't writing songs, and seems to be too far gone mentally to function in a self-reliant manner.

A 1988 album entitled *Opel* collected outtakes and alternate versions from the *Madcap* and *Barrett* projects, as well as some immediate post-Floyd sessions produced by Jenner but abandoned. *Opel* is more than just a closet-shelf carton of single socks and souvenir keychains. It contains some of Barrett's most intimate and affecting music, including the breathtakingly plaintive title track; the delicately rhythmic "Swan Lee"; and two resplendent versions—one vocal, one instrumental—of "Golden Hair," a song that originally appeared on *Madcap* and which features lyrics adapted from a James Joyce poem.

Barrett's nephew Ian consented to an E-mail interview with the Syd-devoted *Set the Controls* Web site around 1995. Ian was respectful of the privacy of his uncle "Roger," and admitted the wayward one's motivations weren't always discernible. "Roger does have a little record player, but he's only got a few records and tapes and they're mainly of classical concerts," Ian revealed. "He really isn't very interested in music anymore. He does have an acoustic guitar which I assume he strums to himself, but I've never heard him play it." Explaining Syd's lack of contact with old friends, Ian said, "He simply isn't interested in going back over a time in his life that precipitated his breakdown and retreat from society. The whole Floyd time is so long ago that he simply wants to be left in peace to get on with his painting and reading and whatever.... He doesn't enjoy socializing and finds it very disturbing to be around large groups of people."

And yet, Ian perceived in his uncle Roger something akin to inner peace. "He is definitely starting to find a sense of contentment that has eluded him since his breakdown," explained the younger Barrett. "He is happy to just potter about at home, watching television and doing a bit of painting or reading.

Having a conversation with Roger is not the same as one with most people as he does have a strange and fragmented way of speaking, so everyday things come out sounding quite abstract. But it all has its own internal logic and it's just his way of expressing himself.... For many people it's easy to block out the real pain the songs put across and convince themselves the songs are just the funny ramblings of a 'rock nutter.' I'm afraid I can't do that."

So, Syd's not coming back. He left behind a gorgeous catalog of twisted childlike folk-pop that his fans will forever enjoy to a degree that exceeds the composer's pride in creating them. Peter Barnes observed, "He's much bigger now as the silent cult figure doing nothing than he was when he was functioning."

Perhaps it's just as well for Pink Floyd. Promoting their 1994 album *The Division Bell,* drummer Nick Mason remarked that the group avoided the cult of personality. "We don't have to promote a Bono or a Mick Jagger," Mason told *Mojo*'s Tim Meekins. "The thing you have to remember is, we're so wonderfully boring."

Unlike Syd, they didn't have to burn out on drugs to get that way.

• 12 •

Eilert Pilarm

THE KING OF SWEDEN

I f the federal government needs yet another scheme to raise revenue from a tax-weary populace, here's a modest proposal: *the Elvis Tax.*

An across-the-board 8 percent surcharge on every Elvis tchotchke: records, buttons, T-shirts, posters, books, costumes, snowglobes, commemorative plates, videos, software, truck decals, and fan club bric-a-brac. Our nation would never experience another budget deficit.

As rockabilly wildman Mojo Nixon once sang, "Elvis Is Everywhere." And where Elvis isn't, there's an Elvis impersonator. Heave a pound of bacon on any American thoroughfare and it's bound to land at the feet of some guy who makes a living bringing Elvis back from the dead.

Then what's so special about Eilert Pilarm?

First, he's the *Swedish* Elvis. Well, one of 'em, anyway. (He claims there's three more.) He's released two CDs of Elvis covers and performs the King's repertoire in Swedish rock clubs.

Second, third, and fourth: does he look like Elvis? *Not in the least.* Does he sound like Elvis? *No way.* Can he move like Elvis? *Forget it.*

Therein lies the *big* difference: thousands of ghoulish, unconvincing Presley grave-robbers are trying their darndest to copy the King.

Eilert, on the other hand, is just being himself.

Eilert (pronounced AY-lert) Pilarm, in his 40s with thinning blond hair, wire-rimmed glasses, and a pudgy, avuncular countenance, wouldn't make the quarterfinals in an Elvis contest presided over by deaf and blind judges. Unlike the King and most of his shadows, Eilert can't sing a lick. And how many Elvis-wannabes vocalize in a thick Swedish accent, delivering lyrics in a

manner that barely approximates English?
How many possess less-than-zero grasp of
the concept of rhythm?

None of these drawbacks have deterred
Eilert from regularly donning the King's
raiment and taking the stage to offer "Love
Me Tender" with passion and sincerity.
Above all, *sincerity.*

Therein lies the charm of Eilert, whose
initials would otherwise seem the only
overt link to his late musical hero.

When Elvis gobbled his final grilled
peanut butter-bacon-and-banana Dagwood
in 1977, the world lost one of its most
potent aphrodisiacs. (The singer, not the
sandwich.) Yet it would be another 16
years before Pilarm felt the calling ("I saw
Elvis in my bedroom") and cloaked himself in sequined robes. Portentously,
Eilert (born April 4, 1953) began his career at roughly the same age Elvis was
when he fatally toppled off his chrome and black leather throne.

Shortly after heeding the call, Pilarm began releasing cassettes titled *Elvis
I, Elvis II,* and *Elvis III,* on which he sang Presley tunes over prerecorded studio instrumental tracks. These tapes were sold after club performances and
through mail order. From this catalog a 1996 CD was compiled, *Eilert Pilarm's
Greatest Hits.* It was reported that veteran BBC Radio One DJ John Peel cited
this release as among his favorite discs. A newly recorded 18-song studio follow-up, *Eilert Is Back,* emerged in 1998. (Both albums are on Green Pig
Records.)

Eilert's Web page, created by friend, fan, and fellow Swede Per-Gunnar
Eriksson, describes Pilarm with needless restraint as "probably the world's
most original interpreter of songs made famous by Elvis Presley." These
include the standards "Hound Dog," "Jailhouse Rock," "All Shook Up," and
"Don't Be Cruel," along with film favorites like "Blue Hawaii" and devotional
ballads such as "In My Father's House." *Eilert Is Back* also features three
bonus tracks in Swedish.

If you're sick of the same old Christmas music, if you've had your fill of
chestnuts roasting, listen to "Silent Night" (on *Eilert Is Back*) as an antidote to
the season's recurrent folderol. Eilert's confidence is unwavering, even if the
melody isn't, and his tenderness is touching. There's a melancholy in his
voice, a longing, and you'll connect. There's no place like Örnsköldsvik for the
holidays.

The music behind Eilert is performed by session-hire Tobbe Karlström, who records the instrumentals over which Eilert lays his vocals. The music is very professional—in fact, it's flawless, generic, and bloodless. It has no pretension, its utility serving one purpose: to put Eilert's singing to bed, which it ably accomplishes. Eilert's not-unpleasant baritone displays a wide range of dynamics: he howls, whines, pleads, and strains his way through a song. He's not always on beat and he's rarely in tune, but as noted elsewhere in this book, "The angels love enthusiasm far more than perfection." When playing Eilert's "It's Now Or Never" on WFMU, I received a phone call from a female New York listener who exclaimed excitedly, "I love it! This man is my future ex-husband!" She rang up the following week when "Release Me" was aired from *Greatest Hits* and averred that Eilert sounded like "the cuddliest man alive."

The charade may seem comical, but it's no joke. "When Eilert started out," Eriksson observed, "I guess he wasn't aware of how he sounded or what he wanted with his singing. It was part of his—at that time—messed up life. He suffered from split personality for over 20 years. Part of his illness was a lot of fantasizing about his childhood idol Elvis."

I spoke with Pilarm via telephone from Sweden. The interview went nicely, despite his admitted "not so well good" English. ("But I can sing a song," he assured me.) He's a very sweet man who lacks attitude, an admirable trait for someone who aspires to fill the King's boots. His real name is Nils Roland ("Like 'Roland Reagan,'" he explained, to clarify spelling) Eilert Dahlberg. He worshiped Elvis as a child and collected his music. Now, he said, he has "all the Elvis" records. "I think I have 50," he attested. When informed that Elvis undoubtedly made more than 50, he concedes, "I don't know how much record he do."

For 15 years before embarking on his singing career, Eilert "worked in wood"—that is, he was a lumberman, cutting trees. Nowadays he's a "cleaner around the paper machine" (he washes office floors).

In clubs, which he plays on an irregular basis, he "has much public when [he] sings Elvis." He chuckled when asked if he's the number one Swedish Elvis. "I think so," he said with some modesty. He has no manager, and performs live without a band. "I sing singback," he explained, meaning he's accompanied by prerecorded tapes.

Eilert took a trip to the United States in 1995, and made a pilgrimage to Graceland. At a hotel 20 minutes from the shrine, he played a small showcase and sang three songs (which he pronounced "Yalehouse Rawk," "Love Me Taynder," and "Teddeh Bear"). It was "wary good," he recalled.

Does he think Elvis is still alive and hiding? "If he lies, I think he is in the hospitile [sic], and he is dying." He believes he himself is Elvis, feels like Elvis, and suffers like Elvis. "I have seen on TV, and I read a book, and I dream of him, many, many dreams," he revealed. "He speak to my dream, he speak to Lisa Marie, and Lisa Marie speak to me. I called her." He insists he talked to Presley's daughter on the phone in 1993, the year of his royal rebirth, and told her, "Your dad telephoned to me, and you have *two dads!*" (Lisa Marie could not be reached for comment.)

Despite assuming the identity, Eilert hoped to avoid some of the King's reckless indulgences, like the horse-dosages prescribed by Dr. Nick. "I don't take drugs," Pilarm asserted. "I have a new medicine now from the doctor, and that's all that I take." He also doesn't fancy the gluttonous diet. "I think Elvis was sick to eat so much," he acknowledged. Does he suspect that Elvis was lonely at the top, that food and drugs filled an emotional void? "No," Eilert demurred. "But when Gladys his mother died, it was a big problem."

As for which Elvis he prefers—young or mature—Eilert declared, "I like Elvis whole time, but he was best to sing when he was old." He enjoys Presley's Hollywood period, despite its abundance of musical dross. Exercising discretion and maintaining his dignity, Eilert has refrained from recording such film soundtrack clunkers as "There's No Room to Rhumba in a Sports Car," "Queenie Wahine's Papaya," or "Do the Clam." "I sing the song I like," he remarked with pride, "the early song and the rock and roll." Onstage, however, he dresses more like the older Elvis, in garish, sequined costumes, overwide belts, and rear-wall collars. He also conceded he does not emulate Elvis's hip-swivel. "I don't moving," he explained. "I sing my style," which he described as basically "standing there."

Eilert may remain fairly motionless, but the audience doesn't. He either lacks the perspective to judge the celebratory impact he has on club-goers, or he's too modest to discuss it.

"I've seen two of his shows, which were pretty much alike," Eriksson recalled, "although one was with a band and one with music on tape and CD. He just enters the stage, says a few words and starts singing." Apart from his shimmering Presleyan regalia, there were no spectacular Vegas-style pyrotechnics. But the vibe sounds similar to the jubilant, revivalist atmosphere of a B. J. Snowden or Wesley Willis club appearance. "The audience is in on the act from the first false note," said Eriksson, "but the crowd is not laughing at Eilert. They're having fun and singing along, dancing and shouting. Eilert looks out at the audience, smiling slightly, but focused intently on the lyrics and singing." There is little between-song banter. "Most of the time he stands pretty much in the same spot," Eriksson continued, "swaying a little from side to side, singing with the mic close to his face."

Eriksson sees Pilarm as part of a quaint Swedish tradition. "In the old days," he explained, "every small Swedish village or town had what we call an 'original'—people who were a bit odd, who dressed and behaved unusually, but who were harmless and were taken care of as part of the social fabric. I'm always intrigued by artists who do it 'their way'—singing or playing really awful, or just very, very strangely. These performers—Eilert is one—aren't destined for greatness, but they have an instinctive belief in themselves that gives what they do a surreal entertainment value. When I heard Eilert's record on the radio, I laughed 'til my stomach ached and I ran out of tears. But when you meet him, his rocking acquires another dimension. He's a pretty level-headed, middle-aged man who does this for real. He's enjoying himself."

Despite his eternal devotion to his idol, Pilarm seems content to keep things from getting out of control. He is apparently in no hurry to scale the Olympian peaks of his predecessor.

"To be honest," Eriksson conceded, "I doubt if Eilert would like to make it really big. He seems content having this singing career, on the level it is at the moment."

• 13 •

Lucia Pamela
INTERSTELLAR OVERDRIVE

neil Armstrong was *not* the first earthling to walk on the moon.
The 1969 album *Into Outer Space with Lucia Pamela* proves that the
woman voted Miss St. Louis of 1926 set foot on that planet before the Apollo
11 team. This eccentric 13-song cycle provides a travelogue of Miss Pamela's
mission exploring what later became astronaut Alan B. Shepard's crater-
pocked golf course.

NASA has refused comment.

Another government cover-up? Art Bell—can you help expose the truth?

Miss Lucia Pamela is the shortest musical route between the Shaggs and
Sun Ra. *Into Outer Space* was originally released on Gulfstream Records, an
obscure Hollywood, Florida, label. Perhaps 500 copies were pressed; few originals have surfaced—on any planet.

Lucia insists she played all the instruments herself, in what sound like half-
a-beat-short overdubs. There's jaunty upright piano colliding with untamed
clarinet jockeying for airspace against daredevil percussion—a musical meteor
shower. Atop this cataclysmic racket Lucia hollers, growls, and stutters her storybook lyrics, yakking away like a tipsy Ethel Merman. The mix is drenched in
extreme reverb, VU meters deep in the red. Imagine an LP of a peyote-
soaked klezmer band, recorded with Joe Meek passed out at the console,
wavering on your turntable between 31 and 35 rpm.

Lucia's performances are spirited and energetic, without an
ounce of self-consciousness. Truly kooky—less schmaltzy than
Mrs. Miller, wilder than Leona Anderson, more rockin' than Florence Foster Jenkins.

DRAWINGS BY MISS LUCIA PAMELA

Miss Lucia Pamela

A childlike positivism flavors Lucia's songs, slathered as they are with her musical peanut butter and lyrical jelly. The subject matter ranges from cows and dogs on the moon to an "Indian Alphabet Chant," and a vertebrae-crunching space-rock dance called the "Flip, Flop, Fly," (no relationship to the Big Joe Turner hit "Flip, Flop, and Fly").

"All of the music is true," Lucia told Neil Strauss in a 1992 *New York Press* interview. "Most of it is from experience."

The stargazing Miss Pamela confides that she recorded her album on the moon. Don't argue. Ask Lucia a direct question about her long, legendary career in show business, but don't expect a logical answer. She may be telling the truth—or embellishing it. A conversation with Lucia is full of cul-de-sacs and curve balls. You may not get a factual response, but you will get an enchanting yarn.

If you believe in fairy tales, you're on this grande dame's wavelength.

I interviewed the gracious and sweet Lucia Pamela at her Los Angeles home in 1991. A grand piano stood majestically in her living room, whose walls were adorned with photos depicting the darling entertainer at many stages of her whirlwind career.

Lucia was born in St. Louis on May 1, sometime during the 20th century (she isn't telling when). She recalls that at age two, while reaching for a fresh-baked cookie on a hot stove, her fingers melted together. The injured child was whisked to a doctor who, she attests, "used a knife to slice my melted hands into 10 fingers. He didn't give me any thumbs, so it made me a better piano player."

The biographical tidbits contained in the original liner notes of *Into Outer Space* are delightfully whimsical. The name "Beethoven" appears three times. Since paraphrasing couldn't possibly do justice to Lucia's poetic flights, here are a few verbatim excerpts (original capitalization, spelling, and punctuation retained):

We would like to give you just a little history of this great star and entertainer; LUCIA PAMELA ...

She started to perform when she was four years old. She is the daughter of a very fine concert pianist, and at her first performance at the age of four she sang and played an Indian Love Song which she herself wrote, music and lyrics. At the age of five, six, and seven years of age, her mother could not take her away from the piano; she had to force her away from the piano to eat.

At the age of seven years, she started to play concerts on the stage with her mother and also played concerts on the stage with the great piano soloist, Charles Kunkel, who was at that time one of the finest concert pianists of the world. He was equal to Paderewski, who was the greatest pianist in the world. He, himself, in person, attended one of the concerts that Lucia Pamela was playing when she was about eight years old. Paderewski was so amazed and so enthused that he went back stage and gave a note written by him to Lucia's mother about her daughter, telling her what he thought about Lucia. In this note one of the phrases was, "your daughter is a natural born pianist, and she will be the finest pianist in the world when she grows up."

Lucia was about twelve years old when she was playing concerts all over with Charles Kunkel who was the first cousin of the great Beethoven. As she was growing up and attending school she won a scholarship to go to college, and she chose to attend college in Germany and the name of this college was, The Beethoven Conservatory of Music and Voice. The people in charge of the conservatory in Germany, after hearing her play the piano and sing, told her mother that her daughter was already so much advanced that there was not much they could do to teach her but, we will be glad and honored to take her under our wing and have her play concerts and continue with her singing, and we would give her advice on anything she would need. This is what was told to her mother by The Beethoven Music Conservatory in Germany, the greatest in Europe....

She was asked directly from the great Flo Zeigfeld to be part of his great follies on Broadway, and to perform her act in the show, which she did.... She did movie picture work with the William Goldman-Skouras Bros. Movie Industry, etc., etc. So the steps on the ladder of success started to go up, up and up for LUCIA PAMELA.

In 1926 Lucia was voted Miss St. Louis; sepia-tinged newspaper clippings in the living room recount her triumph over 2,000 contestants. Around this

time, she says, she learned to drive a car—personally taught by racing champ Barney Oldfield. This has always been a source of great pride. If anyone complained about her erratic driving, Lucia countered with: "Well, who taught you how to drive?"

In a career that spans nine decades, she recalls her performances at concert halls throughout the United States and Europe. She's taken the stage for kings and presidents, and at orphanages and senior citizen homes. Lucia was awarded a Medal of Honor by Congress for her wartime service with the USO for entertaining troops, and she personally knew fellow Missourian Harry Truman. She claims to have been honored in *Ripley's Believe It or Not* for memorizing more songs than anyone in the world: 10,000.

The radiant Miss Pamela, Queen of the Squeezebox

COURTESY MISS LUCIA PAMELA

Lucia reminisces about being a high-profile entertainer in Kansas City, St. Louis, and Fresno. Her all-girl Musical Pirates were the house band at St. Louis's Odeon Theater, where the virtuoso Lucia played 15 instruments. She also enchanted Odeon patrons as "Venus in Spookyland." Celebrants farther west may fondly recall her stint as Mother Goose at Fresno Storyland. She later teamed up with her daughter Georgia, with whom she performed duets as the "Pamela Sisters."

Reaching further back in her memory, Lucia claims to have been "the first person ever on television," though details are hazy. The multimedia star hosted such radio programs as *The Encouragement Hour* in Kansas City, and *Gal about Town*, where she extolled "when, where, and what to do in and about Fresno."

Lucia remains a tremendous fan of the medium. "Radio is great," she says, "for people who don't have a television."

She played concerts with the above-mentioned Charles Kunkel ("cousin of the great Beethoven"), and recalls one fateful incident when Kunkel slumped over at the piano in the middle of their duet.

Did he die?

"Well," Lucia recalls, "no one knew at that particular time. They had a doctor check him to be sure he was gone." Alas—poor Charles had expired! Nevertheless, Lucia resolutely completed the concert.

"Charles," she affirms, "would have wanted it that way."

Just to set history books straight, a few months before Neil Armstrong took his historic stroll on the moon, Lucia visited that celestial satellite. Any doubt that she did in fact travel far out of the earth's atmosphere should be dispelled by her lyrics, which contain eyewitness accounts of lunar life.

WALKING ON THE MOON
Every time I take a trip
I'm sure to meet my friends
From the sky they fly high
this is hello from them
moo-moo-moo-moo moo-moo moo moo-moo-moo!!!!
As I was walking on the Moon
I met a little cow-ow-ow
And this is what she said to me
dah-dah dah-dah-dah-dah dah dah
Moo-moo-moo-moo moo-moo moo moo-moo-moo!!!!
And that's what she said to me

Meow Meow Meow Meow-ow-ow!!!
As I was walking on the Moon

I met a little kitty cat
And this is what she said to me
dah-dah dah-dah-dah-dah dah dah
Meow Meow Meow Meow-ow-ow!!!

In further travels, she encountered a chickadee, a doggie, a "goonie-goon," and a "roo-ooster." Lucia also admits, "I was surprised to find a lot of Oriental people on the moon. I don't know how they got there."

Into Outer Space remains, so far, the only commercially released project recorded on lunar terrain. Lucia explains, however, that in "real life" she doesn't sound the same as she does on the record because "the air is different up there, you know." She also visited Venus, but found the recording environment less to her liking.

In 1976, Miss Pamela self-published a cartoon coloring book, *Into Outer Space with Lucia Pamela in the Year 2000*. It isn't just for children. "It's for everybody," she asserts. "Children aren't the only people who like to color books." One sketch depicts a dog in a spacesuit, smoking a cigarette. At least it looks like a dog. "That was actually a man dressed as a dog," she confides. The book affords a glimpse of Nutland Village, populated by the likes of Monsieurs Walnut, Pecan, and Filbert.

Lucia envisioned an international coloring contest for kids between the ages of 3 and 80. She hasn't yet judged a winner—she's still waiting for last-minute submissions.

That's Lucia's astral vision. A few additional facts have been ascertained, but even a bit of demystification doesn't lessen her charm.

Gulfstream Records was a fairly respected rockabilly label during the 1960s. Michael Arlt, who is creating a Hollywood, Florida, music archive, wrote to me in 1998 that he'd recently met the proprietor of Alpha Records, a local pressing plant.

"This guy used to press for Gulfstream from the early 1960s to the label's demise in the early 1970s when Vince Ferino, the owner, passed away," Arlt revealed. "Vince was this kooky old man who had a habit of recording everything with the sound-on-sound button activated, to get that cheesy echo. He said that was his trademark. In my own collection I have on Gulfstream a Spanish instructional record that was pressed for the Broward County Sheriff's department. It has the same echo. I have a photo of that garage studio at 5614 Taylor Street where *Into Outer Space* was recorded. It looks primitive—we're talking one step from Edison." Arlt also learned that during recording sessions, "Vince had a habit of picking up his tuba and joining in when the spirit hit."

Eight or nine years after *Into Outer Space* was released on Gulfstream, Lucia re-pressed the album on her own L'Peg label, based in her then-hometown of Fresno. (In 1991, it was reissued on an Arf Arf Records CD produced by me. "Walking on the Moon" was included on RE/Search's *Incredibly Strange Music Vol. 2* CD.)

Two of Lucia's compositions, "You and Your Big Ideas" and "In Love, In Love," were recorded by Liberace's brother George, reportedly a longtime friend of Miss Pamela. And in 1994, Laetitia Sadier and Tim Gane of the U.K. band Stereolab penned a tribute, "International Colouring Contest"—including a Lucia voice sample—for their Elektra album *Mars Audiac Quintet*.

The CD reissue of *Into Outer Space* could not be termed an historic rediscovery. The world overlooked Lucia's masterpiece the first time around, and it was never a sought-after collector's item. The album was obscure enough to escape detection almost everywhere, except among those who knew Lucia personally. It should be noted, however, that on their nationally syndicated radio program in the mid-1970s, comedians Bob and Ray reportedly aired Lucia's

"Flip, Flop, Fly" ("When I say 'flip', you flip / When I say 'flop', you flop / When I say 'fly', we'll ALL fly!").

In 1984, a listener of my WFMU radio program recommended *Into Outer Space*, as I had a reputation for exploring exotic, offbeat, calamitous, and visionary recordings—provided the artist was sincere. A cassette arrived in the mail with a note suggesting that Lucia was all of the above—to a *transcendental* degree.

I was astonished at what I heard—Lucia's utter lack of inhibition, the reckless determination with which she careened through her wacked-out interplanetary cabaret-rock. Encouraged by listener phone calls and letters, I aired the tape frequently. But I couldn't locate a copy of the album. Queries at vintage music outlets and record conventions brought blank stares, never a hint of recognition.

On a trip to Los Angeles in June 1988, I met artist and outsider-painting collector Jim Shaw, who owned a Gulfstream edition of Lucia's LP. During an evening of stylus-drops through his archive of strange vinyl, Shaw noted my wistful sighs every time I glanced over at Miss Pamela's album.

Finally he picked up the record—and handed it to me. "Keep it," he declared in a voice tinged with pity. "Seems to mean more to you than it does to me."

In 1989 I wrote to Gulfstream Records, but my letter was returned unopened, marked "No Such Addressee."

Two years later I procured a copy of the L'Peg reissue—same packaging, different logo—and wrote to the label address in Fresno.

A month later my home phone rang.

"Hello, is this the radio station?" inquired a brash female voice.

I was stunned. It was Miss Lucia Pamela. It was like getting a phone call from Syd Barrett.

After making arrangements with Lucia's grandson, filmmaker Chip Rosenbloom, I flew to Los Angeles in January 1991 to meet the charismatic Miss Pamela in person. Several follow-up visits ensued. These were magical encounters, and I plied Lucia with questions, nodding in admiration even when the veracity of her reminiscences was slightly suspect. I didn't intend to do any fact-checking. If she says she played "Venus in Spookyland," go prove she didn't.

On this L.A. jaunt, I also met with Kirk Biglione of North Hollywood. While working as a DJ and music director at KFSR, Fresno, in 1983 and 1984, Kirk had obtained a copy of *Into Outer Space* from a friend at a local record shop, who guaranteed Biglione "the strangest listening experience" he'd ever had. Biglione affirmed his reaction: the album made a stunning impression.

"Lucia became an obsession," Biglione recalled. "I had little or no information about her, and a letter to her record company in Hollywood, Florida, was returned." He made the search for Lucia into a radio promotion stunt. "We offered a reward of five dollars a year for life to the person who provided facts leading to the discovery of Lucia," explained Biglione. "Key bits of information began to drift in. Many remembered her from a long-canceled children's television program. Still others insisted that Lucia was a cosmetic saleswoman."

Finally a listener gave Kirk the address of a local church-sponsored bingo gathering that Lucia reportedly attended on a regular basis. "Several of us from KFSR piled into my Volkswagen and headed to the church," he said. "It was a surreal moment as we entered the bingo hall filled with elderly retired people. After several minutes of trying to explain my purpose, I convinced the number caller to give me his microphone so I could explain the situation to the confused crowd of senior gamblers.

"In perfect form, Lucia jumped up and shouted, 'Bingo!'"

Over the following year, Biglione kept in touch with the frisky Miss Pamela. "We did a number of radio interviews," he noted, "including one lengthy in-depth retrospective of her entire career. Unfortunately the tape of that show has been lost. It's a shame considering all the great information she divulged." Lucia detailed a life of sharing her musical and theatrical gifts with those she loves. That circle of loved ones seems to encompass all creatures of all species in all known—and unknown—galaxies.

"The last time I saw Lucia," Biglione remembered, "she was trying to raise funds to build an amusement park, with a ride that would actually take visitors to another planet. Not such a strange proposition when you consider that she's also convinced her pink Cadillac can fly."

Lucia spends her retirement years in Los Angeles, occasionally racking up frequent flier miles to Moontown. She's always abided by the Golden Rule, and strongly believes in helping people. Throughout her life, she's staged countless shows for charity, performing songs from *Into Outer Space* at schools and senior homes while accompanying herself on accordion.

Though she no longer appears publicly, she remains alert and active with her family and friends. Asked how long she'll be around, she replies without hesitation: "I'm going to live forever." Another claim that no one disputes.

She also remains optimistic: "If the weather is good," she attests, "then everything is good."

THE MAGIC BAND

THE CAP'T

FAST 'N' BULBOUS

The many visages of Don Van Vliet

• 14 •

C a p t a i n
B e e f h e a r t

I N S C R U T A B L E   D R E A M E R

Simpsons creator Matt Groening had an epiphany after he first heard Captain Beefheart and His Magic Band's epochal *Trout Mask Replica*. "When that album came out in 1969," said Groening, "the one high school friend who could stand it along with me, we were jumping up and down, saying, 'If this is what rock and roll is like in 1969, just think what it'll be like in 1984!'

"We had no idea back then that *Trout Mask Replica* would *be* the best album of 1984."

Chris Butler, songwriter/guitarist for the Waitresses, proclaimed, "Beefheart invented an entirely new musical vocabulary. He took the cracked, primitive, electric-country blues of Howlin' Wolf and just kept on going until the 'Delta' he was referencing was not the Mississippi's but a canal on Mars."

As musical outsiders go, Captain Beefheart (a.k.a. Don Van Vliet), thanks to critical darlinghood and rabid international cult worship, has come closer than most to mainstream visibility without ever having been a question or an answer on *Jeopardy*. His albums have never logged impressive sales, and his fearsome mug on a magazine cover would likely depress circulation.

Of course, broad public indifference is a useless barometer of artistic significance. Beefheart, whose influence on subsequent generations of musicians has been enormous, illustrates this maxim.

A casual first-time listener is apt to be confounded by Beefheart's music, with its grating vocals, jerky pulses, and bizarre lyrics. Some of the Captain's recordings suggest a drunken beatnik blathering in tongues while a musical fistfight breaks out nearby. Which doesn't mean he sounds like Yoko Ono. Beefheart's music is challenging. But like a jigsaw puzzle, as queer-cut pieces fit into place, a recognizable panorama begins to take shape.

Beefheart, like his contemporary Iggy Pop, ignited renegade passions in the adventurous souls who bought his albums. He inspired subsequent generations of art-rockers by demonstrating that electric guitar-based subgenres could be less about songs, melody, and heartbeat, and more about Dali-esque subterfuge and free-form unpredictability. Imagine a high-octane Tom Waits with eight cylinders of Ornette Coleman under the hood.

The man's uninhibited approach to dismembering rock tradition is aggressive. His transitional post-blues recordings sound like glued-together shards of vinyl from an earthquake-ravaged pile of psychedelic LPs. *Trout Mask* in particular spazzes out like a series of two- and four-minute crimes against nature. The album's arrhythmic, three-simultaneous key signature mutations are apt to leave the uninitiated wondering if Beefheart's sidemen can't rock—or simply won't. They seem allergic to a steady pulse.

The Captain scattered insurrectionary pollen throughout the punk, DIY, and no-wave movements of the late 1970s, attracting loyal legionnaires in the United States, Europe, and Japan. Pere Ubu, the Fall, and 1/2 Japanese might not have existed without him; Devo, the Residents, and the Gang of Four might not have sounded as interesting. The Clash, Sex Pistols, P. J. Harvey, and the Red Hot Chili Peppers claim indebtedness. Millennial psychedelicists like Olivia Tremor Control display familiarity with the Captain's unorthodox rhythmic tics. And the whole Henry Cow/Art Bears/Slapp Happy family tree is rooted in rich Van Vliet soil.

Beefheart was essentially a self-taught musical sorcerer who crafted an iconoclastic image, behaving, talking, and dressing like a desert-baked Captain Ahab. At times this persona seemed to engulf him, straining relations with his patrons and sidemen and bringing him to the brink of career derailment. He was a control freak who tried to control everything but his own maniacal excesses.

The extent of his potential for *self*-control was debatable, begging the question: outsider or poseur? Discerning motivation in a complex individual like Van Vliet is at best a subjective science. The man has always projected an inscrutable demeanor, blurring the line between stubbornness and monomania. "I don't believe in insanity," he said, perhaps introspectively. "I believe in varying degrees of disconnection." He exhibits many of the impenetrable qualities of outsiderdom, hence his inclusion in this book. The Captain is *out* there, adrift on a raft of idiosyncrasy in the greater sea of public indifference.

The Beefheart chronicles are shrouded in rumors, innuendo, and accusations, peppered with verifiable facts, eyewitness accounts, and faulty memories.

There are half-truths, three-quarter truths, and untruths—many proffered by the man himself.

In a fawning, myth-building May 1970 *Rolling Stone* puff piece, Langdon Winner swore, "This writer considers [*Trout Mask*] to be the most astounding and most important work of art ever to appear on a phonograph record." Throughout that seminal interview, Beefheart came across as a spoiled, self-absorbed artiste, as Winner uncritically accepted anything spewed out in the course of conversation. Years later many of the Captain's associates and Magic Band sidemen attempted to correct some of the disinformation contained in this breakout feature and other early profiles.

Two examples: 1) "Don Van Vliet does not use drugs and does not allow members of the Magic Band to do so either," Winner alleged. This was later contradicted by guitarist Zoot Horn Rollo, who recounted his own, several bandmates', and Beefheart's use of psychedelics and pot. (To be fair, drugs were not a major preoccupation for the band.) 2) "Zoot Horn Rollo and [bassist] Rockette Morton, musicians that Beefheart taught from scratch ..." This is ludicrous, as both musicians were highly skilled players before joining the Magic Band.

Yet Beefheart inspires the defiant admiration one associates with Third World guerrilla rebels. Some Beefheart disciples would probably insist that *Trout Mask Replica* deserved the 700-odd weeks *Dark Side of the Moon* lodged in the *Billboard* charts. His knowledgeable fanboys (Yes, mostly *guys!* See sidebar) seem to be extremely talented, outspoken nonconformists. Make no mistake: Beefheart does not appeal to low-IQ drones. Like their hero, many of his biggest enthusiasts orbit on the cultural perimeter. If not societal outsiders themselves, they harbor outsider sympathies.

The affinity for Beefheart among cartoonists is quasi-mystical. Perhaps, as anyone familiar with his records will attest, Beefheart produces musical comic books: his songs are absurd, childlike, and grotesque. Like the Roadrunner, the Captain's arrangements defy the laws of gravity. His musical textures are panchromatic—not surprising because he's also an acclaimed painter. Besides earning Groening's accolade, *Trout Mask Replica* has been cited with awe and reverence by Kaz, J. R. Williams, Wayno, and Gary Panter. Mary Fleener likes to listen "not while workin', but while cookin.'"

Beefheart has been analyzed, lionized, and curated. There are books, Web sites, music encyclopedia entries, multidisc box sets, tribute albums, and probably doctoral theses exalting his significance. Poetry journals and art quarterlies probe his lyrical and visual creations.

But he's always been too weird for the broader record-buying public. Acknowledging his status as a musical outsider, Beefheart thought some people liked him because his was a hip name to drop. "I feel like a hood ornament on a Rolls-Royce," he told his guitarist Gary Lucas, who added that in the late

COURTESY WARNER BROS./REPRISE RECORDS. DESIGN: CAL SCHENKEL

1970s, "Don thought he was the token weirdo artist on Warner Bros., signed just to prove how sophisticated the label was."

And Frank Zappa, who produced *Trout Mask Replica*, once observed, "I think Don is fantastic, but he's unmarketable."

Though he's always identified as Don Van Vliet, the Captain was born Don Glen Vliet in Glendale, California, in 1941. Glenn Jones, of the band Cul de Sac, said: "The 'Van' in Van Vliet is an affectation, the family name being simply Vliet. But before I ever saw a copy of the birth certificate—which reads: 'Don Glen Vliet'—I approached Don after a show in Boston and asked him to autograph *Trout Mask*. After writing 'To Glen,' he asked if I spelled my name with one *n* or two. I answered, 'Two.' He replied, 'That's the *only* way to spell it!' and added a second, bolder *n* to my name. He started to hand the album back to me, then said, 'Wait; I think I'll give myself another one too,' and appended a second *n* to his signature: 'Don Vann Vliet.' It was only later I discovered his middle name had been Glen, which was his father's name."

TESTOSTERONE

The preponderance of Beefheart bootlegs, post-retirement anthologies, and unreleased-material collections attest to his enduring appeal.

For guys.

Zoot Horn Rollo stressed, "Very few women listen to *Trout Mask*. There weren't babes coming to our shows, trust me." One factor could be that Beefheart's music, from *Trout Mask* on, rarely had any sex groove. Sex is about rhythm, and the Captain's *beatus interruptus* doesn't kindle romantic ardor.

Gary Lucas acknowledged this schism. He recalled Beefheart saying, "My music is for women because they *know*." "But frankly," said Lucas, "it was for weirdos and intellectuals, mainly nerdy boys." Author (*Exit*) and editor (*Seconds*) George Petros told me, "Beefheart's music seems misogynistic. He says 'sex', but he doesn't feel it." This, of course, pre-sumes Beefheart has treated men better than women, which doesn't seem to be the case, to hear some of his players grouse. (Magic Band personnel have all been male.)

For what it's worth, in 1998, an on-line Beefheart discussion group took a demographic poll of its list members in various categories. The by-sex breakdown was:

Value	Number of Responses
Mr.	101
Ms.	3

Admittedly, this could merely reflect a gender imbalance among Web trawlers.

Conduct your own survey. Don't get back to me with the results.

Beefheart had little formal education ("If you want to be a different fish, you've got to jump out of the school!"), but showed an early flair for art. After studying with Portuguese sculptor Augustonia Rodriguez, he won a scholar-ship to further his technique in Europe. However, his mom and dad were con-vinced that art was for "queers" and took refuge with their teen prodigy in the Mojave Desert. The young Vliet supposedly sequestered himself in his bed-room and went without sleep for a year-and-a-half, while his parents slipped meals under his door. "I wasn't neglected enough as a child," he harrumphed in retrospect.

The hothouse adolescent developed an affinity for nature and animals, later reflected in his lyrics and paintings. "When I was three," he told *Spin's*

Kristine McKenna in 1988, "I was very disappointed to open a dictionary and read: 'The great auk—extinct.' That gorgeous bird! The passenger pigeon is gone. These things really bother me." Out of despair, the itty-bitty eco-freak tried to fling himself into the La Brea Tar Pits, but his mother caught him at the last second.

These and other details of his childhood have been retold many times—accounts are readily available from a number of published sources—but how much is true is anybody's guess. Guitarist and Beefheart authority Henry Kaiser cautioned, "People just believe this calculated mythology which goes on and on because of the low level of journalism that existed when most of the writing about this took place. The fan magazines endlessly regurgitate what was [previously written]. Nobody's really done any professional investigation of this stuff."

It's not hard to recognize Van Vliet as a product of his generation—a middle-class hippie enchanted by notions of anarchy, rejection of convention, and salvation through art. But how these rebellious impulses were filtered through a brilliant and perhaps not altogether stable mind is what separated Beefheart from his contemporaries and cast him outside prevailing musical trends.

He was an ardent devotee of R&B, having been weaned on a diet of Muddy Waters, Jimmy Reed, and John Lee Hooker. Washed in the blood of the boogie and Bo Diddley. Steeped in sixties-vintage free jazz like Ornette Coleman and Cecil Taylor. (Zoot Horn Rollo said Don "condemned" jazz giants like John Coltrane, Miles Davis, and Thelonious Monk "for playing notes.")

From his early affinity for classic blues, Beefheart developed a growling, multioctave (anywhere from four to seven-and-a-half, depending on which story you read) vocal style that echoed Howlin' Wolf, or seemed a voice-double for radio immortal Wolfman Jack. He could occasionally evince the tenderness of Otis Redding (e.g., "Too Much Time" on *Clear Spot*). The R&B influence is more evident on his first two albums, *Safe As Milk* and *Strictly Personal*. Sometimes he just sounds like a really fine soul singer (e.g., on "I'm Glad," from *Safe As Milk*). Beefheart could blow a tormented harp ("Owed T' Alex" on *Shiny Beast*) and belch primitive, disjointed squawks on sax ("That's the dolphins speaking through me, man"). But it was that voice, gritty as road salt, coupled with mischievous lyrics and musical clay-modeling that fostered the mystique and attracted the flock.

After the *Safe as Milk* and *Strictly Personal* period, Van Vliet sensed that R&B had been done to perfection by his black predecessors. The only thing left to do was dismember it and use the parts for monstrous recombinant alchemy. It was at this point that Beefheart decided to take a walk on the outside and never came back.

His early record label experiences had been less than encouraging—stylistic no-confidence votes, lack of promotional support, a producer phase-remixing *Strictly Personal* to entice the psilocybin-for-lunch bunch. When Zappa, Beefheart's Lancaster, California, high-school chum, launched his own twin Warner Bros.–distributed labels (Straight and Bizarre) in the late 1960s, Beefheart was afforded a chance to record without creative interference. The outcome was *Trout Mask Replica*—and the birth of a legend.

Trout Mask has a thrown-together quality, an improvised, ad-hoc feel—like someone put the rock and jazz rulebooks in a blender, tossed in several chapters of Harry Partch's *Genesis of a Music* and hit "puree." But the album was, in fact, highly structured, carefully arranged, and long in rehearsal.

Beefheart had no musical training and couldn't read or write notation. He heard strange things in his head, which he demanded his Magic Band mates express instrumentally. He taught parts by hamfistedly pounding passages on a de-tuned piano, or whistling. (Years before Beefheart, this technique had been employed with perhaps greater degrees of sophistication by Raymond Scott and Sun Ra.) Zappa declared that the blues-fugitive had "trouble staying on a beat. Captain Beefheart has no natural rhythm."

"[Don's] creativity wasn't clear cut as far as being very musical," explained Zoot Horn Rollo, whose real name is Bill Harkleroad. "He adopted more of the mentality of a sculptor. His idea was to use sound, bodies, and people as the tools. It was increasingly clear that our job as his band was to turn it into sounds that were repeatable." From a player's standpoint, what Beefheart heard in his head wasn't easy to intuit. As Harkleroad noted, "Because he didn't know shit about music [theory], he sometimes couldn't get things across." Gary Lucas, who played with the Magic Band from 1980 to 1982, endured the same game of musical *Pictionary*. "Gesturing, scat-singing, drawing diagrams and pictures, free-association imagery," said Lucas. "*Anything*. He'd get on the drums, bang a bit, then hand the tape to [drummer] Cliff [Martinez] and say, 'Learn that.'"

Fortunately, his players had the chops to adapt. Beefheart consistently put together remarkable groups of musicians, originally called "His Magic Band," then later, significantly, "The Magic Band," a grudging concession of its members' at least semiautonomous humanity. Players included numerous ex-Mothers of Invention, such as Art Tripp (aka "Ed Marimba"), Elliot Ingber ("Winged Eel Fingerling"), Bruce Lambourne Fowler, and Roy Estrada ("Orejon"); as well as such noteworthies of later renown as Ry Cooder, John French ("Drumbo"), Jeff Moris Tepper, Gary Lucas, and Eric Drew Feldman (who subsequently joined the Pixies). After he'd crystallized his post-blues deconstruction, Beefheart hired eager newcomers weaned on *Trout Mask*. Playing with the Captain conferred cachet; it was an awe-inspiring resumé item. The original Magic Band created the traditions, and later recruits attempted to fill the shoes of their trailblazing heroes.

Harkleroad, a self-admitted "skinny, pimple-faced geek" who as a youth admired Beefheart, joined the Magic Band in 1968 at age 19. He expected to play the fairly straight-ahead R&B he'd heard on *Safe As Milk.* But Beefheart was in transition, and Harkleroad was receptive enough to weird stylistic detours to mesh with Beefheart's musical family. During his six-year tenure Zoot developed a fingering style reminiscent of the intensity of bottleneck and steel guitars in bluegrass and blues, punctuated by abrupt jazz phrasings. His style was approximated to varying degrees by his Magic Band successors.

Lunar Notes: Zoot Horn Rollo's Captain Beefheart Experience (SAG Publishing Ltd., United Kingdom) chronicles Harkleroad's years under the charismatic leader. Words like "generous," "patient," "modest," "diplomatic," "cooperative," and "reasonable" don't appear often in Harkleroad's portrait of Beefheart. Those who enjoy Beefheart's music might be inclined to overlook the man's reportedly graceless and abusive behavior—particularly if they've never had to work with him. Besides being portrayed as a narcissistic borderline psychopath with a streak of musical genius, Beefheart is depicted as a bully, a megalomaniac, and a manipulator.

He kept the Magic Band sequestered in a cottage learning the *Trout Mask* repertoire while he practiced cultlike subjugation. Harkleroad, interviewed after the publication of *Lunar Notes,* told me, "When I first joined the group, Don was going to the library looking up books on how to control people, and literally how to brainwash these young kids. We're talking sleep deprivation, food deprivation." Drummer French told Beefheart biographer Mike Barnes that during the *Trout Mask* retreat, "I remember once going for a month and all we had to eat every day was one four-ounce cup of soya beans."

"I think he believed in his musical abilities and he was using us as tools, rather than human beings," observed Harkleroad. Beefheart, reflecting back in a 1994 interview with the U.K.'s *Independent,* insisted: "People don't like to be used as paint. If they're going to be used by me, that is the only way they're going to be used."

The Captain, looking dapper

The paint analogy—and the controlling character—was amplified by David Greenberger, who played in a 1980s Boston band called Men and Volts, which started as an all-Beefheart cover band. When the Captain learned about it, he was less than thrilled. "Most people who write music want others to play it," said Greenberger. "He didn't. He never liked anyone 'tampering' with his music. His attitude was, 'Leave it alone.' Which is exactly what a painter would do. A painter doesn't want someone else to re-create their work. Unless they were actually *in* the Magic Band, Beefheart's message to wannabe disciples was, 'Stay out of my world; go make your own.'"

At the time of its release, *Trout Mask*'s gleeful vandalism and cooked–Mother Goose nursery rhymes signified a radical departure from prevailing post-Haight-Ashbury psychedelia. Zappa, though listed as producer, tinkered little with *Trout Mask*'s overall sound, content to allow Beefheart artistic freedom. It was released on Zappa's Straight imprint, though Beefheart, according to *Rolling Stone*, "[did] not appreciate being placed on the Bizarre-Straight roster of freaks next to Alice Cooper and the GTO's."

Despite *Trout Mask*'s purported surgical precision, the Captain's vocals have little rhythmic alignment with the band—and for good reason. The instrumental tracks were recorded first, with Beefheart later overdubbing his voice. Zappa suggested that Beefheart wear headphones to hear the playback, as was common studio practice. But Don refused, preferring to howl his lyrics along with sound leakage filtering through the studio's aquarium glass window. "He just shouted free-form," said Harkleroad. "In fact, he rarely ever played with us, except onstage. His vocals were always done after the fact."

Some feel *Trout Mask* is overrated. Veteran music journalist and long-time Beefheart enthusiast Peter Keepnews observed, "*Trout Mask* is always cited as his masterpiece, but I think it has a lot of dross. Like many double albums, it probably has a single album's worth of really prime stuff, surrounded by filler and a few tracks that sound like he's trying too hard to be weird. My vote goes to [the followup] *Lick My Decals Off, Baby*, which is concise and packed with great songs—not a wasted track."

For a true appreciation of Beefheart's recorded achievements, his entire catalog deserves to be explored. From prehistoric, R&B-based Van Vliet; the moonshot of *Trout Mask;* its progressive followup, *Decals,* and sporadic lurches toward semicommercial respectability, *The Spotlight Kid* and *Clear Spot;* the sellout clunkers on the Mercury label; and his comeback-phase funhouse jaunts, *Shiny Beast* and *Doc at the Radar Station.* There's a lot of variety, but a consistent sabotaging of rock proprieties. In a recording career that began in 1965 and ended by self-imposed retirement in 1982, Beefheart cultivated a distinct identity. There are countless flashes of true genius—and times when the Captain and his crew are just scavenging. The two universally

TROUT MASK
EVOLUTIONARY THEORY

My personal—and admittedly crackpot—theory is that Beefheart spent months devising endless permutations to the Music Machine's 1967 hit "Talk Talk." This song could be the Rosetta Stone of Beefheartdom, a blueprint for *Trout Mask Replica*. "Talk Talk" boasts gruff, bluesy vocals, cheap production, and quick and nasty guitar licks, while snaring the decade's Short Attention Span Award for putting the listener through an endless series of hairpin turns and structural contortions in less than two minutes. Of the 28 tracks on *Trout Mask*, six are under two minutes; 17 are less than two-and-a-half minutes. Stylistically, "Talk Talk" sounds ur-*Trout Mask* in a dozen ways.

reviled Mercury albums, *Unconditionally Guaranteed* (1974) and *Bluejeans and Moonbeams* (1975), are considered Beefheart's nadir. These twin releases were unsubtle attempts at harnessing a mainstream pop sound, as close as Beefheart ever came to "normal." Ironically, instead of boosting sales, they alienated his existing fan base.

"I went to see him at [New York's] Town Hall in 1974," recalled Keepnews. "The first Mercury album had just come out, but most people hadn't yet heard it. The old Magic Band had quit and he'd replaced it with a group of competent but uninspired hacks. He played a whole set of his new material, which sounded like bad imitations of the Rolling Stones and Allman Brothers. Halfway through the concert, he was being consistently booed. His response to the heckling: 'I've got a right to win a Grammy!'"

Zappa and Van Vliet fell into several highly publicized feuds, and these two cyclonic forces rarely worked together after *Trout Mask*. In 1975, when Beefheart found himself in financial straits and a legal maelstrom (Zappa: "Don had the ability and inclination to sign any piece of contractual paper shoved under his nose"), they joined forces on a tour and studio sessions that were released as *Bongo Fury*.

From the near career-death experience of his Mercury debacle emerged a strengthened and artistically rejuvenated Beefheart. He went on to create three more superlative albums: *Shiny Beast* (Warner Bros.), *Doc at the Radar Station* and his swan song, *Ice Cream for Crow* (both on Virgin). On these projects, mariachi tints and boogie beats nestle alongside Beefheart's characteristic green-light/red-light rhythms. The title track of *Ice Cream for Crow* is as close as the Captain gets to ZZ Top (with only a fraction of the sales).

Despite Beefheart's tyrannical temperament, Gary Lucas hinted at a certain mellowing over the years. "If you got one-on-one, without other people around when he felt compelled to 'perform' and assume the Captain Beefheart persona," the guitarist noted, "Don was one of the most charming, magical individuals I've ever met. He has a tremendous amount of charisma and personal magnetism."

At Van Vliet's insistence, Lucas undertook the desert rat's management from 1980 through 1984. "At the end, there was a lot of tension between us," Lucas recalled. "The more services I performed in this manager role he'd thrust on me—which I accepted—the more friction ensued, and the more I felt he resented me. That was true with a lot of people who had gotten closer, the inner circle. He would start taking you for granted, and he could be very abusive. But in the early days, he was the utmost in charm and civility. Every time I met Frank [Zappa], he seemed really suspicious, bitter, arrogant, and insecure. But Don could be fantastically relaxed. Generally a warm, big-hearted person."

Nonetheless, Beefheart's erratic behavior still flared up. He could be gracious with friends, then abruptly volatile. Henry Kaiser recounted in his foreword to *Lunar Notes* that he'd invited John French to play drums on one of his

SUN ZOOM SPARK

Beefheart's lyrics have always been a colorful trick-or-treat of puns, wordplay, and evocations of nature, as in "Bat Chain Puller," from *Shiny Beast*:

> Pumpkins span the hills with orange crayola patches
> Green inflated trees balloon up into marshmallow soot
> That walks away in faulty circles caught in grey blisters
> With twinkling lights 'n green sashes
> Drawn by rubber dolphins

His vivid portrait of a "Tropical Hot Dog Night" from the same album evokes "two flamingos in a fruit fight." Van Vliet's jabberwocky represents word-painting of the highest order, the perfect counterpoint to his musical merriment.

A collection of his poetry and art, *Skeleton Breath, Scorpion Blush*, was published in 1987 by Gachnang and Springer, of Berlin, Germany.

albums, to which French agreed. "Knowing the Captain could be quite paranoid," recalled Kaiser, "I mentioned this to Don. He said that was fine; go
ahead. After the album came out, I sent a copy to Don. He called me up and
screamed: 'My drummer, my drums! Send back that painting I gave you! I
don't care if I ever said it was okay! I never want to speak with you again.' And
he hasn't since."

French neatly chronicled the Captain's emotional timeline in a 1994 letter
to *Mojo* magazine. "I spent more time around him than most of the other
band members over a longer period of time," he wrote. "I saw his fiery days as
the young aggressive and sometimes cruel bandleader. I saw him as an almost
broken man shortly after his band left him [1974–75]. I saw him with the *Doc
at the Radar Station* band as the artist mellowed with age and struggling to survive in a rather fickle music world."

After *Ice Cream for Crow,* the Captain called in sick and never returned to
the recording studio or the stage. By then he was earning a better income as a
painter, so he took sanctuary at his Mojave Desert trailer home with the company of his wife Jan.

Following his musical retirement Beefheart rarely emerged in public,
except at gallery shows of his work. It was a simpler life, away from the hustles
of the record biz, the studios, the touring, the marketing. "Perhaps," wrote
Lester Bangs in the *Village Voice,* "he just doesn't have those filtering mecha-
nisms which enable most of us to cope with 'reality' by blocking out at least
80 percent of it."

The Captain also no longer had to deal with musicians. "It's all just paint-
brush to the canvas," he told *Mojo*'s Dave DiMartino in 1993. "And the paint
doesn't say anything. It just allows me to make mistakes." Beefheart didn't
miss urban artist ferment. The trailer galoot dismissed San Francisco as "a
low-budget horror movie." New York, he sneered, "reminds me of a bowl of
underpants. It's filthy there."

At this writing, Van Vliet is reportedly wheelchair-bound and in very ill
health. A number of sources cite complications from multiple sclerosis. The
studio exile this extraordinary artist imposed on himself in 1982—from which
his loyal legions prayed he would someday emerge—seems unlikely to end.

Like the Beatles, Captain Beefheart will only "regroup" in one place. And
it's unlikely he'll sing in unison with any heavenly choir.

• 15 •

Shooby Taylor, the Human Horn

SCAT MAN DO

if you know William "Shooby" Taylor personally, please tell him he's in this book.

Shooby is the world's weirdest scat singer. Known—or perhaps *unknown*—as "The Human Horn," Taylor scats exultantly over records by the Ink Spots, the Harmonicats, and country gospel. Occasionally he's accompanied only by a Farfisa organ. For years, a bootleg cassette of his few New York recording sessions has traveled extensively around the planet, generating a frothing fan base.

But Shooby remains a mystery man, unaware of his growing cult status.

Scatting is an uncatalogued musical Esperanto; Shooby's vocabulary is a whole 'nuther language. Some of his favorite scat syllables are "Raw-shaw," "poppy-poppy," and "splaw," sputtered in a virile baritone vaguely reminiscent of Dudley Do-Right, the chaos-prone Canadian Mountie from *Rocky and Bullwinkle*. (See sidebar "Scatalogue.") A studio engineer who eyewitnessed the sessions reported that while scatting, Taylor played "air saxophone"—hence, the nickname. Shooby might've been attempting heavy-lipped re-creations of John Coltrane or Sonny Rollins solos. His lung capacity is staggering; he never pauses long enough to inhale as he spews out astonishing high-octane vocal runs.

Shooby is 100 percent uninhibited and soulful, in a lovably demented way. His outbursts—there's no other word for his delivery—leave uninitiated listeners shaking their heads. A joyousness permeates these performances, a celebratory quality that serves as an analgesic for temporary relief from existential pain.

Take it from this author, who, if king, would declare scat-singing a public menace on par with drunk driving. I've been known to flee from a room after two notes of Ella Fitzgerald or Sarah Vaughan. Shooby Taylor absolves the sins of a century's worth of annoying vocalists who forgot the lyrics.

"I've played this tape for friends in Texas and down the street," said New York trapeze artist Adrienne Truscott, "and it's an emotional balm. You can't play this tape and *not* feel better. When I listen to it for more than 20 seconds, I'm laughing hysterically. It's so preposterous!" Doug Stone, a producer for the Independent Film Channel, agreed: "If you know anyone who just went through a breakup and you play Shooby Taylor for them, it makes their problems seem completely ridiculous."

Shooby apparently is—or was—a resident of Brooklyn (his current whereabouts are unknown). He recorded at least 14 titles at Angel Sound Studios in New York during the early 1980s before disappearing into the urban landscape. He is rumored to be a retired postal worker—which, one skeptical non-fan observed, "sounds like a diagnostic category."

Taylor begins the tape with a spoken intro, declaring, "Blacks—let's not forget where we came from. Let's learn to love and respeck [sic] each other." He then launches into the pseudo-spiritual "Lift Every Voice and Sing," a once-propagated-but-little-embraced "Negro national anthem" from decades ago. Shooby's repertoire includes "Over the Rainbow," "Tico Tico," "Peg O' My Heart," and "Nearer My God to Thee." He seems particularly fond of a 1980 country gospel album called *Amazing Grace* by Cristy Lane; Taylor dubbed his effervescent scat over Lane's recordings of "Just a Closer Walk with Thee" and "Softly and Tenderly."

The tape's world tour began when a former Angel studio engineer, Craig Bradley, transferred the tracks to cassette and passed along a copy to WFMU radio station manager Ken Freedman. After Freedman aired the tape and it circulated among the staff, Taylor's bizarre stylings inspired missionary zeal in DJs and listeners. The cassette was launched around the international tape-swap circuit, and a legend ensued.

How far has this legend traveled? In the January 1997 issue of *Mojo* (United Kingdom), singer/songwriter Joe Henry wrote in a celebrity survey about personal musical discoveries from the previous year:

> "The most remarkable thing I've heard in a long time is a tape given to me by a keyboard player I've been working with who collects unusual music. It's by a guy called Shooby Taylor. He calls himself 'the human horn.' He was supposedly a retired postal worker from Brooklyn, New York, who developed a cross between scat singing and speaking in tongues...."

"It's unlike anything I've ever heard in my life. A lot of people who hear it think of it like a novelty, but I hear it as a man who's completely come out of a vacuum and developed an approach to music that's as unique as Charlie Parker. No one knows if Shooby Taylor is still living or not; he wasn't ever a professional musician, he just made these remarkable recordings.

"The tape I got was taken from a Dutch radio show, when a DJ from Hoboken aired the tapes when visiting Holland. When I first heard it I laughed all the way through, but now I can't stop listening to it. It's so full of a kind of passion that I can't even begin to describe."

(The "Hoboken DJ" was this author, appearing in 1994 as a guest on *Instituut Schreuders*, a weekly program hosted by Piet Schreuders on the VPRO network. One significant aspect of this 15-minute feature is that it was conducted in three languages: the guest spoke English, the host addressed the audience in Dutch, and Shooby scatted in Taylorese.)

Elsewhere in Europe, the satirical *Adam and Joe Show* on BBC Channel 4 sampled a smidgeon of Shooby in their theme song. Back in the US of A, Tom Waits obtained the tape from his (and Joe Henry's ex-) keyboardist Danny McGough, and became an instant convert. Pop singer and songwriter Marshall Crenshaw was introduced to Shooby's splawdiferousness by one of his sidemen before a Massachusetts gig. Crenshaw pledged undying allegiance, proclaiming Taylor "The King of Farfisa-Wielding, Outer-Space, Lunatic-Fringe Scat Singers."

The now-vanished Angel Sound Studios was located near the old pre-Disney Times Square in midtown Manhattan. The neighborhood was a vortex of porn, pickpockets, greasy snacks, and cheap gin. Anyone—*anything*—was likely to walk into Angel with their life savings in a cigar box and book a session. "Shooby wasn't anything out of the ordinary for the clientele," noted Bradley. "We had this fellow Gary Strivant. He was from Bayonne, New Jersey, I think—a suave character with a crooked rug on his head that looked like a muskrat. He came in and sang 'Young Girl' in a booming, off-key voice while he played piano."

Shooby visited Angel in the early 1980s. He recorded a few sessions with the studio manager, before Bradley eagerly offered himself as board-op for Taylor's follow-up visits. "I was attuned to the unusual," said Bradley. "Shooby was an exciting character, someone you were drawn to right away. He arrived and in a *loud* voice said he wanted to record, and this is what he wanted to do." For each session, Taylor brought along one or two LPs as background accompaniment. He would *only* scat over records; there were no live musicians.

A SCATALOGUE OF SHOOBY DOOBY

Shooby's scat vocabulary echoes Mother Goose nonsense simmering in a rich Afro-Yiddish stew. Here's a few of his imaginative "shyllables":

da-da-shrah

dov-sheddilee-doo-dah

dwee da-da-sah

feedilee-oat'n dwee-bee

la-dah-dah shree, lo poo-pah

lah chilidee-dah-dah-dot, raw
  chidily blah-bah

pa shiddle-ee da-da-la

poppy-da-raw

poppy-poppy dah-shrah, dobby-
  dobby dob-shrah

pwee-dot, dwee-dot, wah e-saw

saw-haw-raw-haw

shleh-do-vey-diddle-ee-doo-zah

shooby-splaw, shabala-raw

shree-shrah-ha, shrabala-rah,
  shala-rah, sada-EEE, sidily-blobby

sidily doot-in-doot splaw

sleh-doo-dah-lava-pee

tweeding-da, tweeding-da ta
  dob-be-dah, lye-ah

we dah-dah sah, pee-pah

Taylor made four or five visits, of which Bradley engineered three. "Like anyone who came in the door, he wanted to get a record contract," Bradley noted. All recordings were first takes. "I think he was just winging it, improvising. So even if we did a second take, it wouldn't be to fix mistakes, it would just be a different version. But he was happy with his performance every time."

While scatting, Taylor mimed air saxophone. "We'd dim the lights to get the right mood," Bradley explained. "Sometimes he'd take off his shirt and stand there, paunchy in his sleeveless 'T,' get comfortable, and wail away on his air sax." Taylor never explained whose style he was imitating, if anyone's. His scatting was a means of self-expression and self-definition. "It was something he did in his apartment," Bradley learned. "It was his identity, his own little world that he'd created. He hung around with his jazz musician buddies in Brooklyn. He considered himself a player, though not of any instrument. Scatting was his thing. He said he'd even played the Apollo a couple of times and was booed offstage."

Rhino Records—after laboring for decades to shake their reputation as a label founded on goofy novelty platters—briefly entertained the notion of releasing Shooby on CD. Rhino's A&R staff eventually came to their senses. (The inherent licensing problems were sufficient discouragement.)

In the mid-1990s, the *Late Show with David Letterman* became intrigued after discovering the cassette in WFMU's (now-defunct) *Catalog of Curiosities* mail-order service. *Late Show*'s liaison claimed to have tracked down Taylor but didn't share the contact information with WFMU. Eventually, a casting exec at *Late Show* had second thoughts, and Shooby was rejected, possibly before an invitation was extended.

To this day, Taylor has not surfaced. "That's a real shame," lamented Bradley. "He'd love to be in the limelight. He isn't aware of the interest in his music. He's a little bit famous, and doesn't even know it."

How Shooby Taylor would wear such fame is rapturous to contemplate. As Bradley described him, "With his fun-loving manner and zest for life, he was probably the kind of guy who got into a lot of trouble. He once told me he got beat up by a woman in a laundromat for being a little too forward. She smacked him around." Taylor was proud of his abilities, and boastful in a theatrical heavyweight-champ sort of way. "He had a loud manner," noted Bradley, "the kind that would disturb everyone in a library. He didn't know how to be quiet."

•15•

Florence
Foster Jenkins

WIDOW'S PEAK

In 1943, soprano Florence Foster Jenkins was riding along the boulevards of New York City in a taxicab. The driver—perhaps momentarily distracted by his passenger practicing her scales—crashed the vehicle, causing injury to Madame Jenkins. After the accident, Jenkins found she could sing "a higher F than ever before." Instead of suing the cab company, she sent the driver a box of expensive cigars.

This was but one incident in the strange, albeit seemingly joyous, life of this majestic and delightfully eccentric diva. Jenkins was a plump New York dowager who loved and lived opera. Her wealth, derived from the deaths of her parents, allowed Florence to pursue a devotion to the high vocal arts despite a dearth of conventional talent.

As a well-regarded and hyperactive heiress, she was never an outsider in the social sense; but in the artistic arena—that's another matter. She was hopelessly off-pitch. She was blessed with a voice that could cut like a knife through *Madame Butterfly*. But what of it? No one ever claimed La Jenkins was anything but earnest.

Jenkins was also not without a droll sense of humor, a dowdy elegance, and an indomitable spirit. If she couldn't hit a certain note, she would swat it, as one would a pesky gnat. If a classic work failed to accommodate her vocal gifts, she had it rewritten; this included the deletion of unreachable notes in the upper registers.

ILLUSTRATION BY CURTIS WOODBRIDGE

Florence Foster Jenkins: a wealth of talent

Yet despite such idiosyncrasies, there is no indication Florence Foster Jenkins considered herself a comedienne, or wished to be appreciated as anything less than a serious artist. Eyewitness reports attest to her sincerity. She obviously wished to entertain; her devotees were *very* entertained. There's no business like Flo business.

Florence Foster was born in Wilkes-Barre, Pennsylvania, in 1868. She descended from full-blooded colonial stock, her paternal and maternal ancestors having settled in America during the 17th century. Her father, the Honorable Charles Dorrance Foster, was a banker, lawyer, and member of the Pennsylvania state legislature. Florence was reportedly a graduate of the Philadelphia Music Academy, and a frequent delegate to Daughters of the American Revolution conferences in the nation's capital.

She apparently caught the singing bug at an early age and took voice lessons for a while. However, her parents objected to her agonizing yelps and attempted to suppress her "talent." But the headstrong girl refused to be discouraged.

In her late teens, Florence eloped to Philadelphia with Dr. Frank Thornton Jenkins, from whom she was divorced in 1902 after an unhappy marriage. Cut off from her parents' financial abundance, she endured great hardship and taught piano to pay the rent. The struggling maiden was rescued by, of all things, the death of her father in 1909. Florence inherited a wad of his estate, and within a few years she had relocated to New York City.

As early as 1916, Madame Jenkins was receiving press attention for her devotion to presenting, under the auspices of New York's Euterpe Club, works of grand opera in English. (Despite her long-ago divorce, society columns invariably referred to her as "the widow of Dr. Frank Thornton Jenkins.") In 1917, she founded the Verdi Club, dedicated to popularizing the composer's works. Her philanthropic largesse gained her much respect in the New York music community.

But Jenkins wished to be known as more than simply a well-heeled matron of high culture. She aspired to be ... an *artiste*.

Her chance came in 1928, when her mother died, bequeathing her an additional fortune. Florence wasted no time embarking on a concert career. She was 60 years old.

Madame Jenkins began staging elaborate and unusual recital programs once a year at New York's Ritz-Carlton Hotel, with a few out-of-town engagements in Washington, Newport, and Boston. The shows starred her alone, with instrumental accompaniment (often by the Pascarella Chamber Music Society). Attendance was by private invitation. These less-than-dignified (and always sold-out) showcases achieved notoriety based on reports that emerged from the rabid loyalists who attended. In addition to the spectacle of Her Royal Tonedeafness valiantly groping for notes in a voice, according to one critic, "tiny to the point of disappearing," the audience would be treated to no less than three costume changes, each more lavish and outlandish than the previous. Her most memorable costume was for the "Angel of Inspiration": a satiny gown of tinsel and tulle with monstrous wings attached at the back. An unidentified New York reviewer described Jenkins's rendition of "Lo, Here the Gentle Lark" as "florid singing, in which the intervals were incorrectly taken, the pitch was nearly non-existent, and the upper notes ... had an infantile quality."

Despite these limitations, Madame Jenkins demonstrated unshakable sangfroid, and her unpolished mannerisms drove fans to paroxysms of hysterics and thunderous applause. "Audiences laughed until they stuffed handkerchiefs in their mouths to stifle the mirth," wrote Daniel Dixon in a 1957 *Coronet* magazine profile.

It may seem unthinkable that Jenkins was oblivious to what most entertainers, professional or amateur, would consider a humiliating audience response. Yet, her accompanist, known as "Cosme McMoon" (actually the great pianist Edwin MacArthur), clarified the peculiar dynamic between performer and patrons: "The audience tried not to hurt her feelings by outright laughing. They developed a convention that whenever she came to a particularly excruciating discord, or something where they had to laugh, they burst into salvos of applause and whistles. The noise was so great, that they could laugh at liberty."

However these reactions affected Madame Jenkins, she was undeterred from further exhibition of her derailed crooning. The incomparable Flo eventually made it all the way to Carnegie Hall—for one performance, on October 25, 1944. The house was standing room only, sold out weeks in advance.

"She was exceedingly happy in her work," wrote Robert Bagar in the *New York World–Telegram*. "It is a pity so few artists are. And the happiness was communicated as if by magic to her hearers." One 1944 un-bylined clipping from an unidentified newspaper noted: "Operatic history... tells of the suicides of failures who drew hisses and missiles instead of approving handclapping on the occasion of their displeasing debuts. Rarely have stampeded beginners recovered from derisive receptions sufficiently to try a comeback, for it takes a brave soul to stand up under such ridicule. The bitter tears of thousands of failures might have been spared had the thwarted singers been blessed with any part of the fortitude of Madame Florence Foster Jenkins."

The tin-throated nightingale considered herself "a God-given coloratura soprano." And, she said, "people expect virtuoso performances from a virtuoso." "Florence Foster Jenkins," wrote Nicholas Limansky, tongue firmly in cheek, "has stood for a certain, occasionally undefinable, degree of excellence in the art of song." Although he never had the pleasure of working with Madame

Jenkins, the legendary conductor Sir Thomas Beecham claimed her studio waxings were among his favorite recordings.

As has happened throughout entertainment history when a performer's determination dwarfs ability, critics go into metaphoric overdrive. One unidentified observer found her "funny as a crutch, without meaning to be so." A reviewer once wrote that the soprano's recording of "Adele's Laughing Song" from Strauss's *Die Fledermaus*—sung in English—promised "more of a kick than the same [price] invested in tequila, zubrovka, or marijuana, and we ain't woofin'!"

The dizzy diva was accompanied for years by McMoon, who, the story goes, was the only one of 20 auditioned pianists who could play along with Jenkins and keep a straight face. For his dignified—if not heroic—support, Madame each year awarded McMoon a gold medal for excellence. It was said that despite Madame's taxi mishap that allowed her to hit the higher F, McMoon was unable to locate the corresponding note on the keyboard.

In 1941, the society songbird was persuaded to record eight selections from her repertoire for private release on 78-rpm disc. They were subsequently licensed by RCA Victor, and seven sides have remained in print on their Red Seal release *The Glory (????)* [sic] *of the Human Voice:* "Queen of the Night Aria" from *The Magic Flute* (Mozart); "The Musical Snuff-Box" (Liadoff); "Bell Song" from *Lakmé* (Delibes); "Charmant Oiseau" from *The Pearl of Brazil* (David); "Biassy" (Bach-Pavlovich); "Adele's Laughing Song" from *Die Fledermaus* (Johann Strauss, Jr.); and "Like a Bird" (composed for her by Cosme McMoon). The eighth, "Serenata Mexicana" (also composed by McMoon), occasionally finds its way into circulation on albums of dubious legitimacy.

Florence was evidently deaf to her own vocal inadequacies. With guests gathered in her parlor, she would alternate discs on the Victrola, then hand out paper ballots, asking the captive audience to judge her recordings against those of competing divas. The visitors would graciously accord their hostess artistic superiority. "Naturally she made comparisons," noted McMoon, "but I do not think she could appraise her own work properly. She really didn't hear the atrocious pitches. She used to sit delightedly and listen for hours to her own recordings."

Jenkins presented just one private New York concert annually, each anticipated as a highlight of the society calendar. She thus considered herself of loftier stature than the world-renowned soprano Dame Nellie Melba, whose performances were open to the public. "Madame Melba is the inferior of we two," Jenkins wrote to Signor Pascarella, "in that she is less discriminating in her choice of audiences."

This was no exaggeration; it was policy. Francis Robinson, Assistant Manager of the Metropolitan Opera, who penned the liner notes to *The Glory (????)*

of the Human Voice, recounted how Madame Jenkins would outfox scalpers by insisting that prospective attendees apply for tickets in person at her lavish suite in the Hotel Seymour. "Toying with the tickets as Rosina might with her fan," wrote Robinson, the following exchange would ensue:

> "Mr. Gilkey, are you a—a newspaper man?"
>
> "No, Madame Jenkins," the applicant replied quite soberly, "a music-lover."
>
> "Very well," the diva beamed. "Two-fifty each, please. Now would you like some sherry?"

Her Carnegie Hall performance coincided with a brash teen-idol's fever-inducing concerts at nearby Paramount Theater. A New York newspaper reviewer, identified only by the initials "P. B.," compared the respective houses: "Only watching an audience listen to Frank Sinatra has this reviewer seen such community of spirit and such simultaneous reflexes as were exhibited last night [at Jenkins's concert]. Not that there is any further similarity between these two artists beyond their common ability to call forth mass exhibition of approval." He noted that Florence's fans were so fervent in their enthusiasm that "the final phrase of each song ... was always drowned in cheers."

"People may have laughed at her singing," said St. Clair Bayfield, her manager for over three decades, "but the applause was real."

One of her resounding crowd-pleasers was Valverde's "Clavelitos." She would emerge dressed in a high comb and mantilla, draped in a gaudy Spanish shawl, carrying a basket of red carnations and prancing a clumsy fandango. One at a time, she would fling the carnations to the audience, each accompanied by a cry of "Olé!" On at least one occasion, she inadvertently flung the basket as well. When this number was encored, McMoon was required to leave his piano post and retrieve the scattered blossoms before the performance could be reprised.

Years later, McMoon recalled her gala Carnegie Hall debut. "The concert went on with the most noisy and abandoned applause. I have never seen such a scene at a bullfight, or at the Yale Bowl after a winning touchdown. When she sang 'Clavelitos,' one famous actress became so hysterical she had to be carried out of her box. 'Adele's Laughing Song' was especially noteworthy. Madame came out in a pastel-colored gown, her eyes were veritable caverns of mascara, with black patches on her face, her head piled high with yellow ringlets of her favorite wig. Besides the 'Ha-ha-ha's'—which people mimicked from the gallery—there was a place in the text that says, 'If my silhouette does not convince you yet, my figure surely will.' She put her hands to her hips, and went into a circular dance—the most ludicrous thing I have ever seen—and created pandemonium in the theater."

A week after her Carnegie Hall engagement, Madame Jenkins suffered a heart attack. She passed away on November 26, 1944, at age 76—presumably with a smile of contentment on her face. She left a legacy of generosity, goodwill, and determination in the face of seemingly insuperable artistic odds.

In his 1995 book, *Eccentrics: A Study of Sanity and Strangeness*, Scottish neuropsychologist David Weeks surveyed "odd" behavior over the centuries and analyzed the relative health, happiness, and creativity of society's peculiar characters. Florence Foster Jenkins was among those briefly profiled in a chapter on "Eccentricity and Creativity in the Arts." Weeks said Flo was to singing what the legendary 19th-century Scots crackpot William "the Great" McGonagall was to poetry. A flattering comparison, in that Weeks felt McGonagall had "limitless belief in his own abilities, and was never discouraged by the relentless scorn of the world."

After her death, Jenkins inspired a school of imitators, but McMoon was dismissive. "Many have tried to give studiedly discordant recitals at Town Hall and elsewhere," he noted, "or tried to make the music funny in that way. But they just make a dismal evening. The reason is that they are not sincere, as Madame Jenkins was. She was inimitable."

Her epitaph indicates that while Florence might have had unflagging confidence in her abilities, she did read the sardonic reviews. Nevertheless, her parting words should serve as an inspiration to the melodically challenged: "Some may say I couldn't sing, but none may say I didn't sing!"

•17•

The Legendary
Stardust Cowboy

WIDE-OPEN SPACE CADET

"**W**e're driving along New York's Taconic Parkway, me and the man who would later be my husband, and in this misplaced effort to impress him, I put on my tape of the Legendary Stardust Cowboy," recalled lawyer Diana Mercer. "I mean, we've listened to the Velvet Underground, Sex Pistols, Captain Beefheart—*whoever,* on this four-hour jaunt. He's at the wheel of my car, and the conversation is at a lull. I'm looking to score some points, so—*what the heck*—in it goes.

"Before I know it, there's flashing red lights behind us, and a six-foot-tall African American policewoman has pulled him over for doing 110 in a 55 mph zone. The ticket cost $310.

"Somebody was trying to tell me something," she sighed, "but I wasn't listening."

The Legendary Stardust Cowboy has been known to make people do strange things. Like sign him to a recording contract. Major labels aren't receptive to weirdness; they're in business to make money, not scare customers. Yet it was Mercury Records who propelled the Legendary Stardust Cowboy (aka "the Ledge") into the marketplace. In 1968, the label released his 45 rpm single, "Paralyzed"—a blast of Texas no-fi wreckage, two-and-a-half minutes of Indian whoops, rebel yells, and caveman cretinism—that forever staked this unforgettable vocalist's claim to fame. The acquisition of this pangalactic buckaroo might have occurred during some Mercury exec's weeklong bender, or during an A&R veep's peyote peak.

Artistically—and psychologically—the Ledge comes across like someone who drove through the carwash with the top down. This bedlam-prone prairie dawg earned notoriety for his uninhibited howling and utter vocal abandon, oblivious to such quaint notions as euphony, rhythm, and restraint. His oral artistry consists of the astonishing number of ways he can emit musical sounds—without actually *singing*. Besides the rebel yell, the Commanche war whoop, and hog hollerin', he's mastered elephant cries, birdcalls, frog croaks, and a menagerie of jungle squawks. The man wails, cackles, and belches; he grunts, growls, and taunts. When the Ledge goes *mano a mano* with a song, melody goes home with a bloody nose every time.

Despite his hyperactive exuberance—bellowing like he's just been goosed—the Ledge isn't threatening or scary. His "singing" voice is a friendly baritone, his vocal chords slightly constricted. Imagine a kiddie-show host whose jockey shorts are too tight. Yet the Ledge speaks in a warm tenor, up in fellow Texan Ross Perot's register. (The comparison stops there.)

There's a lack of attitude in his personality and lyrics, which are imbued with self-deprecating humor. He's lived life as a musical outsider, and been reminded often enough that his "talents" are not welcome in some quarters.

The Ledge's records are sheer fun—if you're ready for a wild ride. "Paralyzed" was described by journalist R. J. Smith as "one long woof of defiance that sounds great at any turntable speed." Along with creek-rocker Hasil Adkins, the Ledge provided stylistic threads for cowpunk and psychobilly, inspiring such voodoo-tinged twangers as the Cramps, Meat Puppets, Butthole Surfers, and Raunch Hands. His more celebrated fans include Brooke Shields and Elvis Costello. Among the Texas roots posse, the Ledge is beloved by Butch Hancock, Jimmie Dale Gilmore, and former school-chum Joe Ely, all of whom proudly call him a friend. Ely, in fact, considers him "West Texas's greatest jazz musician."

The man has left his mark on at least one certified superstar. When David Bowie signed with Mercury in the United States around 1970, the company gave him a stack of 45s as a welcome-to-our-label gift. Among those singles was "Paralyzed." "That was the one he liked best," affirmed Ledge chronicler Tony Philputt, who directed a 90-minute film biography of the Lone Star lunatic. Thus inspired, Bowie appropriated part of the singer's name for his U.S. breakout album, *The Rise and Fall of Ziggy Stardust and the Spiders from Mars*. "Apparently, Bowie was obsessed with this character, and never knew anything about him," Philputt elaborated. "This was up until 1998. A reporter in Chicago who did a story on the Ledge got a hold of Bowie through his management. Bowie still knew nothing about him. He was amazed the Ledge was even alive. On Robert Plant's first solo tour after Led Zeppelin split, before his set, he played the Ledge's *Rock-It to Stardom* album over the hall P.A."

Anyone casually familiar with the musical maelstrom of "Paralyzed" might be surprised to learn that the song has *lyrics*. In the interest of encouraging future audience singalongs, we herewith present:

PARALYZED

I've got a gal, away 'cross town
She won't come to see me unless I pull my shades down
Paralyzed, paralyzed
She puts her arms around me, the way she squeezes me
Makes me paralyzed

When I go to the show
Boy, she does make a fella bestow [sic]
Paralyzed, paralyzed
When I look into her eyes, she makes me paralyzed

I threw my baby in a sack
Threw it over my back
And took off in a big black Cadillac
Paralyzed, paralyzed
She puts her arms around me
She keeps me warm from the storm
She makes me paralyzed

I ran to the 'frigerator
Hungry as an alligator
I opened the door, and what did I see?
I saw my baby starin' right back at me.
Paralyzed, paralyzed
She jumped into my arms
She gave me all of her charms
She makes me paralyzed.

The perpetrator of the feral "Paralyzed" is a relatively mild-mannered pussycat. Before he adopted the guise of the Legendary Stardust Cowboy, he was Norman Carl Odam, born September 5, 1947, in Lubbock, Texas, to Carl Bunyan Odam and Utahonna Beauchamp. He was a shy youngster; he says it took his kindergarten teacher six months to get him to talk. One of his earliest

!PARALYZED!

ILLUSTRATION BY J. R. WILLIAMS

!YEEEE-HOO!

recollections is that at age seven, he knew he "would like to go to Mars instead of the Moon." In school, he distracted himself by scribbling poetry and short stories. He also began developing highly idiosyncratic vocal techniques. "When I was 14," he wrote in a 1969 autobiographical sketch, "I started doing Rebel yells and Indian whoops because I am part Shawnee. I taught myself to do birdcalls and jungle sounds." With this odd array of mouth noises, he began vocalizing around school, hoping to achieve some measure of celebrity with the opposite sex. "I figured that by singing I was able to attract all the girls," he explained. "But I attracted all the boys instead."

The popularity of picker Chet Atkins inspired young Odam to take guitar lessons. He never mastered the Countrypolitan king's smooth fingering, but he did teach himself drums, kazoo, harmonica, buffalo horn, and the rubboard. He acquired rudimentary bugle skills by riffing along with LPs by Herb Alpert and the Tijuana Brass. His early (unrecorded) repertoire consisted of country and western songs popularized by Johnny Cash, Ray Price, and Buck Owens. Along the line to post-adolescence, like a kid tossed from a dimestore bronco once too often, Odam evolved into an authentic frontier wacko.

He also became, from time to time, an unfortunate victim of circumstance. The Ledge's life—like his music—has always been slightly beyond his control.

Joe Ely was a classmate at J. T. Hutchinson Junior High in Lubbock. "The first time I saw Norman," recalled Ely, "he was playing on the steps. He'd get to school 'bout 7:30 in the morning, before everybody else. He'd do a whole set before the bell rang. He just kinda wailed on at the top of his lungs. [Later,] Norman carried on this tradition and played on the steps of the high school." Odam invariably attracted crowds—girls even—and his extracurricular notoriety grew. But he still couldn't get a date. Not all his classmates took his performances seriously. Some considered him a freak. They'd honk their horns, throw dirt clods and Sweet-Tarts. Others flung pennies and peppermints in the hole of his guitar.

At some point in his teens, Odam merged two great obsessions—the wild west and outer space—and decided "The Legendary Stardust Cowboy" suited him better than "Norman." He spray-painted the name—preceded by "NASA presents"—in big gold and black letters across the side of his new Chevy Biscayne (much to the horror of his grandmother, who took a swat at the teen for ruining a perfectly good automobile).

He couldn't get gigs at local clubs, so he obsessively sang in public: at frat houses, outside the Dairy Queen, in the parking lots of the Hi-D-Ho Drive-In and the Char-King. His makeshift stage was the roof of his Chevy, on which he'd painted a map of the moon. His atavistic caterwauling was accompanied by St. Vitus gyrations copied from another hero, Tom Jones. Usually management would run him off the property.

Odam would turn up unexpectedly at parties and give impromptu—and often unwelcome—performances. He occasionally found himself the target of spectator intolerance. When he plied his raucous repertoire in honky-tonks during the late 1960s, he sported long hair and muttonchop sideburns. "Old time country music fans thought I was making fun of them and country music," he recalled. "Owners and managers of clubs had to pull away people trying to get close enough to beat me up." One night at the Hi-D-Ho, an onlooker heaped ridicule on the Ledge's performance, but he ignored her and kept singing. "He either laid his guitar down, or she came up and grabbed it," said Ely. "All I remember is turning around and seeing the front of his guitar cave in, with her foot going through it. It was a sad day. That guitar was his main squeeze."

After high school, Odam resolved to travel in search of fame. Las Vegas. New York. Hollywood. Other planets.

Instead he took a bus to San Diego. Unable to land a paid gig, he moved to L.A. and tried to get on the *Steve Allen Show* and *Art Linkletter's House Party*, but no one was booking unrecorded amateurs who specialized in coyote howls. Disillusioned, he returned to Lubbock, worked in a warehouse, and played local clubs to largely skeptical or indifferent audiences.

In 1968, he tried to contact the best-known musical outsider. "I wrote Tiny Tim a letter," he recalled, "with a picture of myself and musical instruments. I wanted to be on the Johnny Carson show like [him]." Tiny never replied. (Considering the magnitude of his then-popularity, it's unlikely Tiny ever saw the letter.)

With $160 in his pocket, the Ledge aimed his Biscayne at New York. His goal: the *Tonight Show.* He had no manager and no demo tape. He also had zero business smarts.

He never made it to Manhattan—but along the way, the "legendary" part of his name became a reality.

He pit-stopped in Forth Worth, 300 miles east of his hometown. Two vacuum cleaner salesmen, headed out to a local club, spied the Ledge's graffiti-blessed Chevy in a parking lot. They chatted with the driver, and noticed he had what they thought was a guitar. The vac dealers knew the club owner, so they invited Odam along to perform. After witnessing the musical demolition derby that is a typical Ledge showcase, they whisked him to a nearby recording studio, where he auditioned an original song for a young engineer named T-Bone Burnett.

A sense of urgency prevailed—who knew if this transient would be around next day—so they spooled up a reel of tape and hit "record." T-Bone leapt to the drum kit, the Ledge grabbed a mic, and "Paralyzed" was born. The Ledge's aboriginal shrieks and freewheeling bugle brays were underscored by Burnett's furious, not quite-metronomic drumming.

It was an early morning session; the engineers had been up all night messing around, and the whole fiasco seemed half-hallucinatory. "The band was just me on drums, and he had a dobro with a broken neck, so he could only play on the first fret," Burnett recalled. "We just set up two microphones. [The staff was] in a state of sleep deprivation that probably caused us to be more daring than we might've been otherwise. Norman gave me some instructions—'Play drums in the same tempo I'm singing in'—and I said, 'I could do that.' [laughs] Maybe probably. Then he said he was going to take a bugle solo, and he wanted me to take a drum solo, and I found that all agreeable. It was explosive, to say the least."

Upstairs in the same building was KXOL, the only Top 40 AM station in town. Burnett ran upstairs and played the tape for the wake-up jock, expecting a rebuff. Instead the host ranted, "This is it! This is the new music!" The song was aired several times, the switchboard overheated, and T-Bone knew they had a hit on their hands.

"This is something, by the way, to highly recommend Fort Worth," chuckled Burnett, "that the people could love this and embrace it so instantly."

The studio stamped 500 copies on the Psycho-Suavé label. After some initial regional commotion, the single was sold to Mercury Records for national distribution. The deal was brokered by sleazy Fort Worth music impresario Major Bill Smith, who brazenly claimed production credit.

"Paralyzed" embodied some of the most mutant strains ever pressed on major-league vinyl (at least 'til Harry Chapin got signed). It cracked the *Billboard* Top 200—no mean feat for a record that even by the drug-addled standards of 1968 was irredeemably in orbit. It brought the sagebrush spaceman instant fame, if not fortune.

Of course, not everyone "got it." "Paralyzed" frequently hovers near the top of smart-alec rankings of the "all-time worst recordings." British TV comic Kenny Everett compiled an album entitled, aptly enough, *The World's Worst Record Show*; "Paralyzed" shares the LP's furrows with such deeper dumpster pickings as "Why Am I Living?" by Jess Conrad and Dickie Lee's "Laurie." Clayton Stromberger, in a 'zine called *No Depression*, described how "out" the single was: "It was out the window that noted music critic Ed Ward's first copy of 'Paralyzed' went sailing...after his first listen...in 1968. He ripped it off the turntable, pronounced it the worst song he'd ever heard, and flung it as far as it would go. Which of course only added luster to the legend of the Ledge (and left Ward kicking himself years later)."

In November 1968, ironically, the Ledge managed to follow in the footsteps of Tiny Tim by appearing on Rowan and Martin's *Laugh-In*. *Spin* proclaimed the Ledge's performance of his "hit" single among the "25 Greatest Musical Moments in TV History." It could have been—and in certain ways was—a celebratory experience. But some of Odam's friends watching back in Texas were disgusted at what they considered the coast-to-coast humiliation of their guileless chum.

"Paralyzed" was accompanied by Dan Rowan's snide remarks and Dick Martin's slapstick mimicry. Norman just wanted to play his song, and seemed visibly irked at the revelry taking place at his expense. Amid this hilarity, Martin asked his guest to perform another song. Odam kicked into the single's B side, "Who's Knocking On My Door"— just as the zany *Laugh-In* cast emerged from the wings and began clowning on-camera, imitating the Ledge's spastic dance moves and making a mockery of his performance (well, it *was* a comedy show).

How the West was fun: Norman Odam— armed, dangerous, and legendary

"I was confused," the Ledge told me in a phone interview. "I finally got mad and ran off the set. That wasn't part of the act."

Nonetheless, Lubbock's most eccentric export had launched a chart-climbing record and caused pandemonium on the nation's top-rated TV show. Offers quickly followed for appearances on *American Bandstand*, the *Joey Bishop Show*, and the *Ed Sullivan Show*. The "legendary" part of his name seemed assured; the "star" part was imminent.

Unfortunately, within a short while, his dreams were "dust."

Just as the Ledge was set to collect dividends on years of dues paying, a musicians' strike imposed a network ban on live music. Because he'd played guitar on national TV, the Ledge was categorized "union." The variety show offers were postponed.

By the time the strike was over, so was "Paralyzed." It was off the charts. Two follow-up singles flopped. Doppler-like, the Ledge zoomed off the nation's cultural radar as quickly as he'd arrived.

In the aftermath of fleeting fame, the Ledge parted ways with an unscrupulous manager. Mercury Records dropped him. Shortly thereafter, he was arrested and jailed on a trumped-up vagrancy charge. He then learned that Major Bill had purloined a tape of 50 new songs Odam had recorded at T-Bone's studio. Determined to reclaim his work, the Ledge broke into the Major's office

STANDING IN A TRASHCAN
(THINKING OF YOU)

I'm standing in a trashcan thinking about you
As the neighbor's cat goes by
I swallered a horsefly
Happy as I am stepping on a bean can
Just like a frog
Blow my nose on a catalog
Drinking a Dr. Pepper
I'm standing in a trashcan thinking about you
There's TV dinner all over by boots
My spurs got caught in a bowl of soup
I ran outta baloney now I have to eat my pony
I'm standing in a trashcan thinking about you
My own baby found me inside of a trashcan
In some back alley in New York

and retrieved the goods. "I went down to a studio and had the master tape run off onto a seven-inch reel," he recalled. "At the house, I played the songs through, wrote them down on paper, then unraveled the tape down the middle of Henderson Street in Fort Worth so Major Bill—and nobody else—could [sic] get their hands on my music." He later burned the song sheets. "He can't get 'em now," Odam smiled to a friend, "but I still remember 'em."

Next stop was Las Vegas, where he met DJ/entrepreneur James Yanaway, a sincere admirer. "Nobody made the Ledge. He is what he is," noted Yanaway. "There were a few people who were appreciative of what he was doing, and many more who were exploitative. I felt, this guy needs a fair shake." Yanaway had a new label, Amazing Records, for which he recorded the Ledge's first full-length album, *Rock-It to Stardom* (1984). Unlike the skeletal instrumentation on his early singles, this recording (and all his later waxings) employed a band—a cookin' crew. Technique remained parked in the lobby; spontaneity was the prime directive. "He would just start a song," said session drummer Mike Buck, "He wouldn't tell us what key or anything. He'd just start singing, and we'd start playing. Some of it turned out all right, considering the chaotic conditions it was recorded under." The album includes a new version of "Paralyzed," recorded in 1981 with the LeRoi Brothers. As remakes go, it's nearly as vigorous as the original.

Besides an aversion to melody, genteel stage manners don't rank high on the Ledge's list of concerns. He played New York's Folk City around 1985. Diesel Only Records honcho Jeremy Tepper recalled, "The Ledge bounded out of the basement dressing room with a stack of paper plates that he began flinging at the audience frisbee-style. Each of these flying saucers was personalized with colorful Crayola drawings of cacti and desert sunsets." It was just one of several "talents" on display that evening. "Over the course of the show," said dB's drummer/singer Will Rigby, "the Ledge stripped down to his white jockey briefs and cowboy boots, an entertainment gambit not necessarily suited to the music—or his physique. After getting down to scantily-cladness, he was pumping his crotch inches from the face of my friend Naomi, seated at the front table. She's got a good sense of humor and didn't run screaming, but she told me later she was mortified. Or perhaps terrified? He was outside, all right."

Odam left Amazing Records in disillusionment in 1985. The biggest disappointment, Yanaway admitted, was that "I had not gotten him on the *Tonight Show.*" The Ledge didn't just want to appear—he longed to be guest host. Yanaway realized there wasn't much he could do for his client. They parted ways.

A crew of San Francisco–based musicians undertook the honor of backing the Ledge in his Bay area debut in early 1986. Later that year they joined him in the studio to record the album *Retro Rocket Back to Earth* for Spider Records. The repertoire is largely first-take, sloppy but spirited, with no overdubs. Our lost-in-space cowpoke betrays his Luddite leanings, proclaiming in one song title, "I Hate CDs," though it's perhaps less the technology than certain personalities associated with it. "I hate those CDs that Bruce Springsteen put out," the Ledge howls, "He's the number one reason why I hate CDs." The same entourage recorded the *Legendary Stardust Cowboy Rides Again,* but they couldn't find an American company that would touch it. (The album was released on France's New Rose in 1990.)

Aside from a few subsequent singles for Norton Records, not much has been heard from the Ledge in recent years. His fans, however, are committed to preserving his legacy. Besides putting pressure on her car's accelerator pedal, the Ledge impelled Diana Mercer (now divorced from her speed-prone husband) to undertake creation of a Web site dedicated to her favorite musical wrecking ball.

There's also a documentary in the can: *Cotton Pickin' Smash! The Story of the Legendary Stardust Cowboy.* Directed by Philputt, it contains photos from the early years, anecdotes from the Ledge's illustrious circle of friends, the *Laugh-In* debacle, live club footage, and copious chat from the notorious fun-slinger himself. "When we started, we weren't sure if anybody would talk to us," Philputt admitted. "I had to reassure people I wasn't doing this as a joke or to ridicule

COURTESY NORTON RECORDS

him. But almost to a 'T' everyone I contacted was ecstatic that we were doing this. Except his family. They were no help at all. They asked us not to do it."

The project took eight years to complete. At a cost of $22,000, it drove Philputt into bankruptcy (in 1992 he declared debts of $23,300 and assets of $425)—after which he remarked: "I'm glad it's done." It may be dead as well. The owners of *Laugh-In* quoted an astronomical fee for use of the TV footage. "They wanted seven or eight thousand dollars per 30 seconds," explained Philputt, who has pretty much conceded defeat.

Nowadays, the Ledge lives in San Jose and works as a security guard in Santa Clara for defense contractor Lockheed-Martin. "Got a top secret clearance," he revealed. "They designed the Pathfinder spacecraft that landed on Mars." Odam's a meteorology freak—his TV is constantly tuned to the *Weather Channel.* Despite his hatred of CDs, he bought a deck, primarily to listen to his favorite singers: Barbra Streisand, Dinah Washington, and Barry Manilow. "And don't forget Sinatra," the Ledge advised. "He's number one."

The cowboy with the chili-seared synapses doesn't have much money. "It sure would be nice if David Bowie would pay me something for using part of my name in 'Ziggie [sic] Stardust,'" he wrote to webmistress Diana.

He rarely performs in public anymore. And despite his loyal following, the Ledge will always be a taste some folks never acquire. Guitarist Frank Novicki recalled that after one gig, the club owner came to pay the band. "He gave me the money and a good long hard look. Very judgmental," Novicki explained. "He says, 'Are you related to [the Ledge]?' I said, 'No, I just play guitar.' Then he said, 'That is the *worst shit* I've ever heard in my life. Here's your money.' I didn't feel like debating the point. There's a lot worse shit."

Novicki trusts his ears and his heart. "Norman can't carry a tune, and he doesn't really sing in time," he attested, "but you don't have to know any of that stuff to be good at music. Boy, is he proof of that."

Artist and longtime admirer Kevin Teare admits it's not easy evangelizing for the Ledge. "Over the years, the people I've played 'Paralyzed' for—generally the more they knew about music, the better they liked the record," he discovered. "When you play it, some people think you're trying to goof on them. If you don't know a lot about music, you might think it's just a joke. But in terms of the spontaneity of the recording—it's completely lo-fi, the drums are recorded in a way that the signal's breaking up. He crosses a lot of lines in terms of what would be thought of as 'quality.' A painter named Hans Hoffman once said, 'Quality is synonymous with the spirit in which something is made.' And I like the spirit in which this record was made."

The Ledge puts it all in perspective: "Music critics and record reviewers the world over have written about me: that I can't sing, that I can't play the guitar, that I don't know how to carry a tune. Well, neither can Kenny Rogers nor Mick Jagger. All of us are in the same boat."

• 13 •

Robert
Graettinger

SLEEP IN THE GRAVE

Post-Swing Era bandleader Stan Kenton wasn't a formula man. He'd reached the apex of his career as an orchestra director by pushing the genre to its outer limits. His electrifying, bop-influenced recordings extended the form's horizons, yet managed to please a broad audience. In the 1940s, he scored with such hits as "The Peanut Vendor," "Eager Beaver," and "Tampico."

Kenton was also one of the primary exponents of bridging the gulf between the dance and concert halls. He assured listeners that if they didn't feel like jitterbugging, it was OK to sit back and enjoy his tight ensemble's dazzling arrangements. Kenton had broken new ground with such works as "Artistry in Rhythm," an explosive showpiece that stunned the music world. It altered forever the perspective of a young Mexican bandleader named Juan Garcia Esquivel, the later icon of "Space Age Bachelor Pad Music," who claimed he was never the same after hearing "Artistry." Ted Gioia, in *The History of Jazz*, testified that Kenton presented "uncompromising works that defied the conventions of existing jazz harmonic and melodic techniques."

But being a restless nomad took its toll. In late 1948, exhausted by the strain of touring and the pressures of a staggering payroll, Kenton quit music and took a long vacation. His marriage was a shambles, his career in doubt. His wife Violet referred him to a shrink, insisting, "No psychiatrist, no me."

By the time he emerged six months later from this debilitating funk, Kenton had lost the marital duel and embarked on the next phase of his career: the legendary Innovations Orchestra. Dancing wasn't just discouraged; it was near-impossible. "I don't think jazz was meant to continue as dance music," Kenton told *Down Beat*'s Nat Hentoff in 1952. "What jazz is going to evolve into is an American style of—if I can use the word—classical music. And that's what we're trying to do."

Kenton wasn't alone. During the 1940s and 1950s, composers Jimmy Giuffre, George Russell, Dave Brubeck, and the Modern Jazz Quartet's John Lewis, among others, explored the frontiers of what Gunther Schuller termed "Third Stream Music."

For his Innovations project, Kenton gathered such adventurous souls as trumpeter Shorty Rogers, reedman Bud Shank, saxist Art Pepper, drummer Shelly Manne, and a young high-note maniac named Maynard Ferguson on trumpet. Drawing on hypermodernist arrangements and compositions by Pete Rugolo, Neal Hefti, Franklyn Marks, and Manny Albam, Kenton's 40-piece outfit attempted to revolutionize the bandstand by fusing "serious" music and jazz. "From Bartok to bongo drums," sneered critic George Simon dismissively.

Such genre-splicing had been pursued since the "symphonic jazz" movement of the 1920s and 1930s by Gershwin, Whiteman, Grofé, Ellington, even Raymond Scott. But where those earlier progenitors of hybrid forms succeeded in captivating ever larger audiences, Kenton sent his career into free-fall and repelled a sizable share of his remaining fan base. One major reason was his radical approach. In the bandleader's own words, "If you start looking for a melody, you won't find any. We got a great thing out of concocting sound. It's sound concoction." Comedian Mort Sahl, an ardent admirer, quipped, "About that Kenton band—a waiter dropped a tray and three couples got up to dance."

Kenton's musicians and some jazz critics appreciated his pioneering moves. But as Carol Easton wrote in her 1973 Kenton bio, *Straight Ahead*, "the critics were trained and paid to make the effort to meet the music halfway. The audience was not. Droves of Stan's most devoted fans were turned off by the complicated and unconventional harmonies, the flatted intervals, the beatless-ness, and what they considered lack of emotion in much of the music." The classical sector felt little affinity for the "vulgar" jazz pyrotechnics, while jazz buffs cared little for the more cerebral, "highbrow" sheen of Kenton's inventions.

And, in Easton's words, "For many, many loyal fans, the music of Bob Graettinger was the last straw."

Robert Frederick Graettinger was a loner. This gaunt, six-feet-four-inch specter of a man lived in squalid apartments in seedy Los Angeles neighborhoods with little more than a floor mattress, an upright piano, and a stove. He was convinced he could outwit the grim reaper with a steady diet of scrambled

Robert F. Graettinger, ca. 1951

eggs, milk, and vitamins. He was an impotent alcoholic in a shabby wardrobe, with concave cheekbones and a bad complexion. He rarely went to bed. "Sleep in the grave," he'd say. This haunted, cadaverous figure was born, fittingly, on Halloween, in 1923.

Graettinger's childhood in Ontario, California, was reportedly fairly normal. In junior high he played football, an interest eclipsed by music in high school. He studied saxophone and spent summers gigging at mountain resorts, where he acquired a second major predilection: drinking. While in high school he began arranging, purely in the popular swing idiom. Early idols included bandleaders Duke Ellington, and a man often categorized with Kenton, Jimmie Lunceford.

In the early 1940s, Graettinger played alto saxophone with various swing outfits, including those of Alvino Rey, Benny Carter, and Jan Savitt. He introduced himself to Kenton in 1941, approaching the bandleader backstage at the Hollywood Palladium and handing him an original arrangement. It was ambitious, if amateurish, but Kenton was impressed enough to encourage the neophyte to keep working and return to him later.

During a 1942 summer engagement in Phoenix with the Ken Baker band, Graettinger underwent a marked change: he became moodier and more withdrawn, qualities fueled by a more lavish intake of firewater. He also became obsessed with composing. He served briefly in the Army but was discharged for alcoholism.

In 1947 Graettinger offered Kenton a fully arranged composition, "Thermopylae," which the bandleader recorded almost immediately. It was a combative piece of music, lasting under three minutes. As scored and performed, "Thermopylae" unfolds menacingly, pitting the brass against the rest of the orchestra; a dissonant fanfare bellows insistently, nearly drowning out the reeds and rhythm. Kindly put, it was a ponderous work. In a 1974 dissertation, *The Music and Life of Robert Graettinger,* Robert Badgett Morgan noted that the piece employed "the almost constant use of rootless chords result[ing] in an unbroken tension, so that the whole concept of tension and release seems to be negated. The resultant atmosphere is totally depressive." *Metronome* called it "confused writing; the thing gets nowhere." And *Down Beat* shivered that "Thermopylae [was] a moribund, impressionistic thing concerned only with mood—and a depressing one at that." Apparently even Kenton had doubts. He reportedly admitted to friends, "I don't know whether his music is genius or a bunch of crap!"

The 24-year-old "moribund impressionist" was, by this time, no longer a professional musician; he'd given away his alto, telling a friend, "I have more to say than I can say with one horn." In all Graettinger's years on his payroll, Kenton never once saw the man play.

Kenton next began rehearsing an early version of Graettinger's magnum opus, the *City of Glass* suite, a four-part, three-movement tone poem laced with jaggedness and atonality. The work would be revised constantly over the next few years before a definitive recording was made in 1951. While Graettinger was developing *City of Glass,* he was studying composition with Russell Garcia, a well-known Hollywood composer, arranger, and author.

Graettinger's compositions and arrangements are characterized by unrelenting dissonance, polytonality, and colliding rhythms. The instruments seem to fight each other, as if there were an insurrection among the horns. To the uninitiated, the band sometimes sounds like it's tuning up, when they're actually one-third along into the piece. Recordings of Graettinger's arrangements and compositions occasionally suggest a big band with a sour stomach. This is abundantly evident in the opening passages of "Everything Happens to Me" (1949), a gorgeous torch lament sung by June Christy set against a dyspeptic Graettinger background that seems intent on subverting the melody.

Graettinger's music evinces elements of such modern classical composers as Edgard Varèse, Schoenberg, and Stefan Volpe, rather than reflections of the bebop titans who were then laying waste to their jazz forebears' traditions. The critical jazz community isn't usually a united front, but they agree on one thing: that Robert Graettinger isn't one of them. In the "serious vs. swinging" debate over concert-jazz, the jazz sentinels toss his besotted corpse over the fence into the neighbor's yard. The serious side makes no immediate claim on Graettinger—but they don't throw him back.

To many of his works, Graettinger affixed throwaway titles: "Some Saxophones," "A Thought," "A Horn," "An Orchestra," as if having expended tremendous energy on composing and arranging, he couldn't be bothered to worry about clever titles. Some considered the works themselves equally disposable. Barry Ulanov in *Metronome* assessed *City of Glass*: "As music it seems to me to fall somewhere between Schoenberg and Schillinger, but most of all to fall, nowhere suggesting the understanding of atonal or 12-tone composing traditions ... a muddled modern work ill-defined in purpose and not much closer to a work of art than science fiction."

Though Ulanov found it "ill-defined," Graettinger was not averse to a little explanation. From his notes in preparation for the album jacket:

> *City of Glass* derives its inspiration from the interplay and counterpoint of the energies and forces that I see and feel in the world around me. In writing it, my endeavor has been to have the music describe my visions. In this particular work my music has described a city in which the buildings are structures of energy. Structures that are in constant motion and that are transparent so that the motion of one can be seen through the motion of another and many others through these. A city of moving glass-like structures.

Not all reviews were negative. *Gramophone* called *City of Glass* "an impressive piece which deserves to be taken seriously." Rob Darnell in *Down Beat*, after

ROBERT GRAETTINGER

hurling pejoratives like "shrill," "intolerably harsh," "stunts ... beaten to exhaustion," and "needs ... editing," concedes, "He's got something here that's brashly alive and at its best tremendously exciting."

Having discovered Graettinger, Kenton encouraged the lad's excesses, turning his orchestra over to this brooding artiste to use as a canvas for his abstract brushstrokes. Kenton seemed unconcerned about the receptiveness of his audience, who had come to expect maverick moves from the man for whom the term "progressive jazz" was coined. "House of Strings," another early Graettinger work, Kenton found "thrilling." He told an interviewer, "From that time on, everything that Graettinger wrote I didn't contest at all, because I felt that he had arrived and he knew what he was doing."

If few outside the band knew what to make of it, fewer knew what to call it. Graettinger's music had "roots in some unseen dimension," wrote Max Harrison in the liner notes to Capitol's *City of Glass* CD. It was neither jazz nor programmatic orchestral music. It made no pretense of expanding the vocabulary of then-prevailing bebop à la Dizzy Gillespie or Charlie Parker. Yet it was championed by a world-renowned avatar of modern jazz, who had sold millions of records.

Graettinger wallowed in cacophony, as if reluctant to commit to a pleasing melody. You can tap your feet occasionally, but dancing or humming along are largely futile. His music isn't a backdrop suitable for cocktail or dinner, though it could terrorize confessions out of tight-lipped homicide suspects. Graettinger's arsenal is confrontational, and his art doesn't speak to a wide audience. Perhaps it's unspeakable. It's bleak, lonely, and removed—perfectly natural qualities, considering the source. If music resonates within the soul, Graettinger's resounds in a solitary and frightening corner.

As each anxiety-ridden passage unfolds, a new listener is likely to grow increasingly intrigued, or to scream more loudly, "Enough—please!" Considering the effort it takes to assimilate and understand Graettinger's music, let alone *perform* it, his oeuvre will never enter the standard repertoire. Nor will it sell records. For those who seek relaxation and pleasure from music—which is to say, most people—Graettinger is chloroform in the cocktail. His disturbing creations could disperse unwanted guests. Perhaps the only way to effect seduction with Graettinger's music is by taking it off.

Barry McRae, in *The Jazz Handbook*, dismisses Graettinger with one word: "pretentious." George Simon, in *Metronome*, wrote that Graettinger's arrangement of the romantic favorite "You Go to My Head" was "an intense-sounding bit of impressionistic neuroticism that, to put it most mildly, bothers me."

It's telling to consider the two popular songs Graettinger arranged that made it to the recording stage under Kenton: "Everything Happens to Me" and

[171]

"You Go to My Head," both of which reflect aspects of an outsider's mindset. The former is the quintessential loser's lament:

> I make a date for golf, and you can bet your life it rains
> I try to give a party, and the guy upstairs complains
> Guess I'll go through life just catching colds and missing trains
> Everything happens to me.

And "You Go to My Head," while ostensibly a love song, has, for a liquor-sponge like Graettinger, pathologic overtones. His queasy arrangements of these standards were not welcomed by the public. The mayhem Graettinger committed against these songs is analogous to a stranger, invited into your home, who pisses in your fishtank.

The sullen enfant terrible traveled with the Kenton band, but rarely talked with the players. He was usually along for the ride at Kenton's insistence; the bandleader was concerned about his reclusive protégé's utter indifference to his health—notwithstanding Graettinger's prodigious vitamin gobbling. Kenton thought it would be salutary if Bob got "to see a little bit of the outside world."

Observing the band in rehearsal and performance, Graettinger studied each player's technique, the better to compose specifically for each man's style—a practice most commonly associated with Duke Ellington. This penchant for isolating a musician's stylistic nuances was carried to extremes in the case of "A Trumpet" (from his *This Modern World* suite), a showpiece for Maynard Ferguson. Saxist/arranger Willie Maiden told Robert Morgan that Graettinger didn't just observe Ferguson onstage—he studied the trumpeter's backstage warm-up patterns, "what he played when he was just fooling around ... in every dressing room in the country." An upper register solo scale scored by Graettinger for Ferguson, Maiden revealed, was "an exercise that Maynard used to warm up, to get his chops together." Individual parts often had little or no relation to what other members of the orchestra were playing. "You were independent of the guy next to you," said Innovations saxophonist Art Pepper. "If you got lost, you were dead, because there was no way to figure out where you were."

Graettinger's life was as desolate as his music. Comments by Kenton sidemen in Easton's book paint a bleak portrait. Band copyist Clinton Roemer said he embodied "the novel or motion picture version of the starving composer living in the garret." "He was a very *weird* person," observed composer-arranger Pete Rugolo's wife Jan, who added, "he had this terrible coloring—sick." Vocalist-arranger Gene Howard found him "frightening." Art Pepper: "He looked sort of like a ghoul or a vampire ... he had these strange, haunting

KENTON ARCHIVES

Robert Graettinger, year unknown

eyes." Drummer Shelley Manne: "Even though we were on the road with him,... we never really knew him." Saxophonist Bill Holman: "I never had a conversation with him."

Graettinger was paid $25 a week as a staff arranger. When Kenton offered a raise, Graettinger refused. A change in his standard of living was unnecessary; he merely wanted to be left alone to compose in his cheap, dingy garage apartment, soaking up inspiration from Gin Pan Alley.

No one was closer to Kenton's inner circle in the late 1940s than Pete Rugolo, referred to by Easton as "Stan's musical alter ego." Yet even to Rugolo, Graettinger was a looming question mark. "I never really got a chance to talk to him," he said in a telephone interview. "He didn't show up much, didn't socialize. He was a strange-looking fellow. Tall, thin. No color—probably never in the sun. I guess he slept all day. A couple of times I was with the orchestra when he came by. He would talk to Stan, Stan would play whatever he brought, then he'd go back to his little apartment."

Rugolo admired Graettinger's work immensely. "I was trying to write modern music, things that were very classical-sounding, influenced by Stravinsky or Bartok. The band didn't know what to think. A trumpet player would say, 'Hey, I'm playing a B-flat and he's got a B-natural. What's the note?' I'd say, 'No, that's right, that's what I want.' But Graettinger went further than I did. A lot of the players probably weren't real pleased. They would rather play the swinging Count Basie–type stuff. It was challenging. And while some of them liked it, most of them probably didn't. But it encouraged me to go further than I would have."

If Graettinger's music was unconventional, so was his scoring technique, which involved hand-coloring sections of graph paper. The horizontal axis represented time, the vertical designated pitch, and particular colors indicated instruments (e.g., blue for saxophones, red for trumpets, amber for trombones). He learned this system from his mentor Garcia, who called it "painting a score." (The graph system was pioneered by Joseph Schillinger and had occasionally been used by Oscar Levant, Nathan van Cleave, Gershwin, and another Kenton arranger, Franklin Marks.) Particularly aggravating to historians was Graettinger's habit of using both sides of the graph paper for unrelated compositions, with no regard for continuity. Fortunately for musicians and copyists, Graettinger himself transposed these graphs into standard notation. They would otherwise have been unplayable.

Both Easton and Morgan catalogued numerous marginal comments Graettinger scribbled to himself on the colored-coded scores:

Remember walking home last night
    All kinds of inner things poking through
    The open sea and woods and hilltops. Perhaps a big wave, then
backwash during which the cello enters
        immediately a whole golden universe that is brutally interrupted
        Climax is after the peak is reached, then make it to the oblivion
that you so seldom achieve
        those fool birds again
        Clean all of this shit up today

Graettinger lived for two years with an amateur pianist named Gale Madden, a groupie-type who saw herself as inspiring whatever "genius" she happened to be shacking with. As described by Easton, Madden "looked even freakier than Graettinger, in mismatched shoes, [and] men's clothes.... She was volatile and erratic, if not downright psychotic; Graettinger came home one day to find everything dyed pink—bedspread, towels, curtains, clothes, shoes, everything." Easton said one musician tagged Madden "a sexual circus," whereas Graettinger was impotent. She eventually left him for Gerry Mulligan—and others.

Kenton's sponsorship helped Graettinger achieve a degree of exposure he would never have enjoyed with an orchestra leader of lesser renown. It'll never be known how well Graettinger would have worked with a bandleader reluctant to accord him carte blanche with an orchestra, or a chief more protective of a band's reputation. Kenton was the only conductor willing to take a chance with Graettinger, and there's no indication that this human shadow ever sought to arrange or compose for another ensemble. Yet even the blessing of a celebrity like Kenton wouldn't earn Graettinger a shot on the *Ed Sullivan Show*.

Art Pepper, in his autobiography *Straight Life*, recalled the debut of *City of Glass* at the Civic Opera House in Chicago. "It was ... a revolutionary composition, an incredibly hard musical exercise; it was a miracle we got through it. Bob conducted it, a tall, thin guy... he looked like a living skeleton conducting, like a dead man with sunken eyes, a musical zombie. He took us through it, and he finished, and he turned around to the people and he nodded, and the people didn't do *nothin'*. The place was packed; we'd played the shit out of this thing and now there wasn't a sound. They didn't know what to do. We didn't know what to do. I'm looking at Stan and I'm thinking, 'Well, what's going to happen now? What's he going to do *now*?' Stan looked at the audience. I saw his mind, you could see it turning and all of a sudden he *leaped* out onto the middle of the stage, gestured at us to rise, swung his body around again to the audience, and bam! They started clapping, and they clapped and clapped and clapped and then they stood up with an ovation that lasted for maybe five minutes."

But how many actually understood and truly loved what they'd just heard? Trombonist Bill Russo admitted, "A lot of those chords hurt your teeth. Especially your fillings." Capitol Records reluctantly agreed to record the suite after producer Lee Gillette lobbied strenuously for the project. Gillette hadn't even heard the work; he made a case based on Kenton's assurances and the producer's faith in Stan's progressive instincts.

"The night that we completed the album," Gillette told Carol Easton, "I took the dubs home.... I had a record building off from the house. I went out there about one o'clock in the morning and played this whole album, and when I got through and opened the door, I was afraid to walk to the house."

Compared to Kenton's previous releases, sales of *City of Glass* were dismal. Strangely, the LP liner notes contained a comment at odds with Pepper's recollection. After the Chicago performance, the notes conceded, "The applause was sparse and the criticism that followed was severe." The notes further reflected that both Graettinger and Kenton were "sorely disappointed."

This Modern World was Graettinger's sequel. Though nominally consisting of six pieces, it was probably not conceived as a suite insofar as the instrumentation varies radically from section to section. It was never performed in concert and was recorded sporadically over a year and a half. With the possible exception of "A Cello," the various pieces exhibit no more warmth than Graettinger's previous works. John Litweiler, tracing post-bop history in *The Freedom Principle: Jazz After 1958*, remarks that *This Modern World* is "a cold world, cruel in the distant, pure beauty of its saxophone section, the weight of its low brass, and the nerve-racking high extremes of its trumpet passages." Litweiler, who clearly admires Graettinger, sees him as something of an aesthetic hooligan who slowly pulls wings off butterflies, observing that "the threat conveyed by Graettinger's beauty is no less dangerous for its distance and indifference, because it is a threat to our very sanity." Kenton's recording of the "suite" achieved scant critical attention. Nat Hentoff in *Down Beat* was largely unimpressed, labeling Graettinger a "melodramatic Wagnerian."

Although he continued writing, Graettinger left his patron's employ around 1952, when the Innovations Orchestra was disbanded for financial reasons. His solitary ways persisted and deepened. Carol Easton wrote that Kenton would occasionally take the wasted scarecrow for a meal. "Bob would get juiced," recalled Kenton, "and he'd say, 'What time is it?' I'd say, 'It's three A.M.' He'd say, 'Do we have time to go down and look at the ocean?' I'd drive him down to Santa Monica, and he'd sit there and look at the ocean for a while. And then I'd take him home." The hollow log of a man was obsessed with completing his *Suite for String Trio and Wind Quartet*.

Graettinger's music has infiltrated the culture, however indirectly, over the past half-century. His chaotic tints have colored the scores of subsequent composers and arrangers, and if his groundbreaking works now sound slightly less daunting, it's because 50 years of musical iconoclasm have prepped modern ears for his dysmorphic surrealism. Composer/conductor Gunther Schuller declared Graettinger "a complete original." Gert-Jan Blom, leader of Holland's Beau Hunks Orchestra, observed, "Graettinger's music is something of a 'sound-barrier'—you have to break through at high velocity. But once you've done that, you're in a completely new sonic landscape, governed by strange laws and aesthetics. It requires some adjusting for old-fashioned auricles but, boy!—is it rewarding. In this respect Graettinger's musical universe is not unlike that of Harry Partch."

Werner Herbers, leader of Amsterdam's Ebony Band, has conducted Graettinger's compositions and arrangements in concert and recorded two albums' worth. "Since I heard these records back in the 1950s," Herbers acknowledged, "and from the moment I became a professional musician with my own group, I dreamt of hearing Graettinger's music live. He wasn't always successful in presenting his thoughts; in some parts of his work there is a shapelessness, some wandering off into 'unresolved streets.' But for the most part, his music is striking, convincing, and touched by genius."

Graettinger once told a friend, "I live above the timberline, where nothing grows." The air up there must've been as thin as the composer's underfed frame. Graettinger died of lung cancer on March 12, 1957, at Hollywood Presbyterian Hospital. He was 34. The only musicians who attended his funeral were Kenton and Rugolo. Neither *Down Beat* nor *Metronome* ran obits. His string and wind septet was never completed.

By that time, Kenton's days of radical experimentation were over, and he fit more squarely than ever into the jazz mainstream.

• 19 •

B. J. Snowden

MISSION TO VENUS

"Can you autograph this?," asks Fred Schneider of the B-52s. He's talking to an out-of-work, single mom who recorded an album that sold about 100 copies. Schneider's request isn't a joke, and he's not canvasing for votes in a run-off election.

He passes B. J. Snowden a notepad on which are scrawled her handwritten lyrics. "It should be the other way around," she replies modestly. "You're the one on Warner Bros. Records." Schneider grins and stands patiently before the singer-pianist, in the midst of a session at Spa Studios on New York's West 21st Street. A festive vibe prevails. Snowden is recording two Christmas songs, produced by Schneider. Her 15-year-old guitarist son, Andrés, smiles admiringly. B. J.'s silver-haired mother, Virginia, sits in the next chair, waiting to hear the playback of B. J.'s new song, "He's the Santa I Love."

Snowden, in her mid-40s, is optimistic despite her current unemployment. In mid-1998, she was laid off from her music teaching job in Boston. "Every year they called me back. But this year, they didn't," she lamented. "I called about any openings, but the lady said, 'We're not gonna hire you this year, because the principal didn't want to recommend you.' I called the principal, and she said, 'Everybody's proven themselves except you.' So I got laid off."

She wasn't qualified to teach little children about music, but here she is in New York City being produced by Fred Schneider and surrounded by adoring fans.

For a person as sweet and provincial as Snowden, there seems to be some controversy about her talents.

"I think she's a great songwriter who can't sing at all or play the piano," said a fellow known as Ratboy, a clerk at New York's Venus Records shop, where B. J.'s demo tape was first discovered. "Yet the songs are so catchy that once you've heard them, you end up singing them to yourself all day."

During the 1980s, Snowden saved up money and in 1989 taped a demo of original material in a Cambridge recording facility. "I began sending cassettes to music studios, record companies, and different college stations," she recalls between remixes at Spa. "I had a list. Nashville, New York, Los Angeles. I sent out at least a hundred tapes." She got two or three responses—all form letters.

"Then I saw Venus listed as a record store, so I sent them a tape."

To an ultra-hip music outlet on St. Mark's Place this unassuming naïf sent a tape. This was around 1992.

The demo consisted of 10 songs sung by B. J., who accompanied herself on a keyboard synth equipped with a beatbox. Her coordination of these elements—singing, playing, rhythm—is unique, which is to say, the stars aren't always in alignment. The tunes lurch and hobble along in time signatures that can only be calculated in extended decimal percentages. Her phrasing is a bit wobbly, her tone control ragged, her syllabification inexact. As for her keys, Snowden's pleasant, primitive piano suggests Keith Jarrett with finger splints. Her original compositions are delivered in a trenchant, sometimes quavering voice devoid of pretense, marked by occasional garbled enunciation.

The songs also exude the outsider *sine qua non* of earnestness: there's "Ode to Lesley," a lament for a dead cousin; , "U.S. Navy Song," an anthem to

B. J. Snowden at The Cooler, NYC, May 1999

our seabound men in uniform; "In Canada," a roll-call of the Maple Leaf dominion's scenic wonders; and "98," a jaunty tribute to a classic Oldsmobile.

At Venus, Snowden's crude-looking, unheard demo was relegated to an Everest of unsolicited "mystery" cassettes that would be plastic-bagged and sold five-for-a-buck. One day, the curious Ratboy noted the ingenuous, disarming black-and-white cover photo of B. J. and said, "We *gotta* listen to this."

Bob Giordano, a fellow sales clerk, recalled, "Ratboy put it on and everybody was mesmerized. People in the store would stop and say, 'What the hell is that?' They'd never heard anything like it." Venus patrons are among the planet's most ennuyé; they've heard, read, seen it all. How did B. J.'s tape manage to stand out? "It's very genuine," Giordano insisted. "That's what comes across. That's what's so affecting about it."

Fred Schneider was a Venus regular. He was browsing the bins one day when Ratboy popped B. J.'s tape in the store deck. It was love at first listen for the rock icon, who's drawn to outré sonics. Convinced of the tape's peculiar appeal, Venus contacted Snowden—in 1995, three years after she'd sent the tape—and offered to release her songs on CD. With a few additional tracks, *Life in the USA and Canada* came out in 1996 on the shop's in-house DeMilo label.

Snowden couldn't believe it was happening, and Venus played off her excitement. Schneider penned a back cover blurb, calling B. J. a " '90s Renaissance woman. Composes, plays, arranges, and sings the h— [sic] out of a tune." He continued: "I played 'In Canada' for friends in Toronto and they were blown away—this song cements good relations between our two countries forever." One thousand copies were pressed.

It's ironic that an off-axis talent like Snowden would be championed by one of the planet's grittiest record stores, based in the heart of Manhattan's freak ward. Consider the infestation of Lower East Side wannabe bands who've clawed for label deals over the years, and the lengths to which they'd go to attract attention—piercing, tricolor hair, weird gimmicks, convention torched by perversion and blasphemy. And here's B. J.—a stocky, awkward, hopelessly unfashionable but *sincere* proto-nerd from the outback of Billerica, Massachusetts, getting the red carpet.

"I know a band who've been signed and dropped by two major labels," said Giordano. "They wanted so bad to be rock stars immediately, to live the high life. Then there's people like B. J. who don't crave the limelight. They play out of genuine love of music. You can't fake sincerity. She's very joyful and she's not spoiled. It's inspiring to be involved with someone who gets such a thrill from making music. Hopefully in a few years she'll still feel that way. She's sweet, and I value that." When David Grad reviewed *Life in the USA and Canada* in *New York Press*, he noted that B. J. "achieves the lo-fi innocence all the indie kids so crave—but she'd have no idea what you were talking about if you said that to her."

To celebrate the CD release, Snowden was invited to Gotham to serenade jaded art-scum at such caverns of slothcore as Brownies, on Avenue A, and the Cooler, in the notorious West Side meat-packing district. Ever eager to please, Snowden arrived with her usual entourage: son Andrés and beaming mom (who does all the long-distance driving).

Many unsuspecting club-goers, arriving early to see flavor-of-the-week guitar bands, were stunned by Snowden's incongruous presence. With her matronly corpulence, and sporting a coif that was in style 15 years ago—if ever—B. J.'s endearing smile and Jehovah's Witness–strength sweetness contrasted starkly with the sneers and beyond-it-all insolence indigenous to the 'hood. At the drop of a compliment—she heard many in the city—her eyes lit up like a $100 lottery winner.

The guileless B. J. is a roving ambassador of musical goodwill. Like those of her New England compatriots, the Shaggs, B. J.'s songs brim with post-adolescent wonder. Her music radiates a warmth that can keep you snug to minus-20 degrees Fahrenheit, and a magic that undercuts any concept of cool. "New York audiences didn't know what to expect," said Schneider, who introduced Snowden's first gig. "But soon enough, they were clapping and cheering for her."

At her Brownies debut, Snowden used a new Korg synth, though she wasn't fully familiar with its control panel. She spent two or three minutes between songs programming rhythms, chattering nervously to sustain audience attention ("Please bear with me—maybe in another year I'll have it together") as she intently studied a settings diagram, twirled knobs, and flipped switches. The apologies were unnecessary; New York had never offered a more forgiving, doting audience, who waited patiently, slightly amused—even after the fifth and sixth delay—'til Snowden announced she was ready to proceed with the set. They requested "In Canada," and many sang along. She thanked the audience for anything and everything—for clapping, for behaving, for coming to the show, for the encouragement. She overflowed with gratitude, often to the point of speechlessness. Then she muttered to herself, leaned over the keyboard, squinted through her glasses and started flipping switches to find the next song's programmed beat.

While B. J. was in New York, Venus landed her two spots on MTV's now-defunct *Oddville*, where she performed "In Canada" and a non-CD song called "School Teacher," which she dramatized with blackboard and chalk.

Before her newfound celebrity, Snowden had only been to New York to visit cousins. "I thought it was a cold city," she admitted. "People in general were very unfriendly. They wouldn't even give us directions." How surprising,

B.J. Snowden

Life in the USA and Canada

DeMilo
Records

To Cedric

B J Snowden

Thank you

for everything!

then, that her tape would be warmly embraced by a bleeding-edge record store in the East Village. "The people from Venus were dynamite," she exulted. "Even though they're from New York, they're very nice."

When she arrived for her first club date, did she fear that urban sophisticates would laugh and consider her a rustic relic? "I was nervous," she confessed. "I was thinking, 'Wow! I'm playing New York!' That's one of the big wishes of people in Massachusetts, to play New York. Bingo! I did it!" Now Fred Schneider, a world-renowned musician from a Grammy-acclaimed band, is pestering her for an autograph.

When Schneider first heard Snowden's tape, he liked "that someone was writing and performing their own compositions totally outside the mainstream, and with a sense of humor." He's long been a connoisseur of musical underdogs and weirdness in general. "I'll buy records just for the cover in the hope that the music will be just as wild," he said. "B. J.'s not your typical rock 'n' roll or pop. She's joyous, and the audience just gets pulled in."

The famed vocalist's admiration took Snowden by surprise. "When I first visited Venus," she said, "They promised me that when the CD was pressed, it would be endorsed by Fred Schneider. I said, 'Who's Fred Schneider?' I'd heard 'Love Shack' on the radio, but I never knew who the group was. Later, when I found out Fred was in that band, I felt kinda stupid." (She's still never heard "Rock Lobster.") But it was inspiring that someone famous cared; it symbolized an achievement. Schneider has lavished tons of support on Snowden; at the Christmas session, he told me he thinks "Brian Wilson should do a duet with her."

Her full name is Bertha Jeanne Snowden, and you can find her in the *World Who's Who in American Women* (she answered a mail solicitation and paid the requisite fee). In her hometown of Billerica, Massachusetts, she shares a spacious house with her mom, son, and brother Donald. "My family's been in town for five generations," she boasted. "My grandmother was the first African American to graduate from Billerica High School in 1915. My mom worked in a factory, doing wiring and soldering." Her dad hailed from nearby Malden.

Though B. J.'s parents weren't musicians, her grandmother played piano. Bertha Jeanne started fingering the ivories at age three but didn't take her first lesson until age twelve. Growing up, she absorbed classical music, along with Motown, Elvis, Ellington, and country. Sensing a budding star, her father paid B. J.'s way through a four-year program at Boston's Berklee College of Music, where she obtained a degree in 1973.

That same year she married Alan Lee Wilson, with whom she had Andrés, born in 1983. Sadly, Alan and B. J. were divorced in 1992. Her song "From the Chapel (to the Courtroom)" chronicles the disillusionment. "Now," she explained, "I go by my maiden name, 'Snowden,' because my parents worked hard to have me." "U.S. Navy Song" was also about Alan, who served in that branch of the armed forces. "I wrote that when I was in love with my ex," she revealed. "Now I can't stand him, so I don't play it anymore."

When her father passed away in January 1998, she composed a song, "Love, Love, Love, the Angel of Love," about him.

These days the main man in her life is Andrés, who travels with B. J. to gigs and accompanies her on electric guitar for several numbers each set. Andrés, who's fond of playing *loud*, admits to an Eddie Van Halen fixation. "I like it when he plays good music," his mom declared. "But I don't like it when he plays heavy metal. He can play the blues loud anytime."

B. J. knows the importance of passing along musical appreciation to the next generation, which is one reason she enjoyed teaching. It hurt when her appointment wasn't renewed. Didn't it mean anything to the school administration that this instructor had a record released by New York tastemakers with genuine street-cred, that her disc had been endorsed by that avatar of cool, Fred Schneider?

"The music supervisor was turned on about it," she said, "and he's trying to get me back in the system. But for now I'm just collecting unemployment." She's using her free time to write new songs, and betrays ambivalence about returning to the classroom. "In the educational system is too much bureaucracy," she asserted. "There's these principals who think they're so great, and they don't really give a darn about the kids, but they pretend they do. When I'm tryin' to teach the kids different things, they come in and criticize. But I know I'm doing right. Because I know my music and they don't know anything about music."

Bob Giordano sighed, "I wish I had a music teacher like her when I was in school."

Her original pre-CD tape gave thanks to, among other people, the Postal Workers of Billerica. Coworkers? Neighbors? Fan club? "No," explained Snowden. "It was a mistake. They said they were going to buy a tape from me if I thanked them on it. So I did. Later when I went in and told them that my tape was out, you know what they said? 'No soliciting.' Now I wish I hadn't thanked them." It's enough to make an entertainer go ... *postal?*

The sensitive side of B. J. comes across in "Ode to Lesley," about a close cousin driving home from work late one night who was killed in a head-on collision with a drunken motorist. "We were good friends," sighed B. J. "I'd just seen her at a wedding, and we were going to get together. But she got killed. She left two children."

ODE TO LESLEY
You were born when I was five
I'll tell you that's no jive
We loved you and it was true
You were such a friend
Friend, friend, you were such a friend
Life has come to an end, you were such a friend

You were the only girl, and it's the same with me
Being the baby of the family, to me it's plain to see
Friend, friend, you were such a friend
Life has come to an end, you were such a friend

Life is not predicted
Nobody knows what life has in store for us
Until it shows
Cousin of mine, you are
And time must move on
Never procastinate [sic]
No one, no one knows their fate
Friend, friend, you were such a friend
Life has come to an end, you were such a friend

On a happier note, a number of years ago Snowden vacationed through Canada with her son and mom (who, again, did most of the driving). Some Americans choose to view our neighbor to the north the way New York sees New Jersey: a tacky, inferior wasteland. Snowden attempted to build a bridge between the two nations. Her immortal anthem, "In Canada," pays tribute to each of that country's provinces and the dominion's natural beauty:

IN CANADA
The cities very clean you see
Their people welcome you and me
It is a home away from home
It's Canada, in Canada

[chorus]
In Canada
Folks treat you like a queen
In Canada, they never will be mean
In Canada, they treat you like a king
You'll feel welcome
It makes you wanta sing

Newfoundland, Nova Scotia is always green
The scenery is like a dream
And PEI waters are blue and clear
In Canada, it's really near

[chorus]

New Brunswick and BC coastal shores
Manitoba and Ontario Lakes are wide
The rivers do flow from side to side
In Saskatchewan, in Canada

[chorus]

You'll see West Edmonton Mall
Where fun parks and stores stand tall
You'll see the ice rink glow
To the Water Parks kids can go

In Canada, la-la-dah-dah-dah-dah
In Canada, la-dee-dee-dee-dee-dee
In Canada, whoa-ho-ho-ho
Canada, Canada

There's a music video of "In Canada," featuring images of mounties, hockey rinks, pancakes smothered in maple syrup, caribou, and beer—all the things that make the place great. Except maybe the athletes. "I don't like hockey players," B. J. confessed. "They're crazy. They take their sticks and start bashing each other with 'em."

Snowden appeared on a Boston cable TV show, which broadcast the "In Canada" video. Asked by the host to sum up the music business in one word, Snowden furrowed her brow with ponderous intent, leaned into the microphone, and declared: "Humanistic." Afterward, she claimed, the station lost the original copy of the video (she doesn't blame the program host). When she tried to retrieve it, "They claimed they had those videos down in the basement and there was a flood and it ruined the tape," she recounted. "They lied about it."

As typically befits someone orbiting on the musical outside, B. J. is largely unconcerned about what amounts to a journalistic distinction. Do people say she can't sing, her cadences are out of sync, her songs amateurish, her playing clumsy? "I don't really get that," she mused. "But some people don't think I can sing. They think my music and words and playing is good, but my singing's not that good."

Would she like to sell a million records?

"Of course," she laughs. "I'd love it."

B. J. received some performance royalties from radio airplay, but not enough to quit her day job—if she had a day job to quit.

What do fellow Berklee alumni think of her achievements—having a record released by the hippest record store in Manhattan and having it endorsed by the coolest guy in the B-52s? "They send me a form letter each year asking what I'm doing," she said, "and I always write back and tell 'em something."

But they haven't invited her to speak at commencement?

"They only do that for real famous people," she sighed. "I'm not there yet."

Wild Man Fischer in his "studio"

• 20 •

Wild Man
Fischer

RITUAL OF THE SAVAGE

rhino Records became a megamillion-dollar enterprise during the 1990s by indulging the Boomer reissue market. Psychedelic nuggets, discomania, and kiddie TV theme packages rolled off the label's assembly line in a capitalist twist on the feel-good trend of recycling.

Oddly, Rhino's first release was a shoestring 7-inch single by a jobless, homeless, certified-psychotic street singer named Larry "Wild Man" Fischer. Wild Man's 45 rpm spinner, "Go to Rhino Records," was pressed in 1975 to hype a store, not a label. There was no label until this novelty disc was shipped from the pressing plant.

Less than a decade later, after Rhino (the label) had released three full albums by Fischer, Rhino (the store) had to eject him from the premises for bullying patrons to buy his records.

Fischer epitomized the Mental-Illness-Can-Be-Fun school of songcraft. As a clinical case, he wins the Triple Crown: manic-depressive, paranoid, schizophrenic. Larry also likes to throw things—sometimes verbally, occasionally overhand. He has a publicly unrestrained potty mouth and is prone to sporadic fits of violence.

He's a pioneer, too: Allegedly, back in the late 1960s Fischer was one of the first virtuosos of the Air Guitar. And at a 1971 National Guard Armory gig in Kalispell, Montana, after offended staff powered down Larry's amplification system, he continued his performance—foreshadowing the *Unplugged* trend by 20 years.

In his checkered career, this lithium-fugitive has hung out with Tom Waits, Linda Ronstadt, Janis Joplin, and Jim Morrison, and he's recorded with Devo's Mark Mothersbaugh and pop icon Rosemary Clooney.

Fischer was discovered by Mothers of Invention mastermind Frank Zappa, who found the demented drifter howling his ragged serenades along L.A.'s Sunset Strip during the height of hippiedom. In 1968, the same year the Mother Superior released *Trout Mask Replica*, a double-album of Martian blues alchemy by Captain Beefheart (see chapter), Zappa unveiled the two-disc *An Evening with Wild Man Fischer*.

Zappa often echoed defiantly a charge about the Mothers made by a Columbia Records exec, that the group had "no commercial potential." With Wild Man Fischer he seemed determined to produce an album with *negative* sales appeal. Fischer was an obvious, albeit likeable, nutjob. He couldn't carry a tune in a dumptruck—not that he would've been permitted to operate heavy machinery.

The gatefold album's 36 titles are a developmentally arrested cycle of fun-loving lunacy and deranged autobiography. The back cover proclaimed: "Wild Man Fischer is a real person who lives in Hollywood, California. He used to be very shy. He didn't have any friends. One day he decided to be more aggressive. He would write his own songs and sing to people and tell them he wasn't shy anymore. When he did this, everyone thought he was crazy. His mother had him committed to a mental institution twice."

True. But it wasn't just *singing* that landed Wild Man in the psycho-pen.

Lawrence Wayne Fischer was born in Los Angeles on November 6, 1945. Facts about his pre-Zappa days are sketchy. His father passed away in Larry's youth. As a teen, he apparently assaulted his mother, Pearl, one or more times, earning two institutional stays. His psychological disorders were organic and possibly drug-aggravated, though no one seems to know for sure. Statements by Fischer on the matter are contradictory and unreliable.

"My mother used to scream at me all the time," Fischer told artist J. R. Williams in a 1997 telephone interview. "She'd say I was never gonna do anything, so I started writing songs. The more she'd yell, the more I'd write all these songs. And I'd sing all over the place, every day. I wouldn't stop. I got thrown out of high school for it, I got thrown in the mental hospital for it. I just sang constantly. And I got attention. I figured I could be a rock star and impress my family. I'd be as big as the Beatles, or Dylan. People said I looked a little like Dylan."

Fischer claims to have gotten his nickname from R&B singer Solomon Burke. "He discovered me in a closet [sic] and he said, 'Knock 'em at the park [sic], wild man.' And I kept the name," Fischer explained to Williams. "He took me on tour for two shows before I even made records. But that didn't last. He said, 'You certainly talk a lot for a white guy.' [laughs] He said, 'I never knew they made white people like you—with so much soul!' He actually thought I had a lot of soul."

By 1967, Larry was a familiar character on the bacchanalian Sunset Strip freak circus. For Fischer, adopting hippie ways was the natural path of least resistance since it entailed not working, not paying rent, panhandling, and abnegation of personal responsibility. Curious passersby who flipped Larry spare coin were regaled with a song du jour. (One customer, a young British bluesman named Eric Clapton, was so impressed by Fischer's antics that when he attended the Grammys in L.A. decades later, the guitarist reportedly inquired of a Warner Bros. exec about Wild Man's whereabouts.)

In 1968, Zappa launched his twin WB-distributed labels, Straight and Bizarre. On the former, he released Beefheart, Tim Buckley, and Alice Cooper, among others. The Bizarre catalog featured his own solo albums, as well as LPs by the Mothers and Fischer.

The critical perspective on *An Evening with Wild Man Fischer* reflected the split typically rendered about certain outsiders. Some considered Wild Man's uninhibited, id-driven crooning a refreshing alternative to overhyped, commercial drivel and gushed over his sincerity and lack of pretense. Others felt Zappa was exposing a guileless and vulnerable mental patient to merciless public ridicule.

Zappa wrote the following proviso on the record jacket: "Please listen to this album several times before you decide whether or not you like it or what Wild Man Fischer is all about. He has something to say to you, even though you might not want to hear it." The front cover depicts a dashiki-clad Larry grinning idiotically, holding a steak knife near the throat of a life-size cardboard cutout of an elderly woman. A placard around her neck reads: "Larry's Mother."

The double LP, a documentary of one man's chronic madness and its artistic manifestations, is divided into four side-long perspectives:

1) "The Basic Fischer," consisting of a cappella songs and dialogue fragments captured on the street in front of the Strip's Whiskey-A-Go-Go and Hamburger Hamlet (Fischer: "Hey, would you like to hear an original song for a dime?" Passerby: "No thank you."), underscored with studio improv percussion by the Mothers' Art Tripp; and a cannabis-logic dialogue between arrested adolescent Kim Fowley and KROQ jock Rodney Bingenheimer offering prophecies about Fischer's future.

2) "Larry's Songs, Unaccompanied," consisting of off-key, berserker nursery rhymes howled in a disturbed, semi-hysteric style. On titles such as "I'm Working for the Federal Bureau of Narcotics" and "Monkeys Versus Donkeys," Fischer veers from crackpot crooning to hyperactive yammering as

he bellows his way through over a dozen lost-in-space song shards. In his own self-unaware way, Fischer cranks out more than a few catchy melodies and some revealing lyrics: "Think of me when your clothes are off / think of me when your clothes are off / think of me when your clothes are off / 'cause I'll be thinking of you."

"Some of his songs, rudimentary as they are, to my ears sound as good as most of the stuff being played on the radio in those days—or, for that matter, *these* days," said music journalist and Zappaphile Peter Keepnews. "They sound goofy because his voice is so bad and he's singing a cappella, making 'doot-doot' noises where instruments should be, and also because his sense of time is inconsistent. But if someone had taken the time to arrange the tunes for a band and try to make professional-caliber recordings—as Zappa in fact did for 'Circle' and 'The Taster,' which sound great—the songs and the singer wouldn't have seemed so far from the mainstream. As far as I'm concerned, 'Merry-Go-Round' is a great song by any standard." (Larry performed this last number on *Laugh-In*, and his recording of the tune was used in the 1969 film *Medium Cool*.)

3) "Some Historical Notes," including "The Taster," which features Larry backed by the *We're Only in It for the Money*–era Mothers, along with more underdeveloped song scraps, autobiographical logorrhea, and meshugginah philosophical observations buffered by compulsive giggling.

4) "In Conclusion," featuring the most poignant material on the record, "The Wild Man Fischer Story." The tape rolls as Larry sings and dramatizes, year by year, his adolescent travails ("In the year of 1965, I was committed to the mental institution again"), punctuated with impersonations of his parents, school principal, and taunting coworkers.

Side four's final track, "Larry Under Pressure," is as nakedly confessional as it gets. In response to Zappa's query, "Don't you like to make records?," Fischer replies: "Yes, but I've been under strain lately, unexplainable strain.... Despite how happy I was in '61 and '62, I was committed to back-to-back mental institutions. I was raised with the fact that I was crazy, I was raised with the fact that I had to sleep with old men who pissed and shit in [sic] the floor, and I was raised that you're crazy, you'll always be crazy, and I never dug that. I can't be happy anymore when I sing, that's the main reason. The fuckin' bastards—they're all fuckin' bastards, Frank."

Dick Kunc, who engineered a number of seminal Mothers/Zappa-related albums, worked on *An Evening With*. In an interview with Bill Lantz, Kunc recalled, "That was a trip. My first task was to literally follow [Fischer] around the streets for several days, carrying a Uher two-track [tape deck], chronicling whatever madness he got into. Parts of that mission were plain scary! Larry was truly certifiable then. The basement sessions were very strange, as you might guess. Frank was gentle, encouraging, yet demanding of Larry—as Frank was with all who toiled under his baton. Later, with the roving and basement stuff in hand, Frank and Larry and I went into the studio and hammered together that album."

By the estimates of one WB exec, *An Evening With* miraculously sold around 12,000 copies—platinum by outsider standards. The album served as a long-term calling card for Fischer, endearing him to subsequent generations of outré music enthusiasts. Wild Man's singing also was a big influence on the song stylings of *Sesame Street*'s Oscar the Grouch. Skeptical? Listen to "I Love Trash" on the mangy Muppet's album *Let a Frown Be Your Umbrella*. The similarities are spooky.

Larry performed live with the Mothers a few times, but eventually Fischer and Zappa became estranged, and Wild Man retreated into the local freak scenery. He resurfaced with an occasional TV or L.A. club appearance, his cognitive disconnect seemingly intensified. Busking for handouts remained a vocation. The singer with the Silly Putty cortex also added greatly to his legacy of outlandish behavior. Just ask Dennis Eichhorn.

Eichhorn was a young counterculturalist living in Spokane, Washington, in 1971, when he booked Wild Man for a local concert. The ensuing escapades, covering several years, were recounted in *Real Stuff*, a comic periodical (Fantagraphics Books) written by Eichhorn in collaboration with numerous artists. (J. R. Williams illustrated the Wild Man saga.)

Eichhorn described picking up Fischer at the airport and driving him to a fast-food eatery, North's Chuck Wagon. There, the deluded singer *loudly* invited a waitress to "suck my dick" backstage after the upcoming show. Following the concert, which was a financial and—all things considered—an "artistic" success, Fischer camped in Eichhorn's living room for several weeks. His routine was to stay up all night counting his money and improvising new songs. During the day, he'd throw abrupt temper tantrums, re-count his money, and pig out in the fridge.

One afternoon, Fischer wandered into town for lunch. After a typical junk food chowdown, he was denied use of the snack bar's rest room.

Urgency mounting, he canvased the neighborhood ringing doorbells, hoping "one of his many fans" would let him use their toilet. A local resident named Dave—not a fan but someone who recognized Fischer from a concert poster—charitably acceded to the request. Eventually Dave grew suspicious when Fischer remained upstairs for three-quarters of an hour. Ascending to the second floor to check on his visitor, Dave found Wild Man unloading a steaming heap in a clothes closet. The host was shocked—but turned entrepreneurial. Realizing a "celebrity" had squatted and dumped in his home, Dave sprayed the pile with polyurethane and charged friends admission to view the shrine.

Another incident depicted in *Real Stuff* involved Fischer barging into the bathroom while Eichhorn's wife, who had just gotten her period, was inserting a tampon. She barked at the intruder, "What the hell do you want?" Fischer replied, "This!"—as he wrenched the tampon from the stunned woman's vagina and ran out into the street, laughing uproariously and twirling the bloody cotton mess.

"All the stories in my comics are absolutely true," Eichhorn told me. "The tampon, the shitting in the closet—I could show you the house in Spokane—all of it." Besides being a chronicler of Fischer's offstage capers, Eichhorn was a genuine fan of his onstage antics. "I saw him perform in Moscow, Idaho," he recalled, "and it was the funniest performance I've ever seen. I was in stitches, laughing uncontrollably. Fischer's manic energy really emerged, and the result was pure comedy. I wish I had it on video."

Staffers at the Rhino shop were fans of the original Zappa-produced album. They also knew Larry, who continued circulating his dime-a-song sideshow in L.A.'s hipper precincts. In 1975, Harold Bronson, the store's then-manager (and the label's managing director since its inception), got the idea to employ Fischer as a singing sandwich board for the business. The result was the now-legendary 45, which launched a cottage enterprise that eventually revolutionized the reissue industry.

The early days of Rhino (the label) are littered with odd 7-inch discs: rockabilly parodies, power pop, one-off Dr. Demento–type novelties. "To think of us then as a label—even to look back on it now—is somewhat humorous to me," recalled Gary Stewart, Senior VP of A&R and a former clerk and manager for the store. "We just put out some records by friends. We did Wild Man's single for fun, and eventually we started selling it."

Bronson decided to produce an album, *Wildmania*, in 1977. Fischer's Rhino long-play debut bears the prestigious catalogue number "RNLP-001." More song-structured than the Zappa project, *Wildmania* is a charming collection of semi-controlled lunacy, with most tracks sung a cappella, and a few employing rock band accompaniment. The album sounds spontaneous, though not improvised; these melodies had obviously been pinballing through Fischer's miswired synapses for a while.

His other albums for Rhino were *Pronounced Normal* (1981) and *Nothing Scary* (1984), both produced by Dr. Demento mainstays Barnes and Barnes.

The *Nothing Scary* tracks were recorded in a studio, at parks, in tunnels, and over the phone. Many are drenched in period synths, others are just bare vocals. The overall variety of the arrangements and imaginative backings make it Fischer's strongest outing—a pure pop record, though posing no chart threat to Wham!. (Gerry Beckley and Dewey Bunnell of the group America composed two songs for the album.) Snatches of unfettered candor in tunes like "Oh God, Please Send Me a Kid" ("Oh God, is there a female in this world who will have my baby?") and "Outside the Hospital" ("Inside the hospital / people eat lousy food / there is such a somber mood"), delivered in Fischer's childish caterwauling, foreshadowed such oracles of EEG overload as Wesley Willis and Daniel Johnston.

"When recording *Pronounced Normal* and *Nothing Scary*," recalled actor Bill Mumy (who coproduced as Art Barnes), "Larry would tell my partner [Robert Haimer, also known as Artie Barnes] and I where and when to pick him up. Many, many times, we'd drive to the location and wait ... and wait ... and wait. No Larry. If we knew where he was staying, usually at inexpensive weekly hotels, we'd go look for him in his room. He was often asleep."

But Mumy was patient and saw the projects through because he genuinely likes Fischer and recognizes his talent. "When Larry's inspired," said the producer, "when he has what he calls the 'triple pep,' there isn't a more dynamic or soulful performer in the world!"

Tom Brown, Rhino's longtime customer service manager, had his share of Wild Man sightings. "He'd come in from time to time and cause a scene, demanding his royalties," Brown recollected. "I saw him once almost threaten bodily harm to Gary Stewart. He *demanded* to speak to Harold. Scared the shit out of the receptionist. She was trembling. Harold finally came out to calm him down. The last time I saw Larry was in the warehouse at our old location on Colorado in Santa Monica. I could smell him—he looked *really* dirty. He was taking a bunch of LPs off the shelves, and he said, 'I'm takin' these albums. Richard [Foos, Rhino founder] said I could have some albums.' I offered to help load them in his trunk, no problem, just to get away from him as quickly as possible. It's tragic. He's genuinely insane."

Looking back, Stewart has regrets. "Frankly, I feel a little bad about the whole thing," he admitted. "Larry's life has been tough. There's extreme mental illness there. He was paranoid. He would go around saying, 'This album could be the next *Sgt. Pepper's*.' If he saw you in public, he would follow you around. At the time, we thought all this was hysterical. When you're immersed in alternative, post-glitter, underground punk culture, there's humor about certain things that aren't actually funny. His song, 'I'm the Meany' [from *Wild-mania*] has a line about, 'She told me she was pregnant, so I hit her in the stomach.' During a period of nihilism, smart-assedness, and less morality, I used to think that was hilarious. But when you realize stuff like that really happens, it's not funny anymore."

Bronson recalled the time Fischer was ejected from the store. "Every once in a while Larry would come in and as usual overstay his welcome. It would be cute for 20 or 30 minutes, but three or four hours later it was past obnoxious. Once we asked him to leave—after he'd been there maybe eight hours or so."

Fischer resents his Rhino experience as only a bug-eyed delusional can. He ranted to interviewer Jay Allen Sandford: "They never promoted me! Even though I was their biggest star, back before they started just re-releasing old albums by has-beens!... Rhino would screw it up every time. They hate me, you know. If it wasn't for them, I'd be the biggest thing right now. Bigger than punk, Weird Al. Do you think he's funny?" The question was rhetorical, as Larry denounced the goofy satirist: "He stole my act. Guys like [Weird Al] have a lot of nerve, ripping off old pros like me. I could've had him messed up, if I was that type of person. Which I'm not. I'm an artist, you know?"

Fischer was just getting started, as he spewed invective about his original patron. Zappa, he fumed to Sandford, "hates me. He's jealous, 'cause I got so famous so fast after he did my album. I mean, we used to hang out, whistle at girls, do all the clubs and stuff. One day, I was over his house. And he said something rude, I forget, like: 'Why don't you put your money in the bank?' He was bugging me because I wasn't, like, as rich as he was and living in a big old house. So I got pissed, you know? I threw a jar or something at him [one report says a wooden toy, thrown at Frank's toddler son Dweezil]. And it missed him, but he was still all yelling at me and everything. His wife or daughter came in, and he said I almost hit them, and then he kicked me out. Frank's a mother, that's all."

But Fischer's recording days weren't quite over. Around 1986 he taped a duet with Rosemary Clooney. "It's a Hard Business," written and produced by Barnes and Barnes, is a synth-rocker about the tribulations of trying to succeed in the music industry. According to Mumy, when Clooney heard "Oh God, Please Send Me a Kid," she was so touched that she contacted Larry and began a telephone friendship. The session was her idea, resulting in one of history's more incongruous pairings. Strangely, Rosie and Wild Man exhibit a magical rapport. For years, bootleg tapes of this track circulated thanks to sporadic airings on Dr. Demento's syndicated radio program.

Fischer's albums were largely unavailable despite appeals by his fans to record companies. Rhino rolled out a limited edition two-CD set entitled *The*

Fischer King in 1999 to inaugurate its Web-only imprint Rhino Handmade. The package contained 100 tracks (15 previously unreleased, including "It's a Hard Business") and a 20-page booklet. Fischer's original albums remain consigned to the high-priced collector's market.

Now an industry outcast, Wild Man reflected on his glory days. "David Byrne talked about me in a magazine once," he exclaimed to J. R. Williams, "about me and Captain Beefheart being influences on him. He named my album and *Trout Mask Replica*—that these were great records. All I can tell you is David Byrne made it a lot bigger than me."

Wild Man spotter Mark McFadden posted a number of vignettes to Brian Belovarac's Fischer Web site. "Larry had friends all over Hollywood and environs, usually within walking distance of the Boulevard itself," wrote McFadden. "People would look out for Larry, making sure that he ate, lending him a couch to sleep on for as long as they could stand to have him around. That sounds cruel, but Larry was very hard to be around. He was manic, monomaniacal on the subject of music, and prone to breaking and throwing things when frustrated.... [One time] Larry got mad at his alarm clock and threw it out the window. That was so much fun that he threw everything else he owned out the window. This sort of behavior is what got him blacklisted at most every hotel in Hollywood.... Let me hasten to point out that Larry's circle of friends was large, and no matter how annoyed they got with him, after a cooling off period he was inevitably invited back in."

Occasionally someone expresses reservations about whether Larry's music-biz handlers fed delusions of stardom that were unsustainable, considering his far-gone mental state. "It was hard to escape the feeling that everyone was partying at Fischer's expense," observed Neil Nixon in the *Rough Guide to Rock*. With a history of psychiatric lockup, Larry was a walking landmine. His unpredictable, destructive behavior served notice that while he might not be a menace to society as a whole, he could imperil those in his immediate vicinity, especially those closest to him, who were offering help.

Fischer may not have control of his temper or his destiny, but he's not without a certain awareness of his plight. In 1968, on the brink of Zappa-pegged notoriety, he sang, "Will I end up a bum, will I end up a crumb, will I end up in hell, will I end up in jail, will I end up in Jesus, will I end up in trees?"

His early brain-derailing maternal clashes provoked odd later-life searches for foster care. "When Larry had some money," said Mumy, "he bought a year pass to Disneyland. He used to call me from the Magic Kingdom all the time. He went there 'to soak up family love.'"

It's easy to ascribe virtue to a simple-minded savage like Fischer, and to discern essential truth and beauty in his uncivilized behavior. "Would that there were more Wild Man Fischers in the world," wrote one fan on Belovarac's Web site. "It would indeed be a better place." Such sentiment is appropriate scribbled in yearbooks, but not in real life. Wild Man's volatile impulses provided over-the-edge entertainment for thousands of fans who didn't have to stick around and pick up the pieces. While spreading joy through his records and chaotic performances, Fischer seems to have inflicted a modest degree of misery on those closest to him and wallowed in a bit of it himself. The adult-child who earned the sobriquet "Wild Man," and whose behavior embodies the name, will always be dependent on those with the maturity and patience to provide guidance, sandwiches, and the occasional couch. If more folks were like Fischer, more of us would be sleeping on subway grates. One Wild Man is enough. Would that there were more people to take care of human wreckage like him.

Mumy remains a close, quasi-custodial friend, in contact with Fischer almost daily. "Larry is a unique artist with a one-of-a-kind mind," he observed. "He literally combusts with songs. His melodies are primitive and memorable. His lyrics are heartfelt, ranging from great pain and angst, to the most innocent, genuine love imaginable."

Fischer remains haunted by his days walled off in mental hospitals. "That's why he avoids seeking medical help for his emotional problems," Mumy explained. "Whenever things start to 'happen' for him, like recording, gigging, or doing promotional work, or people in general take an interest in his music, he gets paranoid. That's the biggest reason why he doesn't make more music or gig. He retreats from the world and show business for good reasons. He's a sweet and difficult man, who hasn't received enough love and support from his family or the music industry."

Fischer no longer considers himself part of the business. "It became a dream that turned into a nightmare," he conceded in 1997. "I don't have much of a career anymore. I've given up. But they're still talking about that album I made in 1968. Is that pretty good, or what?"

Fischer now lives in a room in the Hollywood area, occasionally drifting around Cahuenga Pass. He keeps to himself, and judging from the lack of headlines, largely stays out of trouble. "Larry has very little money," explained Mumy. "He lives poorly, but with dignity. Most of his time is spent in his room, making phone calls to a very small amount of people in his 'inner circle.' He also walks around a lot.

"If you ever meet him," advised Mumy, "tell him you like him. Talk to him. Maybe buy him a meal or a soda. He's worth it."

• 21 •

Snapshots
in Sound

ELSEWHERE IN THE
CURIOUS UNIVERSE

"Way lost no-fi monsterdom."
—RON MOORE

Old, new, available, or out-of-print—for further adventures in outsider music, explore recordings by these artists ... if you can find them.
Or—select 25, do some research, and write Volume II!

Hasil Adkins
Nasty, atavistic creek-rocker; seminal influence on the Cramps. Deserves a book by himself. Not hard to find his albums; if not in stores, try junkyards. Has recorded for Norton, A.R.C., Personal, and Hunch from the 1960s through the 1990s. Nick Tosches asserts: "Like the Bible and toilet paper, the music of Hasil Adkins belongs in every household."

Leona Anderson
Daffy but charming chanteuse who released LP *Music to Suffer By* (RKO Unique/ca. 1953). Tunelessly shrieks "Rats in My Room," "Limburger Lover," "(Friday Is My Day for) Fish" (78 rpm, B side), and other comic numbers backed by carnival calliope or full orchestration. Perhaps more commonly thought of as a comedienne, there's something a little spooky about Miss

Anderson in a house-of-mirrors sort of way. Artist Paul Bacon, who knew Leona, said, "I'm not sure whether she knew she was funny—but I have my suspicions."

Obvious prototype for the later *Tonight Show* shenanigans of Mrs. Miller, though Anderson displays greater sophistication and subtlety. Lamentably, no known collaborations ever took place between Anderson and her contemporary Spike Jones, though she did share soundstages with the Bil Baird Marionettes.

Arcesia

Johnny Arcessi was a Rhode Island big band belter in the 1940s and 1950s, who moved to California and underwent lysergic revelations in the late 1960s. He reinvented himself—at age 52—as Arcesia, a navel-gazing acid folk-rocker, and hooked up with a Doors-influenced band that backed his psychedelic lounge-rock histrionics. Around 1970, he recorded one legendary and now astronomically priced collectible LP called *Reachin'* (Alpha Records).

The too-earnest Arcesia over-emotes in an unnatural, hysterical manner—half-singing, half-sobbing—and rarely returns to a relaxed register. The album title could, in fact, refer to the high notes he strives for but fails to hit. This record was a cry for help—from more than just potential customers.

The song "Butterfly Mind"—a "butterfly equals beauty" allegory—includes the trenchant plea: "Don't let a wasp grab you / don't let a hand nab you / don't let a net get you / and make you a beautiful dead thing for all his friends to see." On "Mechanical Doll," this acid-glazed Tom Jones sings about an angel that flew into the room, who "dropped her wings and gassed everyone there."

"When I first discovered the LP in 1988," said collector/archivist Paul Major of Parallel World Records, "I had to find this guy. Eventually I tracked down some of Arcessi's relatives who had a 'junque' shop in upstate New York. Nobody seemed to know much about his exploits in L.A. It's a total mystery to them why he did what he did. They had four original copies of the album, which he'd sent from the West Coast." Major said Arcessi's family thought the record was "strange."

The original LP cover was plain white; the printed artist's name and album title were its only identifying features. Whether this was a nod to the Beatles' *White Album* or simply a budgetary constraint remains part of Arcesia's unknowable, sphinxlike aura. No personnel or recording info was included on the jacket.

Reachin' was reissued in 1997 on Germany's Ten Little Indians label in a limited vinyl pressing with a different cover, but it has never appeared on CD.

Major has been unable to locate any musicians who played on the sessions. Arcesia died around 1978, at age 60. His relatives said that after he split to the coast, they never saw him again.

David Arvedon

Arvedon's oeuvre should be mandatory listening for fans of obtuse music. After sharpening his teeth with a Brandeis U. sixties rock combo, the Psychopaths (one archetypal 45 in 1968), Arvedon focused on studio recording. He hired seasoned session vets and an engineer/arranger groomed during the Sinatra/Tin Pan Alley era, creating an artistic conflagration ignited by his own bizarre musical vision. The result was not dissimilar to MSR song-poem madness.

After exhausting the possibilities of this ill-conceived nexus, Arvedon hired a bunch of greasy, long-haired, $$-hungry rockers, resulting in more out-of-sync, convoluted sounds. Trying to teach a horde of proto–Spinal Tap dingbats his full-length rock opera about teeth (songs include "Mr. Decay Germ" and "Living in a Cavity") had strange musical ramifications.

After a decade-plus sabbatical, Arvedon rekindled his artistic sensibilities and recorded a trilogy of songs in the early 1990s under the moniker Psycho's Psychopaths. He made select appearances onstage (including Karaoke bars) in Boston, creating a modest stir among hipsters and post-punks who knew little of his past. The two-CD set, *In Search Of The Most Unforgettable Tree We Ever Met*, represents Arvedon's complete studio recordings from 1968 through 1974.

Penn Jillette is a huge Arvedon fan.

(by Erik Lindgren)

Frances Baskerville (aka Frances Cannon), the Singing Psychic

File under "Chicks Who Levitate and the Songs That Launch Them." Baskerville not only psychically predicts and sings—she's Texas's foremost finder of lost persons!

A 1987 LP, *Frances Cannon, the Singing Psychic*, featured 16-track synth-rock backing as Fran talk-sang in a loopy Lone Star drawl about UFOs, miracles, and earthquakes destroying California. (An out-of-print 1985 LP, *Songs from Cannonville*, was unavailable for review.)

Her 1999 CD, *Songs from Beyond*, was decidedly lo-fi, featuring a renamed Frances Baskerville (her middle name) sounding more like a pubescent Southern belle coyly singing karaoke-style over recognizable instrumental records that were unrelated to her daft lyrics.

On "JFK—I Was Their" [sic], our colorful clairvoyant describes eyewitnessing Kennedy's assassination from the grassy knoll—while the melody of "Ode to Billie Joe" percolates in the background. "Legend of Killer Whale" [sic] is delivered over the old Bobby Darin chestnut "Splish Splash." On "Star's Ghost," the infallible Frances forecasts: "Marvin Gaye he's coming back oh yeah / he forgives his dad for what he's done doin' him in." The song also signals, inexplicably, that Martin Luther King and Michael Landon will accompany Gaye's Lazarus shtick.

From her Web site: "Fran discovered her psychic abilities after a near death experience involving an 18-wheel truck."

"This happened in 1979, when I got these powers," Fran told me over the phone. "But at the time I didn't know it was called 'psychic'—I just thought I got a lot smarter." She was in a Chevy Impala, stopped by a beauty shop in Princeton, Texas, when a lumber truck backed into her passenger side. "I was stuck on the back of this 18-wheeler, me and my car," she recalled. "I was in lumber from my waist to the top of my head. And it was kind of like, I divided, and part of me went into this tunnel. I saw a bright light. I could see my father, who'd passed on—he wore a plaid shirt and khaki pants. And there were angels. Then I could see everything I'd ever done or heard. I saw all these people, but we talked with our hearts, not our mouths, and we knew each others' thoughts. Suddenly, I just knew *everything*—the past and the future. I heard the voice of Jesus Christ. It was real amazing—for a moment. Then the angels helped me rejoin my body in the car."

Though she suffered broken ribs, a damaged neck artery, and had "pinholes of lumber" in the retina of her eye, Fran survived the standoff with the truck. From that day, like a certified member of the Justice League of America, she decided to apply her new-found clairvoyant powers to the forces of good, engaging in "psychic detective work and ghostbusting."

Her firm, Baskerville Investigations, specializes in "missing children, insurance claims, and surveillance." Her Web site boasts that BI has found over "9,000 missing persons, more than anyone in Texas." It's a huge state, with lots of places to hide—but *not from Fran!*

"Basically, I just feel that God leads me to things," Fran acknowledged. "Without him, I couldn't do anything."

Baskerville has appeared on *Good Morning, America* and the *David Letterman Show*. She also makes frequent call-ins to the *Howard Stern Show*, on which she sings prognostications and is often busted for the inaccuracy of prior predictions.

Fran's in a league with Lucia Pamela—a lovely, loveable screwball, brimming with élan. She's bound to leave listeners shaking their heads, with big smiles on their faces. Private readings are available.

Brute Force

Off-the-mark, incomprehensible cabaret-rocker who recorded one bizarre album, *Confections of Love* (Columbia, 1968), featuring songs like "To Sit on a Sandwich" and "Tapeworm of Love." Real name: Steven Friedland, a New York cosmic-tripper who inexplicably snared a major label deal for this landmark release. Produced by the eclectic John Simon, which says *a lot*. Brute later got roped into Beatledom for a one-shot novelty 45 on Apple, "The King of Fuh" (Get it?). In a previous incarnation, wrote brilliant pop tunes for 1960s chart-climbers the Cyrkle and the Chiffons.

The Chipmunks

Seemingly harmless, helium-voiced trio of fur-lined singing sibs—but in the rodent community, they are considered *far outside* the mainstream.

Christian Con Man

The ancient Zen riddle, "What is the sound of one hand clapping?" was devised to free the mind of the constraints of rational thought. In the same spirit, the cassette-only release, *Christian Con Man Goes Hawaiian,* begs the question, "What is the sound of one tongue flapping?" Lee Edwards, apparently Chicago-based, is Christian, but not overtly evangelical, though he professes the "con man" derives from his "total confidence in the Lord Jesus Christ as [his] savior." His gushing, romantic story-songs begin with awkward, Neil Hamburger–grade jokes, which evolve into organ-accompanied, choked-up paeans to his wife and family, before careening inexplicably into emotional climaxes. CCM rambles like a man who scrupulously observes the nine-drink minimum.

Michelle Boulé, cohost of WFMU's *Incorrect Music Hour,* sees CCM's poetry as "bringing new meaning to the term 'blank verse,'" and points out that his weepy ode to "Grandsons Pat and Lee" is a direct rip of Dick Whittinghill's egregiously sappy "Apology at Bedtime."

Ken DeFeudis

Unmelodious but earnest New England home recording klutz who's been distributing homemade cassettes for years. Dubbed "Mr. High on Life," DeFeudis shouts needlessly as if trying to communicate verbally with the deaf. Melody jumps the tracks in the first 15 seconds and careens uncontrollably down a musical embankment, coming to rest three minutes later in a twisted, smoldering wreck of verses and choruses. Sings originals ("Run for Cover Lover") and standards ("You Are My Destiny," "New York, New York"). Hammers away at keyboard synths, rarely varying timbres from factory pre-sets. From his press kit: "He believes in allowing creativity to flow. This belief can be com-

pared to the difference between a trimmed bush (neat and round) and a beautiful natural bush allowed to burst forth in its best array—free to grow.... His awareness is superb."

A profile accompanying the tape refers to DeFeudis's "relentless abilities." Those abilities include making the world a safer place to live: the profile states that DeFeudis "devised an improved automobile braking system that he feels could save thousands of lives which he presented to an automaker but says he has to re-present it in order to try to overcome their 'cost effective mentality' with a 'life effective mentality.'"

Del Rubio Triplets

"Three gals, three guitars, one birthday." Gracefully aging sisters—Milly, Elena, and Eadie, never too old for go-go boots, miniskirts, and *big* hair. Not as anthropologically compelling as the Shaggs, though chromosomal links to the Wiggin sisters are worth investigating. Based in California, the DRTs toured for decades in a station wagon named "Bambi," racking up 400,000 miles while they entertained at up to 20 hospitals and nursing homes a week. "This is a vocation," noted Milly. "God has chosen us to sing to the sick and retirees."

These wonder-sibs made several Dr. Demento–worthy novelty records during the 1980s, doing Ladies' Rock Auxiliary covers of "Walk Like An Egyptian," "Neutron Dance," and various pop standards. Also performed on *Pee Wee's Playhouse* and the *Pee Wee Herman Christmas Special*. They claimed to know "1,000 songs in six languages." Constant touring kept them young. Said Elena: "Men at retirement homes think we're in our thirties!" (Eadie passed away in December 1996, curtailing the band's activities.)

Roky Erickson

Former leader of 1960s psych-blowouts 13th Floor Elevators with subsequent legacy of deranged but righteously rockin' solo records on such labels as Pink Dust, Restless, Trance, 415, and Emperor Norton. Richie Unterberger, in *Unknown Legends of Rock and Roll*, quotes Henry Rollins in *Rolling Stone:* "Only a Captain Beefheart or a Roky Erickson could write something like 'Click Your Fingers Applauding the Play.' Mick Jagger couldn't come up with something that brilliant. Yet he'll make $47 million this year, while Roky lives in a dump." Erickson is cited as a pioneer of Lone Star psychedelia and a much-admired songwriter, but LSD eventually fried his synapses, leading to hospitalization for criminal insanity. Big fans R.E.M., ZZ Top, and Butthole Surfers, among others, participated in a 1990 tribute album to help Roky pay legal bills resulting from arrest for stealing a neighbor's mail. "In Austin," writes Unterberger, "he's an institution, revered on the same level as his old friend and one-time Austin resident Janis Joplin." (Unterberger's book contains an entire chapter on Roky.) Erickson's powerful songwriting should transcend any preoccupation with his fragmented personality.

Judson Fountain

The Ed Wood, Jr. of radio drama; his records recall the golden age of radio—after a dozen bong hits. Not specifically musical, but if this book doesn't mention him, none will. Jackson Brian Griffith, in *Pulse*, summed up: "Imagine paint-sniffers aiming for the Firesign Theatre and hitting *Plan 9 From Outer Space*."

Though he was between 16- and 20-years-old when his "reddio drammers" (as he pronounces it) were recorded and released on the Sanders label in the late 1960s, Fountain was captivated by old-time radio theater that had vanished from the airwaves by the time he was born. His simple, derivative plotlines deal with Halloween kitsch—spooks, witches, haunted houses—as vehicles for morality plays about redemption through honesty and damnation as punishment for evil-doing. Dementedly amateurish scripting, egregious ethnic accents, inept editing—all seasoned with generous needle-drops of shrieking ladies and wolf-howls from that classic Elektra Sound Effects library.

If you can find any of these vinyl rarities, they should be—but aren't—worth thousands of dollars, and oughta be reissued on CD. Tapes of Fountain's "drammers" have achieved legendary stature among tape-swapping cartoonists. If these relics survive Armageddon for future generations to behold, it will give our descendants even greater nightmares about pre-apocalypse civilization.

Bingo Gazingo

Cantankerous, retired street poet from Flushing, New York, who recorded an album at WFMU radio studios in 1997 with a strange array of session rockers (including R. Stevie Moore, Chris Butler of the Waitresses, and Dennis Diken of the Smithereens). The eponymous CD reveals Gazingo as a dazzling wordsmith of Beefheartian proportions, whose wry lyrics reward close scrutiny on a literary level. Also like Beefheart, he recited his lyrics without

listening to what the band was playing behind him, causing an arrhythmic disconnect between words and music. Titles include "Up Your Jurassic Park," "I Love You So Fucking Much I Can't Shit," "Two Pack Shaker," and "Oh Madonna (You Stole My Pants)."

Sri Darwin Gross (Dap Ren)

Then-living Eckmaster warbling spiritual anthems he composed "in the [popular] idiom of his day" (1972) on LP, *It Just Is*. Imagine *Goofy Sings the Phil Ochs Songbook*. SubGenius overlord Rev. Ivan Stang calls Eckankar™ "the Stupidest Cult," and "the Ultimate 'Duh.'" It's about the ancient science of astral projection—soul travel—in which you rack up frequent flyer miles levitating through the cosmic flux. Imagine an album of *songs* about it!

ECK-xotica—not to be confused with *real* music

But beware—*powerful stuff!* The liner notes include this caveat: "If listened to with half an ear, [these songs] seem to be no different that [sic] what one might hear on the daily radio. However, if that is what one has heard, he has been caught by the living ECK Master in the ruse of Rumi. He has slipped some of the highest, most profound wisdom to be found on the planet over on the listener as he vaguely tapped his foot and half listened to the comfortable familiar sounds of today." Like anyone would mistake "Oh, How I Love the Blessed Sugmad" for Bachman-Turner Overdrive.

Oddly, Gregg Turkington of Amarillo Records found a 1986 LP called *Golden Thread*, which is Gross performing instrumental lounge-jazz versions of the songs from *It Just Is*, minus any references to Eckankar on the cover or in the track titles. Had Gross undergone an epiphany? Been defrocked? Or simply succumbed to gravity?

Intrigued, I E-mailed Turkington.

IRWIN CHUSID: "Instrumental lounge-jazz" versions of IT JUST IS?

GREG TURKINGTON: Yup. Darwin Gross on vibes instead of vocals. He gives credit to the people who did the color separations for the front cover, the pressing plant—even to Pagemaker for being the program used to typeset the liner notes. Yet the other musicians are credited only as "free spirits"!

IC: A new genre: ECK-xotica!

GT: GOLDEN THREAD is on the "Sounds of Soul" label. I'm glad I was able to figure out what the hECK it was, as the front cover doesn't clue you in.

I wish the Eckankar community would get it together to reissue IT JUST IS on CD. Have you ever tried to read one of Paul Twitchell's Eckankar sci-fi books? They're even crazier than Gross's music. A lead character in one of them is named Peddar Zaskq. They're completely baffling, yet stone-cold boring.

Peter Grudzien

In his obscure-pop compendium *Underground Sounds,* Ron Moore refers to certain records that embody "Grudzienesque" qualities (see Kaplan Brothers). The neologism refers to the low-fi, junk-for-joy sonics of home recording artist Peter Grudzien.

It does *not* refer to Grudzien's standing as an openly gay country music artist. This particular subgenre might fill new-release bins in San Francisco and New York nowadays, but Grudzien came out in song 40 years ago, when it was decidedly dangerous to declare such sexual orientation in public.

Peter Grundzien

The tall, cadaverous-looking Grudzien grew up in Queens, New York, in the 1950s. After hearing a duet by Kitty Wells and Webb Pierce in 1953 on his parents' car radio, he became obsessed with country. His fixation eventually compelled him to visit Nashville, where he met one of his heroes, Johnny Cash. He began writing songs inspired by Hank Williams, and was deeply influenced by Bob Dylan, who Grudzien saw performing at small Greenwich Village clubs in the early 1960s. Around this time, Grudzien recalled, "my country music began becoming openly gay and still is to this day. I guess I'm in my own bag doing overtly gay country music, but it is what I like doing best."

Grudzien's own entry in *Underground Sounds* contains the following thumbnail: "NYC eccentric country psych with bluegrass picking. Very special 'real person.' Home studio compilation with tons of claustrophobic sounds in thick [demented] mix. Dreamy psych aura over basically country [-bluegrass] style playing which tends to stagger rhythmically. Amazing songs about hard-luck gay romance and hallucinatory religious visions with an upfront sincerity that's breathtaking."

Peter took part in the original 1969 Stonewall Riots that launched the Gay Pride movement. His 1974 album *The Unicorn* addressed religious-Christian-sex-redemption themes—all the biggies. Longtime Grudzien enthusiast and friend Paul Major reissued *The Unicorn* with bonus tracks on CD in 1995 (Parallel World). The album's songs were recorded over many years, the earliest dating from around 1960. Jello Biafra described the album as "madhouse hillbilly from the *Twilight Zone.*"

Grudzien lives in the Astoria, Queens, house in which he grew up; his nonagenarian father has one floor, Peter has the other, with a recording set-up. "Inside, the place hasn't changed much in forty years," noted Major. "Peter collects budget classical records from the 1950s on the Plymouth label, which he says sound horrible because they were pressed on old melted black telephone plastic."

For years, Grudzien seriously believed he'd been cloned by the government—and wasn't sure if he was the original or the copy. He also suspected Johnny Cash had a clone. He went backstage after a Cash concert to give his icon one of his own CDs, but when Grudzien became convinced it wasn't the real Johnny, his gift-giving spirit wilted. "Why should I waste the CD on a clone?" he insisted.

In a ragged, nasal baritone Grudzien delivers original songs that are candid, soul-baring, and at times a bit twisted ("Don't Come Feelin' Up My Doorknob Anymore"). The millions who've driven Reba and Garth megaplatinum probably wouldn't care much for Grudzien's take on country themes. His song "Hunky Honky" includes the lines: "I'm a hunky honky in a honky-tonk bar / Where the boys look like girls, and the girls look like boys." The jaunty "Candy-Ass Lover" was written about a longtime companion who, Grudzien says, "taught me to drive stick shift." And his topical "Star-Spangled Banner Waving Somewhere" is a plea for gays in the military : "Though I realize I'm homo, that is true sir / don't judge me by my preference in sex / Let me show Uncle Sam what I can do sir / Let me help to take the terrorists down a peg."

"Peter doesn't realize exactly how his music is perceived as being so strange," explained Major. "He's still trying to break into the Nashville country scene in a normal sort of way." Grudzien continues to make home recordings, which he sells on cassette out of a briefcase at his rare live gigs.

Dora Hall

Solo Paper Cup heiress and wannabe singer-starlet who recorded more often than necessary in the 1960s and 1970s, Hall's mail-order releases were available only through proof-of-purchase seals printed on Solo product packaging. Every time the dentist gave you a little white paper cup and instructed you to rinse 'n' spit, you helped underwrite Dora's showbiz ambitions.

Hall looked a bit like a better-preserved Minnie Pearl, the Grand Ole Opry lady with price tags on her hat. Deep-pocketed Dora's multigenre clumsiness included forays into rock, pop, country, kiddie, and show tunes. Never had the phrase "Get a life!" pertained with such urgency. A too-rich diva with copious time on her hands, Hall lured such Branson-bound leftovers as Frank Sinatra, Jr., Rich Little, and Phil Harris into her orbit for godawful medleys and so-called "TV Specials" such as 1968's *Once Upon a Tour*. This was pre-public access, begging the question of what station aired these stunningly inept debacles?

Hall passed away sometime in the late 1980s.

Kenneth Higney

Kenneth Higney's legacy rests on one self-produced and largely self-performed album, *Attic Demonstration* (Kebrutney Records, 1977). "Among outsiders," said Paul Major, "Higney is the Shaggs of loner-folk. There is no calculation to his art." Major described Higney as a "Bayonne, New Jersey, trucker who sold his rig to put out this record, which went nowhere."

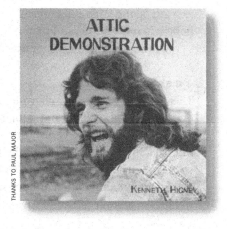

THANKS TO PAUL MAJOR

Ron Moore, in the colorful collector's jargon typical of his spiral-bound compendium *Underground Sounds*, describes Higney as follows: "Open wound real person basement psych damage strums with buzz fuzz burst. Mix of Spencian [as in 'Skip'] floaters and warped rhythm ravers. At times sounds like 1/2 Japanese doing Modern Lovers outtakes. Way lost no-fi monsterdom."

"Every song, no matter how it starts out," said Major, "by the end he's singing about his pain and the morbid world. Everything goes dark." The track "Children of Sound" begins with "Children of my beautiful wife / you were raised enjoying your days / now you're rich not poor"; but by the tune's conclusion, Higney warns: "Do you realize you'll only die / in this world of hate."

Great line from the song "Let Us Pray": "hidden in the grass was a three-fingered glove." And in "No Heavy Truckin,'" Higney's plight sounds typically dire: "I've got one ticket left in my tunnel book / I can't go anywhere."

In a 1977 article in New Jersey's *Aquarian*, Gene Kalbacher noted that Higney made these mostly first-take recordings "to induce major artists to re-record them." Whatever such "inducements" entailed, the profile notes that "Higney's 'Can't Love That Woman' was considered by Waylon Jennings's management for six weeks before plans were aborted." And in a testament to U.S. postal carriers—at least—the article avers that "Lucy (sister of Carly) Simon was sent demos of his ballads." Kalbacher's surprisingly candid assessment describes Higney's art as "monochromatic, almost atonal music.... The obvious absence of harmony renders the vocalizations flatter than they actually are. And the singing is flat—if not downright disarming. Mixing is nonexistent." Wonder why it took Waylon's managers a month and a half to nix the project?

When he released *Attic Demonstration* in 1977, 26-year-old Higney printed 500 covers but only pressed 300 discs. Major met Higney in the 1980s and filled the leftover covers with newly pressed copies of the album stamped from the master plates.

When Major got married, Higney gave him a copy of the original pressing as a gift, along with a note that said, "Dear Paul, Good luck in your marriage. I hope it is more successful than my record career."

Within a few years, Major was divorced.

Jessica Kane

Theatrically volatile, yet charming, Brooklyn-based unsinger-nonsongwriter, performance-poet, film- and puppetmaker wacko. On the cover of her *Varicose Days* CD (Mekkatone, 1996), the very comely Ms. Kane poses stark naked—full frontal—with two plastic baby dolls, each suckling a nipple. The CD's 44 tracks are deliciously vulgar in a sweet, post-nubile sort of way, and Ms. Kane's playful tape manipulation and musical deconstruction cast her as Larry Flynt's wet-dream answer to Laurie Anderson.

Kaplan Brothers

The Kaplans were a Chicago-based lounge act who did the Jewish nightclub circuit for a while, even played the White House as guests of Nixon. At some point, perhaps overcome with angst, they began performing and recording strange cover tunes with a *big* message in mind. Of their three known albums, *Nightbird* is on Paul Major's Top 10. "It's one of the ultimates in sincere weirdness," said Major. "It contains a 'psychedelic symphony' with keyboards—including Mellotron. The whole LP is a 'Meaning-of-Life'-melodramatic masterpiece." The brothers had deep, deep basso profundo voices, adding to the gravity of their meta-cabaret pomposity. A highlight of *Nightbird* was King Crimson's sinister, overblown "Epitaph."

Ron Moore, in *Underground Sounds,* painted a broken-mirror portrait of *Nightbird:* "Low rent genius schmaltz kings proggy ballad supperclub Holiday Inn moves, Arcesiaesque vocals. These guys were the real thing. Complete lack of self-awareness kitchen sink symphony with Grudzienesque production. It's apparently a concept LP but you'll never figure it out sober.

Tinkling piano, synth washes, flutes. Lots of sounds which have no business being there."

Kids of Widney High

Album *Special Music by Special Kids* (Rounder, 1989) features rock music by developmentally disabled children who suffer from epilepsy, Down's syndrome, cerebral palsy, and muscular dystrophy, and many of whom have behavioral problems. A vertiginous groove, and an artistic triumph. *Not* for poking fun at.

David Koresh

Album *Voice of Fire* recorded in the Branch Davidian compound was posthumously released on the Junior's Motel label in 1994. Royalties *do not* benefit the Children's Defense Fund. Writer Mykel Board expressed ambivalence: "A Mormon or Janet Reno—sometimes it's hard to know where to put your proper hatred."

Ray Korona Band

Jersey City–based folkie recorded the $5 *Working People's* [sic] *Music Tape* in 1998; then, according to the press release, "as unions and community groups continue to order hundreds of tapes weekly," he released a special CD edition. Korona's 1960-based baked earnestness will have you cringing along to such toe-tappers as "We Will Have Dignity (Sweatshops, Globalization, Child Labor)," "(If There's Sexual Harassment, I'm) Calling the Law," and "Jobs For All." Korona's quest for justice exceeds his grasp of catchy songwriting, and his lack of singing ability could explain his sympathy for out-of-work laborers. In Korona's world, as long as kids are starving, the poor are exploited, and workers downsized, *no one's gonna enjoy any good music!*

Little Marcy

Sinister-looking Christian puppet whose strings were pulled and vocals dubbed on perhaps 35 to 40 Word Records albums in the 1960s and 1970s. Ever see the *Twilight Zone* episode where a cuddly plastic doll with a mind of its own threatens to kill dad (Telly Savalas)—and eventually does? Little Marcy is that doll's evangelist sister. A frightening little goblin. She's coming for you, your children, and—on *Little Marcy Talks with the Animals*—your pets! Long-time Christian puppet fetishist (and cartoonist—see Legendary Stardust Cowboy) J. R. Williams enucleates the Marcy phenomenon: "Imagine a geriatric, senile Betty Boop, institutionalized in a Catholic nursing home, spending the remaining years of her 'second childhood' singing out for the Savior to come and take her away. Lord have Marcy."

Luie Luie

Herve Villachaize-soundalike invents discombobulated dance called "El Touchy," which today could be indistinguishable from many forms of sexual harassment. On album *El Touchy* (Penstar, circa 1980), Señor Luie plays all instruments, including guitars, drums, horns, and worst synths ever, in disjointed syncopation guaranteed to rupture vertebrae. Delusional liner note excerpts:

A Master Musician, LUIE LUIE will make you come—and glad you came. A Superb Showman, he will sting you with his searing songs, and pierce your innermost with his pearly Trumpet. He will caress you. He will force your feet to fidget and seduce your silent hands. His beat will bow your head.... This tall Music Matador oozes his music from ten fingers, two feet, two knees, his mouth, and a thousand brains, and in this all inclusive posture combination of mind and body and muscle and spirit, overwhelms the strong, the meek, regardless of age, sex or religious relationships.

Find this record!

Fergus macRoy

"This is a record of Fergus macRoy's religious revelations to date," says the rear cover of the LP *Mystic*. Backed by a competent piano-organ-bass-drums quartet, the enigmatic macRoy imparts less wisdom than confusion. His jaunty ditties explore alienation, the limitations of human knowledge, and hell on earth—but the delivery isn't as heavy as it sounds. macRoy's albums come across as entertaining, low-key jokes on—if not shared with—the listener. But then again, he could be on the level. Hence, the mystery of these albums. Sample lyric from "His Eyes":

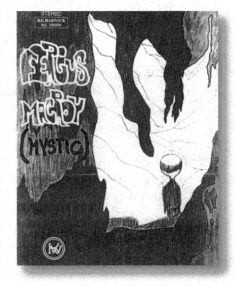

"His eyes are odd / green and blue and odd / seeing them I think of God / and pray." Liner note explanation for this song: "Dead serious—what the experience was we don't know." Vocalist/composer Fergus and lyricist brother Angus are identified as "middle-income Nova Scotia fishermen" (if the irony-laden liner notes can be believed).

Notes also claim a first album, *Fergus macRoy at the Homestead Upright*, did not sell, that the vinyl "sits in boxes," but they decided to do a second album: "We aren't going to praise these songs or sell them on any basis whatsoever. We just know in our souls that they are important and what the world needs now is important." The lyrics occasionally lapse into non sequiturs, like someone reading aloud answers to a crossword puzzle. Art archivist Glenn Bray turned up two LPs, listened closely, and wrote: "Real? A gag? Wha?"

Constance Mallis

In November 1998, California composer-singer Tommy Jordan (of the Luaka Bop band Geggy Tah) hailed a shuttle limo at the Portland, Maine, jetport. While enjoying the New England scenery en route to a record mastering facility, Jordan struck up a conversation with the driver, Michael Mallis, who realized his passenger was a musician. Mallis unfolded a tale about the secret legacy of his deceased father, Constance, with whom he had had a difficult relationship. Mallis explained that his father had left behind a wealth—thousands!—of a cappella recordings of original songs and quasi-operatic works.

"There must be some great stuff there," Jordan conjectured.

"Well, no," responded Mallis.

"Have you listened to it?" asked Jordan

Michael had. He wasn't too excited about it. He'd saved the entire cache but didn't know what to do with it.

"I'll take it," offered Jordan.

"But it's *bad!*" explained Mallis.

This heightened Jordan's intrigue. He affirmed his sincere interest and gave Mallis his address in Pomona.

Shortly thereafter, Jordan received a shipment of two briefcases and a cardboard box, containing dozens of tape reels, cassettes, dictation discs, Edison cylinders (used decades after they'd become obsolete), handwritten sheet music, and typewritten librettos. The material spanned the early 1960s to the early 1980s. It represented the legacy of one very eccentric, self-assured, paternally negligent, and grotesquely "talented" musical closet case.

Michael had attached a little note: "Tommy—don't die reading this stuff. Lots more."

On the tapes reviewed by Jordan thus far, Constance Mallis speaks in a pompous British accent and sings in an absurd basso profundo, phrasing with bombastic operatic flourish. He sounds like an English music hall performer with run-down batteries. The recordings are plagued by cheap tape hiss, low-frequency rumble, and occasional sound dropout.

Before delivering each work, Constance announces his own systematic folio references, for example, "This is number 1,064 of the series."

The Mallis oeuvre is weirdly moving, the atmosphere rather haunting. His titles include "The Garden of Eden, or The Original Sin: A Drama," "Oh Youth, Where Is Your Destiny?" and "Lulla-Lulla-Lullabye." The elder Mallis wrote music and words under many assumed names, including "Alex Los Angeles," "Guy Puck," and "Rex Oberon." His lyrics allude to "this silky airy pageant world" and "a canopy of dust and worms." Some tapes feature poetic recitation in which Constance speaketh: "Napoleon, protect us with his mighty sword!"

Mallis's voice brims with self-confidence. "He's fearless in tackling this material," noted Jordan. "He concentrated on his work. He was driven." In the middle of one tape, a woman is heard walking into the room and muttering, as if searching for a garden tool. Constance continues singing, oblivious to distraction.

Designer and WFMU listener Laura Lindgren commented, "Mallis reminds me of the Beckett play *Krapp's Last Tape* gone terribly wrong."

As Michael explained to Tommy, the Mallis family had inherited a fortune and occupied a mansion near the jetport. His father used this affluence to underwrite his solitary home recording obsession, indifferent to conserving the Mallis bankroll. Constance (or "Constantine," as some manuscripts indicate) didn't work and had little interest in his family. He simply wanted to write and record, sequestered in a fantasy realm. He never approached record companies, didn't perform in public, and made no attempt to publish or publicize his work. He was Charles Ives without the insurance gig. Mallis spent decades immersed in creative autism, pouring his soul into cruddy microphones, while capturing countless hours of idiosyncratic melodic invention on disc cutting machines, antiquated cylinder technology, and tape decks.

After his death, the family had to sell the mansion to avoid poverty.

For all his obvious eccentricity, Mallis exhibited great intent. He went to extraordinary lengths cataloging his output, archiving it for posterity as if this private endeavor would someday merit great public concern. Perhaps he was recording soundtracks for some future Henry Darger art exhibit.

Jordan is attempting to match typewritten manuscripts with the corresponding tapes. "We're just beginning our exploration into this material," he noted. "The deeper we go, the better it seems to get." Jordan hopes to eventually release an album of Mallis's claustrophobic self-expression.

Brooklyn musician Brian Dewan is helping Jordan sort and organize the material. "I can't help but think that Michael was subconsciously fishing around for a home for this stuff," observed Dewan. "He didn't want to do anything with it himself, but at the same time he didn't want it destroyed or lost to oblivion."

Serendipitously, in Tommy Jordan, Michael Mallis encountered someone with the proper degree of curiosity to preserve the hothouse musical legacy of his late father.

Charles Manson

Unlike his later-namesake, Marilyn, who was accused of merely inspiring atrocities among his youthful followers, Charles was a more proactive role model. (His homicidal mayhem is recounted elsewhere, if you need a reminder.) Another distinction between the Mansons is that Marilyn's records—which some consider equally, if differently, atrocious—wear the platinum mantle, whereas Charlie's sold only to those handful of curiosity-seekers who fetishize art by murderous psychopaths masquerading as messiahs. Any number of Charlie's recordings have been released on various fly-by-night indies over the decades following the 1969 Tate-LaBianca killings: *Lie: The Love and Terror Cult* emerged on LP within a year; *Unplugged 9/11/67* is an acoustic Manson-only solo tape; *The Family Jams* features members of the Manson litter recorded in 1970 singing their leader's songs while Chuck languished in prison; *Commemoration* is a collection of recordings made by Manson in the tank from 1982 through 85.

On *Lie,* Manson's acid-tinged crooning is backed by various Family followers. One of his songs, "Cease to Exist," was later, uh, "borrowed" by Dennis Wilson, retitled "Never Learn Not to Love," and recorded by the Beach Boys on their album *20/20*. "I make music," Manson once said. "What other people do with it makes trouble."

A. J. Marshall

Strange, ageless crooner who emulates Al Jolson—not during Al's prime *Jazz Singer* period, but rather toward the end of the Big Ego's career after throat surgery lowered his range. Stranger still, Marshall doesn't perform Jolson-era songs that would best suit his style; he instead attempts to bridge the generation gap by interpreting modern standards such as "This Guy's in Love with You" and "I'll Never Fall in Love Again." Recorded at least one album, and several singles. A 45 rpm cover photo depicts Marshall, who appears to be wearing leased hair, surrounded by a bounty of glamourbabes who look young enough—collectively—to be his daughter. They seem genuinely excited to be in A. J.'s presence.

Buddy Max

Lecanto, Florida–based flea market troubadour and ex-taxidermist whose heart is gold even if his records aren't. Self-released albums and singles from the 1960s to the 1990s on the Cowboy Junction label include "Tribute to the Challenger" (about the ill-fated space shuttle) and the seven-minute "Birthmark Story," about a strange congenital skin blemish. *Roller Derby* 'zine says Max "fuse[s] the stylistic legacies of Hank Williams, Sr., Bill Monroe, and Lawrence Welk as well as Jandek into a lonesome oompah loompah you'll never find anywhere else."

Rod McKuen

Yes, *that* Rod McKuen. Outsider! Note his wobbly vocal performances and sincere hippie kitsch on numerous albums. Rodney Perkins, writer and strange-music enthusiast in Houston, Texas, explains the enigmatic phenomenon: "What separated Rod McKuen from his more esteemed contemporaries was his marked inability to express himself. His casual hodgepodge of hipster jive, romantic sap, and subdued perversion sounded deep to the casual reader or listener. His use of generalities and vague terms allows the latitude for one to read almost anything into the poems. People identify with him because he is just as they are: full of emotion and passion but unable to articulate these feelings. Here we have the strangest of paradoxes: a man whose inability to express himself endears him to millions of others who are unable to express themselves."

Ray R. Myers

A gaunt but handsome man, Myers is pictured on the cover of his 10-page, self-published (circa 1941) autobiography, *Life Story and Picture Album,* sitting in a stiff-backed chair, a guitar laying horizontal on the floor before him. His bare feet are positioned across the strings.

But something's missing. Two things, in fact.

Myers, according to the pamphlet, billed himself as "The World's [sic] Famous Armless Musician." He claimed to be "known the world over." But beyond this modest piece of literature, written in the third person, there aren't many extant clues about his career.

He was born armless on January 2, 1911, to a Lancaster, Pennsylvania, farm couple, whom he identifies as "Mr. and Mrs. William Myers." He dedicates the booklet to his mom and includes two photos of "Mother Myers"—

but never once mentions her first name. His parents had eight other children, "as normal as any child could be." As a youth Ray learned to use his feet in a prehensile manner, eventually becoming an expert rifle marksman and obtaining a legal driver's license. He played trombone in the high school band.

Myers then obtained a Hawaiian guitar and "with ambition that only the Good Lord can give, he learned to play using his feet. With the toes of his left foot he held the steel bar to note the guitar and with his right foot he held a very small pick to strum."

In 1933 Myers played the Chicago World's Fair, then returned to the Lancaster area to broadcast on WGAL. His singing and plucking eventually landed him gigs on WWVA (Wheeling, West Virginia), WEEU (Reading, Pennsylvania), WHAS (Louisville, Kentucky), and WSVA (Harrisonburg, Virginia). As Ray tells it, he was quite popular on radio and in concert.

JUST A PLEASANT PASTIME

He married Eleanor Jane Sturm in 1937, and they had a son, Ronald Nelson (born with all appendages intact). Besides putting his pedal to the metal, Ray wrote songs. Several are reprinted in the booklet, though only one is actually attributed to him by name. Lyrically they reflect common hillbilly themes: cabins, mines, mother, and Jesus. The title of one—about being reunited with his mom in heaven—is touching in its irony: "Shake Hands with Mother Again."

If Myers ever recorded, no evidence has emerged, hence we don't know what his foot-playing technique or vocals sounded like. No country or bluegrass history books in my research mentioned him. I surfed the Web and couldn't find a blessed thing. Finally I consulted the Lancaster County Historical Society. Jack W. W. Loose, county historian for over thirty years, had never heard of Myers, but offered to do some detective work.

"There isn't a record of Ray R. Myers in Lancaster County after 1941," wrote Loose. "The Polk directory people only started listing the part of the county outside the city in 1963. Since Ray wasn't listed in the city, that suggests he lived out in the country, as did his son. I found a listing for a Ronald N. Myers living most recently near Leola, a village in Upper Leacock Township. Ronald, if he is the son, was captain of the fire police at Leacock/Leola in 1994. That suggests he was retired by then. He's not listed in the current directory. He may be dead. I have made inquiries, and will let you know if I find any information."

Loose received no replies. But his sleuthing continued.

"I drove out in the country to Leola/Bareville to hunt down the home where Ronald Myers lived according to the 1998 Polk directory," Loose wrote two months later. "No telephone is listed. I found the place and couldn't get any response at the front or back doors. I visited the neighbors on both sides. They were Vietnamese, and their English was rather unintelligible, but they said they never see anyone going into or leaving the house. The lawn and property looked well-tended. I visited the local post office, where the clerk—upholding the privacy act—refused to say whether or not Ronald Myers lived at that address. I told her I sent a first class letter to Myers, but it was neither returned nor answered.

"Next I visited the local firehouse where Ronald supposedly was captain some years ago. I met a young fellow so new on the job he didn't know of anyone named Myers. I then visited an old friend at the local hardware store, and he never heard of Ron Myers. So I got absolutely nowhere."

What became of Ray R. Myers is a mystery. But what remains of his legacy at least made it into this book.

Jim Noste

Avuncular septuagenarian home-improvement mogul adenoidally croons his way through the Tin Pan Alley songbook on self-released LPs *Songs for You, Vols. 1–3* (circa 1980s). Noste is backed by a competent Nashville ensemble no doubt paid out of company profits. Cardigan-clad Noste founded the Island Home Center in Union, New Jersey, in 1953. (The name, according to the album, refers to the "showroom [that] is located on the center island of Route 22, one of our state's most busy highway [sic].") Having developed this thriving family enterprise, the album liners attest, "[Noste] never lost an equally strong interest for music. He keeps his love for singing solely as a hobby.... [This] album gives him an additional sense of pleasure and excitement within his musical realm." The sense of excitement Noste summons up for storm windows, vinyl siding, soffits, and Verosol shades (all pictured on the LP back cover) gives an idea of the thrilling nature of his vocal stylings. With a microphone serving as his metaphorical van, Noste delivers such household fixtures as "The Lady Is a Tramp," "Misty," "My Way," and "I Write the Songs" with all the élan of—well, of a gentleman who has spent 30 years in the home improvement business. He's a charmer all the way.

Nicolas (Nikolai) Obukhov (Obouhov)

Obscure Russian composer (1892–1954) and religious fanatic turned expatriate bricklayer whose rarely staged or recorded works frothed with mystical intensity and feverish morbidity. The composer typically instructed his performers to sing and play "in the anguish of death," and he poured a lot of his own blood—literally—into his work.

Obukhov's pre-WWI experiments with 12-tone harmonies pre-dated Schoenberg. In 1918, he fled the revolutionary ferment of his native land and emigrated to Paris.

In France, he constructed one of the earliest electronic instruments, the "Croix Sonore" (Sonorous Cross), which was similar to and contemporaneous with the Ondes Martenot. The device was intended to be used as part of a large-scale work that took Obukhov about 20 years to complete—*La Livre de Vie* (*The Book of Life*), a magnum opus numbering approximately 2,000 pages.

While developing the work, the burly Obukhov lived in poverty with his Russian wife and scraped by on a bricklayer's wages. In their tiny apartment, he built a shrine that sheltered *La Livre*'s score, which had been notated with bar numbers printed in red Maltese crosses and tempi etched in the composer's own blood. The work lay under candles that burned round the clock. Obukhov's wife, in a fit of anger, once sliced up the manuscript, leaving the composer to carefully bandage the dismembered work while tracing all cuts with yet more of his own blood.

La Livre had other peculiarities. For the musicians, Obukhov designed mystical robes emblazoned with crucifixes, and he arranged the orchestra in a cross pattern for the performance, which was designed to take place in an outdoor temple. The composer believed that if *La Livre* were performed correctly and in its entirety, it would invoke the return to power of the last Russian emperor, whom Obukhov believed wasn't dead, but in hiding. Movements were performed, but the work was never staged in its entirety. (Too bad—the emperor remains in seclusion.)

Obukhov wrote other, more modest works, which nonetheless dripped with gothic embellishments. Score notations challenged performers to sing or play their parts "with ecstatic horror" or while "groaning and shrieking." Instructions to vocalists might include whistling, performing "with an insane smile," delivering words "with malignancy," or giving the appearance of "suffering furiously." It was not uncommon for his music to change time signatures eight times within a few bars.

This unconventional composer earned the respect of Ravel (who called him a genius) and Honegger (who wrote a preface to Obukhov's book *The Treatise of Tonal, Atonal, and Total Harmony*, and asked him to notate some of his work). In his 30s Obukhov gained a patron in the French countess Mme. Aussenac de Broglie, who set him up in a house and supported his artistic endeavors for the rest of his life.

Upon his death, Obukhov left over 75 works, which are rarely performed and most of which have never been recorded.

(by Robin Edgerton)

Congress-Woman Malinda Jackson Parker

A loveable Liberian eccentric whose hard-to-find recordings conjure up a heavenly hash of Nina Simone and Lucia Pamela. The late "Ma Parker" of Marland County was a member of Liberia's House of Representatives during the administration of President William V. S. Tubman. The daft yet elegant Parker sang, wrote, and published her own songs, possibly two or three albums' worth. She accompanied herself on grand piano, which she pounded mercilessly as she revamped folk songs and addressed cultural concerns with a freewheeling half-sung, half-narrated storytelling style.

The one album that's come to my attention (courtesy Lou Smith), *Tubman Goodtype Songs of Liberia by Congress-Woman Malinda Jackson Parker* (circa 1971), appears to be a U.K. vanity pressing. It contains uninhibited odes to bush cow milk, the disease-spreading propensities of mosquitoes, and the blessings of palm trees. On the first of two versions of "Cousin Mosquito," she utters the

word "cousin" 204 times within the song's three minutes and 27 seconds. The second version is based on Rachmaninoff's *Prelude in C Sharp Minor*. In the song's intro, she pronounces the composer's name "ran-uh-MAN-ov," ran-uh-MAN-yee-ov," and "ran-uh-MAH-ni-nov."

Smith gathered some biography about MJP from a Liberian chat list. She was by reports kind, generous, and beloved; dressed in a flamboyant manner; and was never without a bag of candy to bestow sweets upon little children. She appeared to have a measure of independent wealth. Though there was no known familial connection, the congresslady was referred to as the Parker Paint Company's best customer because of her cosmetic overload.

Charles S. Neal, III, wrote: "She was a female Tom Lehrer. 'Cabbages and Scronions.' Wow—what a lyricist!!" Frank J. Stewart, Jr., wrote: "I don't know a lot about Parker, only about the terrible makeup she wore in the city of Monrovia. But she was a legend. People had a lot of respect for her. In fact she was one of Tubman's best friends. Everyone loves her song, 'Chicken Is Nice with Palm Butter.'"

Washington Phillips

A bit of a mystery man, about whom very little is known aside from his few late 1920s recordings. In fact, more is known about the peculiar musical mechanism that made his recordings so special. Discovered in Texas in 1927 by Frank Walker, a blues A&R scout, George Washington Phillips played a unique instrument called the "Dolceola." This celestial-sounding keyboard-harp was invented around the turn of the century by Ohio piano tuner David P. Boyd. It consisted of a zitherlike frame with 60 wire strings and a miniature keyboard encompassing 25 chromatic notes; it was simultaneously keyed and strummed, and produced a delicate, chimelike resonance. Boyd produced about 35 Dolceolas, which he packed in his automobile before heading to California. Despite ads in prestigious music publications, the Dolceola never caught on; by the time Phillips acquired one in the 1920s, Boyd was probably long out of business.

Phillips delivered gospel tunes in a raw, but gentle voice, accompanied solely by the Dolceola. His singing is passionate, humble, and haunting. Over several studio sessions in 1927 and 1929, he recorded 16 hymns of stern, unflinching moralism (for example, "Train Your Child," "The Church Needs Good Deacons," and "Mother's Last Word to Her Son"). Shortly after the second session, he died of tuberculosis. Today, very few Dolceolas exist. The instrument has rarely been recorded, and when it has, no one could approach the stunning mastery of Phillips, whose hands were guided by divine forces. A Yazoo CD, *I Am Born to Preach the Gospel,* contains his complete recordings.

1907 ad for a Dolceola

Palmer Rockey

Scarlet Love is the soundtrack LP to Palmer Rockey's 1980 independent film feature that was shot in Dallas, but never commercially circulated. Paul

Major describes Rockey as a "hustler, lounge lizard, and flimflam man" who gigoloed production financing from Dallas socialites during the 1970s. After 10 years of filming, Rockey hired top-rank session players for the sound-track recording—which featured his abysmal vocals and sleazy, depraved lyrics.

After screwing the socialites, probably literally, Rockey did a figurative jel-lyjob on the musicians, none of whom got paid. The film had a lavish Dallas premiere—which flopped. Rockey reportedly split town the next day, and no one in Dallas ever saw him—or the film—again.

Rockey sings like an even goofier Harvey Sid Fisher. He feigns rockabilly and lounge attitudes, but he's a sub-karaoke amateur with zero personality. He sounds like he's laying down a reference vocal for the *real* singer, who apparently never made the session. That this talent-free charlatan convinced wealthy matrons to underwrite his artistic pretensions shouldn't surprise. Money and good taste don't always comfortably coexist.

At least four variations of the soundtrack album have surfaced, with minor differences in jacket art and song styles, and two are retitled *Movie Album*. Cover photos depict Rockey as a creepy, sinister-looking bulldog, in snazzy threads.

After discovering the album and developing a fascination, Major enlisted some friends for investigative prowls around Dallas. Locals who recalled the film debacle said that Rockey had a chauffeur-driven Rolls and often sported a fur coat in 110 degrees Texas heat. He was reportedly a follower of Satanic buf-foon Aleister Crowley.

Years later, Major tracked down Rockey in California and phoned him about the project.

Rockey's reply: "Don't ever call me about this again."

"Dusty Roads" Rowe

The world's most unique clarinetist, whose playing—about three notes—cov-ers a very small parcel of real estate. Offers rambling blues- and gospel-based vocal workouts reminiscent of Lionel Hampton (the *singing* Hampton, that is). Abundant fun here. At least one known LP, a vanity pressing called *Always Raring to Go Hope You Will Enjoy This Album as He Travels to and Fro* (no label). Probably from Washington, D.C., judging from clues on the album jacket. On side one, "Dusty Sings Folks [sic] and Spiritual Songs"; on side two "Dusty Sings Pop and Ragtime." No personnel listed, but Dusty's affiliations are— AFTRA, BMI, AGVA, IBPOE, a Washington, D.C., Musicians Local, League of the Sacred Heart of Jesus, and others.

Modern-day vaudevillian and Fortean scholar Doug Skinner paid four bucks in a New York thrift for what could be the world's only existing copy of

Always Raring. Impossible to tell from the cover art or playing when this album was recorded. "The package design is so rudimentary it could have been done at any time," said Skinner. "It could be Early Rudimentary or Late Rudimentary."

"Dusty has all the style and grittiness of an old bluesman with none of the musical ability," mused Skinner. "He has a great voice but no sense of pitch. His exuberant wailing has no relation to anything." About Rowe's minimalist clarinet squawks, Skinner observes, "He kinda locks into a little few-note groove and goes back and forth. He makes playing the clarinet sound easy."

Michelle Boulé calls Rowe "real drinks-thru-the-nose entertainment."

San Lucas Band

Guatemalan mountain village orchestra, recorded on legendary ABC Command LP (1975), *The Music of Guatemala.* World music equivalent of Portsmouth Sinfonia: out-of-joint, listless, unable to come to grips with rhythm. Musical delirium tremens—like a Salvation Army band that fell off the wagon. Leading indicator of colonial-vestige talent gap between developed and emerging nations.

William Shatner

Shatner, as James Branch Cabell once said about Mencken, "is a phenomenon somewhere between electricity and influenza." His sole album legacy, *The Transformed Man,* (Decca, 1968), tags him as the Elvis of Golden Throats. Musical outsider? Give this album a listen.

How it came about is revealing. Dennis William Hauck's biography, *Captain Quirk* (Pinnacle Books, 1995), tells how Shatner was motorcycling through the Mojave Desert with friends in summer 1967, when his Suzuki Titan 500 hit a rut. Shatner was tossed, and he blacked out after the heavy chopper landed on him. His buddies never looked back. After Shatner regained consciousness, he sensed the presence of a "shadowy phantom" and was "infused with fresh energy." He righted the cycle, but couldn't trip the ignition. He was stranded in the midday desert, in 110 degrees heat. Disoriented, Shatner began pushing his cycle—which "seemed to acquire a mind of its own," wrote Hauck. "He could push it in just one direction," as if guided by "an unseen force." On the horizon, Shatner glimpsed "a mysterious dark figure waving him on." Hours later, he arrived at an old gas station, where he looked up and "observed a pie-pan shaped object glistening in the sky." His three friends, after a frantic search, found Shatner "relaxing with a cool drink at the gas station." Hauck concludes, "He almost certainly would have died had he not been guided to safety by the unknown presence."

Shatner became convinced that superior intelligences in the universe could interact with humans. "I can't prove UFOs exist," he conceded, "but anyone who denies they exist is as foolish as the person who denies God exists." Shortly thereafter, Shatner recorded *The Transformed Man,* his artistic statement about his desert UFO encounter. He's given no indication, in any subsequent interview or public confessional, that he was anything less than serious about this tour-de-force of umbilical contemplation. "The thrill I got from making this album," he once boasted, "was deeper and more satisfying than anything I have ever experienced. I was really in orbit."

Major Bill Smith

Forth Worth eccentric who produced two number-one hits ("Hey! Baby" and "Hey Paula") and one number-two hit ("Last Kiss") during the early 1960s,

Major Bill Smith claims Elvis lives and has recorded a duet on his label with Kelli...?

then went overboard with Elvis-Is-Alive jag during 1980s. Wrote exposé novel, *The Memphis Mystery,* and released requiems and fishy Elvis soundalike productions on Le Cam label. Smith contended that Elvis faked his death to escape the pressures of stardom, adopted the name of his stillborn twin, Jessie Garon, then skied off to a private island to live in peaceful seclusion. Smith made other recordings: his anti-abortion spoken-word elegy, "Cry of the Unborn Child," only served to convince pro-choicers that *Roe v. Wade* should be extended to works of art.

Joseph Spence

Bahaman, acoustic guitar-picking master of the rhyming spiritual; lyrics often unintelligible, as if mumbling to himself. Spence (1910–1984) was acclaimed for his unique interpretations of native folk and dance songs, gospel, and disorienting American pop covers. He recorded extensively for Arhoolie, Folkways, Rounder, and Ryko from the 1960s through 1980s. His "Sandy Craws is Comin' to Town" should be a seasonal staple on every jukebox in the friggin' universe, and should displace every Mel Tormé record in existence.

Skip Spence

Alexander "Skip" Spence was the original drummer in Jefferson Airplane. He'd never played drums in his life, but was supposedly hired in 1965 and assigned the kit by singer Marty Balin, who felt Spence "looked like a drummer." Skip departed after JA's debut LP. In 1967 he was recruited as guitarist for overhyped but doomed folk-psychedelic outfit Moby Grape, for whom he wrote a few songs, including the classic proto-cowpunk "Omaha."

Following his (possibly inadvertent) ingestion of plutonium-grade LSD in 1968, Spence busted up New York's Albert Hotel with a fire axe. This little frolic earned him six months in Bellevue psychiatric hospital and commenced a 30-year schizophrenic odyssey. Some friends blamed the oversized acid dosing; others felt the hospital stay amplified the initial damage. Skip became irrational and prone to violent outbursts. He wore upside-down crucifixes and gouged devil horns in his guitar finish. Meanwhile, as the doctors were probing, prescribing, and peering at his EEG, Skip wrote a bunch of songs.

Slightly recuperated and bailed out by a friend, Spence motorcycled to Nashville in 1969 and recorded for Columbia a solo album entitled *Oar*. It was a curious blend of quirky, unpresumptuous folk and off-the-hinge roots rock, a sort of mountaineer Syd Barrett. Considering Spence's galvanic acid spike and the period during which the album was recorded, *Oar* was surprisingly anti-psychedelic. It had the loose, pastoral feel of a Smithsonian indigenous field recording. Producer David Rubinson told Richie Unterberger in *Unknown Legends of Rock and Roll*, "If there's such a thing as a naïf movement in rock and roll, *Oar* would be the first of its kind. It's guileless." Moby Grape bandmate Peter Lewis said the album "delved into the darkness of the soul." Modern listeners might say it sounds a bit like Beck, but without the arty self-consciousness.

Alexander "Skip" Spence

A Sony A&R exec told me the original *Oar* LP sold around 600 copies, which is mailroom floor-sweepings for a major label. Fact is, the album was all but ignored by Columbia as a commercial impossibility. Skip spent the ensuing decades intermittently homeless, committing sporadic acts of mayhem, and under occasional clinical lockup for paranoid schizophrenia. His chronic hard drug use was aggravated by alcoholism. Yet Spence was generally the object of great affection among his friends and fellow musicians, who saw him as a wayward, but essentially harmless and loveable overgrown kid. He was "a mouse without his cheese," Lewis told *Mojo* magazine in 1999. "He had trouble staying focused.... He was, I don't want to say surreal, but he lived in a heightened state of awareness."

In July 1999, *More Oar: A Tribute to the Skip Spence Album*, was released on Birdman Records. It featured Alexander the Grape's songs covered by such fans as Tom Waits, Robert Plant, Mudhoney, Son Volt, and Robyn Hitchcock. Early production had been held up because many artists couldn't decipher

Skip's often-mumbled lyrics. Publishing administrator Lynn Quinlan offered to transcribe the words if Spence would help. Quinlan told *Mojo* magazine that Spence replied, "Let me get this straight. I recorded that thing about 30 years ago in Nashville in three days in my pajamas, got on my motorcycle, and drove back to California.... Now you want me to remember the *lyrics?*"

The album was released about three months after Spence died of lung cancer in a Santa Cruz hospital, two days short of his 53rd birthday. The U.K.'s *New Musical Express* reported that just hours before he expired, Spence had listened to an advance tape of the tribute. That same year, *The Complete Oar Sessions*, featuring the original album and unreleased tracks, was issued in a landmark edition by Sundazed.

Peter Lewis told *Mojo* about the sheer strangeness of Spence's having written *Oar* while undergoing complete psychological collapse. "The songs were just from the *zone*," he opined. As for whether the songs were "good," Lewis chuckled and conceded that the word was "not enough to describe what they were to me. They were just ... *accurate*."

Supie T.

Spit-prone punk ranter Dan Theman, under the name "Supie T.," has attracted a bemused following around Cleveland. A shell-shocked Vietnam vet, Supie records his own a cappella rhythmic harangues, passes out tapes, and occasion-

ally performs in local taverns and on low-watt radio stations. His indignant, foul-mouthed street "jams" (as he calls them) deal with the fucked-up music business ("Please Tell Me What Color"); tennis champ Monica Seles; Supie's tour of duty in Southeast Asia ("After My Buddies Got Killed in 'Nam"); and Guinness Stout. He also offers the occasional cover song, such as Bacharach and David's "Don't Make Me Over," which Supie calls "the funkiest jam Dionne Warwick ever did." He accompanies himself with beatbox mouth noises, whose sonic similarity to flatulence is purely coincidental. His propensity for saliva-spewing, however, should be investigated for possible public health risks.

"I'm not a rapper, that's not the kind of jams I do," Supie said in a radio interview. "I do alternative rock, and I try to be as versatile as possible." He occasionally records with local musicians, and the resulting gestalt of voice, guitar, and salivary discharge is passionate, if chaotic.

Pete Seward, formerly of Cleveland, wrote: "Dan used to visit a cartoon art studio where I worked. He didn't have a job, and received some kind of government check. He would grace us with performances, which he was always quite excited about. He'd be drunk and lots of spit would fly. Downtown, he'd walk around with something stuffed in his crotch to attract girls. Our best guess was a potato. His name, 'Dan Theman,' could be read as 'Dan the Man.' He is fixated with all-girl groups and wrestling.

"Live, he is something to behold. He is quite serious."

These sentiments were echoed by Doug Gillard, Guided by Voices guitarist, who has backed Supie on studio tapings. Gillard attests, "Supie is very serious about his art and his songs. He sings about direct life experiences and the resulting pain or joy. His observations are unflinchingly earnest. His stories never involve a fictitious character, and he feels every word he sings, as is evident in his live performances. Supie is the real thing in a world of bullshitters."

Robert C. Banks made a documentary film about the Midwest's master jammer, *You Can't Get a Peace of Mind*. Supie also has a CD, *Getdown Airwaves: Coming to a Radio Near You*.

Which isn't likely. Unless you live in Cleveland.

The Talent Show

Bewildering but charming recording of a 1981 combined Boston youth group/nursing home talent show released on an Arf Arf CD in 1996. Sweet, post-Alzheimer crooners, stage-frightened preteens, and geezers who haven't learned a new song since the heyday of vaudeville take their turns at the mic without pretense. Captured for posterity by David Greenberger, of Duplex Planet endeavors. (See Jack Mudurian chapter.)

Jan Terri

The Windy City–based Terri's synth pop is frothy, if unexceptional, but her VHS compilation should be sought and studied by fans of the burgeoning field of outsider music video. Terri has less charisma than a DMV clerk; her production values reflect someone who got her first video cam as a birthday present and hasn't yet figured out what to do with it. Terri and her sidekicks (possibly her family) are clueless regarding how to act in front of a camera—and therein lies the viewing fun. Atrocious lip-synching: mouth movement has no correlation to the lyrics, as if her singing was dubbed in English to mask a foreign language performance.

A correspondent who prefers to remain anonymous writes: "Jan has released three CDs. In the studio, she hums the songs to her 'music guy,' who arranges them and plays accompaniment. At her 'concerts' she simply plays her CD on a boombox and sings solo. Her retired father, who does Elvis and Sammy Davis, Jr., impressions in bars, frequently acts as her 'opening band.' Witnesses have reported seeing numerous jars of pickle juice in various rooms of the Terri household. Until her musical career takes off, Jan works as a limousine driver."

Yo La Tengo covered her "Rock and Roll Santa" at a 1998 Christmas appearance in New York City.

Think
Album entitled *Encounter* (Laurie Records, 1972) tries to bridge generation gap in unintentionally hilarious way. Legendary single, "Once You Understand," dramatizes how when teens can't communicate with their elders and vice versa, kids will take drugs and OD. So goofy it sounds like a parody—*but it's not.*

Gordon Thomas
Charming, albeit incredibly clumsy singer and lyricist backed by competent jazz sidemen who probably owed him favors. Thomas played trombone with Dizzy Gillespie in the 1940s. Decades later he recorded perhaps a half-dozen LPs on his own Samhot label, featuring his joyful, loony-tuneless vocals. Always depicted on LP covers with his trombone, which he *never* seems to play on his albums. Over 50 percent of his original song titles are women's names, though it's uncertain if these were lovers, ex-wives, favorite waitresses, or simply his way of personally thanking each customer who purchased a previous album. Has a strange fascination with the word "good"—as a qualitative measure, it occurs in his lyrics with alarming frequency.

Three Peas in a Podd
Apparently a trio of American Legion Hall troubadours from Michigan, featuring drums, Farfisa organ, and trumpet. The Podds's horn player transcends avant-garde, with wild, uncontrollable high-notes. They sing and play—*transform,* really—such standards as "If I Ruled the World" and "Misty."

Tangela Tricoli
Tricoli, according to a correspondent, was one of the first female jet airliner pilots. And while we don't know if she received salary parity with her male col-

leagues, she apparently earned enough to finance recording a solo album of her songs.

Her 1982 launch, *Jet Lady* (no label), is a musical flight without a crew. Sort of an acoustic Patti Smith with anti-gravity shoes, Tricoli bounces untethered around the musical ionosphere. Melody occasionally vanishes from the radar, and her singing suffers engine trouble attributable to serious structural flaws at the manufacturing stage. Her unforgettable canine diatribe, "Stinky Poodle," steals the show.

Tricoli appears on the LP cover wearing a pilot's cap and officer insignia. The album experiences frequent turbulence and unexpected loss of altitude. As someone once said about Phil Ochs, Tangela plays guitar as if her hand were webbed. There is something (David) Lynchian about this woman.

Herve Villachaize

Two grating, hyper-adenoidal vocal performances on *Children of the World* benefit album (Epic, 1980) hint at career crossover prospects cut short by tragic suicide.

Wayne

Liner notes in their entirety: "After 35 years hitchhiking the homeless highway—and seven more years traipsing the hallways of academia—and still looking good after more than 50 years of hard living—the hobo's first CD: *Wayne—At Last!*" Those hallways of academia—turns out he was sweeping them. In a dispirited but game voice, Wayne sings odes to chiggers, a 1968 mining disaster, and smoking. CD gives phone number for booking information, presumably when it won't interfere with this West Virginian's custodial commitments.

Les Wilson

Loveable, septuagenarian cowgeezer from Portland, Oregon, whose long-term post-WWII military-related mental disorder serves as the perfect excuse for his disorderly recording. A colorful character, Wilson has for years polished a corner barstool at a local pit called Wimpy's. His countrified CD, *Take Me Home*, captures his failed-breathalyzer takes on "Blue Moon," "Jambalaya," "Guadalajara," and other western favorites. Wilson is a tenor who sounds like he shares DNA—and possibly a vocal coach—with the Legendary Stardust Cowboy. He doesn't so much murder a melody as tenderize it with the wooden mallet of

TODD CHATALAS

his voice. Ain't even close to a key, but doesn't seem to care. Technique isn't the point; passion and spirit are.

An early 45 rpm single, recorded with the "Hollywood Hills Orchestra" (say what?), featured a cross-eyed medley of Tin Pan Alley standards "Sleepy Lagoon" and "Tonight We Love." Michelle Boulé testified that when she first heard a tape of this single while being driven to the airport, she laughed so hard she "wet her panties."

Wilson ran for U.S. president in 1976 (according to history books, he lost) and campaigned for Portland City Council President in the late 1990s. His platform was "to legalize prostitution and certain drugs, tax them, and use the proceeds to fund the schools"—proving his politics are more grounded in reality than his singing. The president of his fan club, "Gas Man" Dick Siegler, resigned because he couldn't stand Wilson's music. Apparently, neither could Wilson's fellow residents at the Mt. Scott Adult Care Center where he was transferred in 1997. Harmless cavils, shrugs Les. Life is good: he has an album, a Web site, and a warm barstool waiting at Wimpy's, where his CD is always on the jukebox.

More Candidates for Immortality

All these artists have made at least one record or noteworthy cassette that has been discovered by the outsider collecting network. Remember the names—seek the music.

Trude Adams
Rev. Alecia
Ali Mapo and His Girls
Alvaro and his Singing Nose
Amazing Delores
Amway Singers
Herbie Angell
Anselmo
Kal Anthony and Impalas
Anton Maiden
Tom Arico
Adolph Babel
Kali Bahlu
Tammy Faye Bakker

Jack Barrett
John "Bowtie" Barstow
Owen Baxter, King of Irish Country
   and Western
Edith Bouvier Beale
Steve Bent
Y. Bhekhirst
Bobbejaan
Jerome Bongiorno
Bongo Joe (George Coleman)
Sylvia Boshers
Patricia Brady-Danzig
Calvin Braxton
Stewart Brodian

Patti Brownell
Tex Cameron
James Cannings and Faith
Jerome Carlson
Ellis Chadbourne
Ann Chase
Sharon Cook
Cosmic Lightning
Norman Cox
D'Bush
Daddy Bob
Gert Daigle
Lillay Deay
Jimmy DeSorbo and the Country
   Casuals
Dixon DeVore
Pamela Dickinson
William Dominoe
Donzelli's Group
Arthur Doyle
DQE
Patty Duke
Anne El Bandito
Debbie Ferrar
Isadore Fertel
Howard Finster
Kathy Fire
Giggling Psychopaths
Officer Larry Gillespie
Boruk Glasgow
Ed and Alice Gorin
Roy Henry Alexander Gover
Jess Grant
Melissa Griffith
Arthur G. Grundig
Hansadutta Swami
Troy Hess
Don Howard
Louise Huebner
Abner Jay
Jon

Jr. and the Soulettes
Dania Kara
Fireman William Kieswer
Corey and Richard Klender
Dee Knack
James Kochalka Superstar
La Loca
Sharon LaPrade
Anton Szandor LaVey
Michelle Lemay
Sylvia Lipson
Sam Lipton
Little Lisa
Smiley Manvoor
Marty's Misfits
Ed McMahon
Dean Milan
Rickie Miller
Kadish Millet
Hayley Mills
Queenie Montgomery
Paul "Super Apple" Moralia
Freda Moss
Eddie Murray
Mysterious Clown
Lisa Noto
Larry O'Neill
Don Ohman Sr.
Omo the Hobo
Gen Orange
Dennis Pedevillano
Margie Pet
Richard Peterson
Pneumershonic
Poet and the Picker
Red River Dave
Red Shadow
Nilda Luz Rexach
Jeannie Reynolds
Elvis Don Ringo
Rick Rondone

Nathan Russell
Sam Sachs
Jimmy Sapienza
Telly Savalas
Reed Senta
A. K. Sharif
Frank Sinatra, Jr.
Wooshie Spkamoto
Winston Smart
Rosie Smith
South Bay Surfers
J. D. Sparkman
Michael Owen Sullivan, the Singing
    Irishman

Cookie Thomas
Barry Tiffin
Time Masheen
Bobb Trimble
Up with People
Jimmie R. Vestal
Kay Weaver
Mikey Wild
Gary Wilson
Tom Wilson
Ya Ho Wah 13

AFTERWORD

If you've read this far, it's safe to assume you're a fairly unusual person, inquisitive, perhaps a bit "outside" the mainstream yourself, because outsider music, by definition, offers little of interest to the vast majority of your fellow citizens. They have neither the time nor the curiosity for it.

The spectrum of music to which the average person is exposed—versus the variety of available sonic art—is extremely limited. Yet I don't subscribe to conspiracy theories about the music industry suppressing uncommercial (or *non*-commercial) artists; nor do I believe that the government, the Trilateral Commission, hi-tech audio firms, *Billboard*, radio programming consultants, agents of the Nine Elder Bankers, and David Geffen are in collusion to prevent anyone from exploring the nether reaches of musical marginalia. These lumbering Goliaths aren't concerned with Jandek or Shooby Taylor.

Most consumers simply do not have adventurous taste in music. They're preoccupied with families, careers, and paying bills; home improvements and car repairs; personal vices and health crises; and getting a good night's sleep. Insofar as music plays any role in their lives, they prefer the comfort of familiar artists and recognizable formulas. For that, no one should be faulted. It's a filtering process, necessary to avoid sensory overload. A person who can't appreciate music beyond Air Supply or Jimmy Buffett may have an appetite for exotic food, fine art, or extreme sports. But when they or their progeny get married, they want the festivities resonating with the strains of Billy Joel, Sinatra, Motown oldies, and Madonna. Weddings and bat mitzvahs are not occasions for expanding one's musical horizons, or those of your guests. And yet music provides an important ritualistic function, and I harbor little doubt that pop standards played or performed at these events have great significance to all involved. Captain Beefheart's "Neon Meate Dream of a Octafish" or Wesley Willis's "Shoot Me in the Ass" just won't do.

Yet outsider music does have its place—an intimate, dimly lit enclave. *Songs in the Key of Z* has attempted to air out the dusty attics and damp cellars of the greater music community, while introducing some of the dizzy aunts and eccentric uncles about whom your parents rarely spoke.

Does this book contend that outsiders are "better" than their commercial counterparts?

Of course not.

Are outsiders more "genuine"? This is arguable and hinges on the measure of one's cynicism about packaging and marketing as practiced by the music business. How sincere is Whitney Houston? Megaplatinum stars like Garth Brooks and Mariah Carey are often bad-mouthed by jaded sophisticates as "shallow" and "manufactured," though the same accusation is rarely leveled at a rapper who moves 10 million units and is considered an authentic "voice of the street." Are we to presume that artists who have achieved explosive commercial success did so by accident? That there was no compelling aspiration on their part to become rich and famous?

No one honestly believes that.

So—no, I don't feel that outsiderdom is the exclusive provenance of authenticity.

Nor is ambition solely characteristic of "inside" musicians. Most outsiders would *love* to be certified gold. Some recognize the unlikelihood of such acclaim, others anticipate triumphant breakthroughs any day, and still others seem totally oblivious to the broader public.

The difference rests in the "fingerprint" factor of packaging and selling music. For those exploited through conventional music channels, by the time their product reaches the market it will have been revised, remodeled, and re-coifed; touched-up and tweaked; focus-grouped and Photoshopped. It's Music by Committee.

Consciously commercial releases are targeted at an imagined audience that must be second-guessed: "What will appeal to *them*?" and "Will they *buy* this?" If CDs acknowledged all the cubicle cattle who contributed to production, the list would be endless, like the five minutes of eye-blurring credits that scroll at the conclusion of a motion picture.

Most outsiders don't have a committee at their disposal—and many don't have much of a target audience. Autonomy is often the prevailing modus, the process intensely solipsistic. Outsider efforts thus reflect greater individual control over the final creative contour. This is partly attributable to the low-budget operations of many outsiders, and in some cases to their inability or unwillingness to cooperate with or trust anyone but themselves. It's ironic that the less corporate money at an artist's disposal, the more *singular* the vision.

In this, the outsider represents greater creative purity, something closer to a natural state. Equally ironic, because many outsiders sound perfectly "unnatural." Perhaps "visceral" would be a better adjective to describe the enigmatic outsider process.

This inscrutability—our inability to fully comprehend the internal calculus of outsider art—partly explains its charisma. Art under the microscope, art denuded, is art demystified.

We can listen to outsider music. We can analyze, appreciate, and extol it. But we can never fully understand the odd compulsions and stupefying inner visions of those who create it.

Mainstream and outsider perspectives can be contrasted with two fundamental questions.

To the mainstream artist, the question is: "Where do you get your ideas?" The artist may have an answer, or may not.

As regards the outsider, the question—never asked directly, but always to a third party—is: "What were they thinking?"

This question holds a key to appreciating outsider music. Because it's not really a question—it's a statement in disguise, implying, "The mind that created these unearthly sounds is beyond my grasp."

Hence, "What were they thinking?" can probably never be answered.

Perhaps we should dispense with the question altogether and just listen and enjoy.

AN INCOMPREHENSIVE DISCOGRAPHY

Some LPs have been reissued on CD; for the most part, entries below indicate first issue, regardless of format. Singles, EPs, and compilations containing artist tracks are omitted, unless vitally pertinent. If two years are listed, the second indicates a reissue. For a genre this slippery, an accurate discography is impossible. Did the best I could. Missed a few? Shoot me.

The Shaggs

Philosophy of the World (LP)	Third World	1969
Philosophy of the World (LP reissue)	Red Rooster/Rounder	1980
Shaggs' Own Thing (LP)	Rounder	1982
The Shaggs (CD)	Rounder	1988
Philosophy of the World (CD)	RCA Victor	1999

Tiny Tim

God Bless Tiny Tim	Reprise	1968
Tiny Tim's Second Album	Reprise	1968
For All My Little Friends	Reprise	1969
The Eternal Troubadour	Playback	1986
Tiptoe Through the Tulips/Resurrection	Bear Family	1987
Rock	Regular	1993
I Love Me	Ponk/Seeland	1995
Songs of An Impotent Troubadour	Durtro	1995
Tiny Tim Live in Chicago (with New Duncan Imperials)	Pravda/Bughouse	1995
Tiny Tim's Christmas Album	Durtro	1995
Prisoner of Love	Vinyl Retentive	1995
Girl (with Brave Combo)	Rounder	1996
Unplugged	Tomanna	1996
Live in London	Durtro	1997

Jack Mudurian

Downloading the Repertoire	Arf Arf	1996

Joe Meek

The Joe Meek Story, Vol. 1: 1960	Triumph/Line Music (UK)	1991
I Hear a New World (with the Blue Men)	RPM (UK)	1991
The Joe Meek Story: The Pye Years	Sequel (UK)	1991
The Joe Meek Story, Vol. 2: 1960–61	Triumph/Line Music (UK)	1992
304 Holloway Road—Joe Meek: The Pye Years, Vol. 2	Sequel (UK)	1993
Work in Progress: The Triumph Sessions	RPM (UK)	1994
The Musical Adventures of Joe Meek	Kenwest (UK)	1994
It's Hard to Believe It	Razor & Tie	1995
Joe Meek Presents 304 Holloway Road	Sequel (UK)	1996
Let's Go: Joe Meek's Girls	RPM (UK)	1996

MSR Singers/Song Poems

Beat of the Traps	Carnage Press	1990
The Makers of Smooth Music: MSR Madness Volume 2	Carnage Press	1995
I Died Today: The Music of Rodd Keith	Tzadik	1996
The Human Breakdown of Absurdity: MSR Madness Volume 3	Carnage Press	1997
I'm Just the Other Woman: MSR Madness Volume 4	Carnage Press	1997

Jessie Cherry

"Fair Columbia"	private 78 disc	ca. 1901

Jandek

Ready for the House (as The Units)	Corwood Industries	1978
Six and Six	Corwood Industries	1981
Later On	Corwood Industries	1981
Chair Beside a Window	Corwood Industries	1982
Living In A Moon So Blue	Corwood Industries	1982
Staring at the Cellophane	Corwood Industries	1982
Your Turn to Fall	Corwood Industries	1983
The Rocks Crumble	Corwood Industries	1983
Interstellar Discussion	Corwood Industries	1984
Nine Thirty	Corwood Industries	1985
Foreign Keys	Corwood Industries	1985
Telegraph Melts	Corwood Industries	1986
Follow Your Footsteps	Corwood Industries	1986
Modern Dances	Corwood Industries	1987
Blue Corpse	Corwood Industries	1987
You Walk Alone	Corwood Industries	1988
On the Way	Corwood Industries	1988
The Living End	Corwood Industries	1989
Somebody in the Snow	Corwood Industries	1990
One Foot in the North	Corwood Industries	1991
Lost Cause	Corwood Industries	1992

Twelfth Apostle	Corwood Industries	1993
Graven Image	Corwood Industries	1994
Glad to Get Away	Corwood Industries	1994
White Box Requiem	Corwood Industries	1996
I Woke Up	Corwood Industries	1997
New Town	Corwood Industries	1998
The Beginning	Corwood Industries	1999

Daniel Johnston

Songs of Pain	Stress (cassette only)	1981
Don't Be Scared	Stress (cassette only)	1982
The What of Whom	Stress (cassette only)	1982
More Songs of Pain	Stress (cassette only)	1983
Yip/Jump Music	Stress (cassette only)	1983
Hi, How Are You	Stress (cassette only)	1983
The Lost Recordings Vol. 1	Stress (cassette only)	1983
The Lost Recordings Vol. 2	Stress (cassette only)	1983
Retired Boxer	Stress (cassette only)	1984
Respect	Stress (cassette only)	1985
Continued Story	Stress (cassette only)	1985
Merry Christmas	Stress (cassette only)	1988
Yip/Jump Music	Homestead	1989
Jad Fair and Daniel Johnston (with Jad Fair)	50 Skadillion Watts	1989
Live at SXSW	Stress (cassette only)	1990
1990	Shimmy-Disc	1990
Continued Story/Hi, How Are You	Homestead	1991
Artistic Vice	Shimmy-Disc	1992
Fun	Atlantic	1994
Dead Dog's Eyeball: Songs of Daniel Johnston (by Kathy McCarty)	Bar/None	1994
Rejected Unknown	Which	2000
Why Me?	Trikont	2000

Harry Partch

Plectra and Percussion Dances	Harry Partch Trust Fund	1953
Oedipus	Harry Partch Trust Fund	1954
Plectra and Percussion Dances	Gate 5	1957
Thirty Years of Lyrical & Dramatic Music	Gate 5	1962
The Wayward	Gate 5	1962
Plectra and Percussion Dances	Gate 5	1962
Oedipus (rec. 1954)	Gate 5	1962
The Bewitched—A Dance Satire (rec. 1957)	Gate 5	1962
Revelation in the Courthouse Park	Gate 5	1962
Water! Water! Rotate the Body...	Gate 5	1962
U.S. Highball	Gate 5	1962
And On the 7th Day Petals Fell...	CRI	1967
The Music of Harry Partch	CRI	1967
The World of Harry Partch	Columbia Masterworks	1968

SAN DIEGO ENSEMBLE

New Music for Trumpet (includes "Ulysses Departs from the Edge of the World")	Orion	1971
The World of Harry Partch (Quadraphonic)	Columbia Masterworks	1972
Delusion of the Fury (rec. 1969)	Columbia Masterworks	1972
The Bewitched—A Dance Satire (rec. 1957)	CRI	1973
Harry Partch / John Cage (one side devoted to each composer)	New World	1978

AMER. MUSIC THEATRE

Revelation in the Courthouse Park	Tomato	1989
The Music of Harry Partch	CRI	1989

NEWBAND

Play Microtonal Works by Partch & others (includes "Studies on Ancient Greek Scales")	Mode	1990

AMER. FESTIVAL OF MICROTONAL MUSIC ENSEMBLE

Between the Keys: Microtonal Masterpieces of the 20th Century (includes "Yankee Doodle Fantasy")	Newport Classics	1992
The Composer/Performer CRI retrospective (includes "The Letter")	CRI	1994

NEWBAND

Play Microtonal Works by Partch & others (includes "Daphne of the Dunes")	Mode	1994
Enclosure 2: Historic Speech—Music Recordings from the Partch Archives	Innova	1995

TED MOOK/STEPHEN KALM

17 Lyrics of Li Po	Tzadik	1995

KRONOS QUARTET

Howl (includes *Barstow*; arranged by Ben Johnston)	Elektra Nonesuch	1996

NEWBAND

Dance of the Seven Veils (includes "Castor and Pollux")	Music & Arts	1996
The Harry Partch Collection, Vol. 1	CRI	1997
The Harry Partch Collection, Vol. 2	CRI	1997
The Harry Partch Collection, Vol. 3	CRI	1997
The Harry Partch Collection, Vol. 4	CRI	1997
Gay American Composers Vol. 2 (includes "Ulysses at the Edge")	CRI	1997
Enclosure 5: On an Ancient Greek Theme	Innova	1998
Enclosure 6: Delusion of the Fury	Innova	1999

Wesley Willis

Radiohead	Wesley Willis Records	1993
Prisonshake	Wesley Willis Records	1994
Rev. Norb	Wesley Willis Records	1994
Rev. Norb 2	Wesley Willis Records	1994
Machine Gun Kelly	Wesley Willis Records	1994
Double Door	Wesley Willis Records	1994
Mr. Magoo Goes to Jail	Wesley Willis Records	1994
Dr. Wax	Wesley Willis Records	1995
Rock Power	Wesley Willis Records	1995
Spookydisharmonious Conflicthellride (The Wesley Willis Fiasco)	Urban Legends	1995
Drag Disharmony	Wesley Willis Records	1995
Wesley Willis' Greatest Hits, Vol. 1	Alternative Tentacles	1995
Wesley Willis, Wesley Willis	Fuse	1995
Fireman Rick	Wesley Willis Records	1995
Daren Hacker	Wesley Willis Records	1995
Delilah's	Wesley Willis Records	1995
Atomic Records	Ghetto Love	1995
Jason Rau	Wesley Willis Records	1996
Tammy Smith	Wesley Willis Records	1996
Fabian Road Warrior	American	1996
Black Light Diner	Fuse	1996
Mr. Magoo Goes to Jail Vol. 1	Wesley Willis Records	1996
Mr. Magoo Goes to Jail Vol. 2	Wesley Willis Records	1996
Mr. Magoo Goes to Jail Vol. 3	Typhoid Mary	1996
Rock 'n' Roll Will Never Die	Oglio	1996
New York, New York	Wesley Willis Records	1996
Feel the Power	American	1996
Metal Clink Punishment Jail	Wesley Willis Records	1997
Rock 'n' Roll Jack Flash (Wesley and the Dragnews)	Wesley Willis Records	1998
SMD Promotions	Fuse	1998
Wesley Willis' Greatest Hits, Vol. 2	Alternative Tentacles	1999
Joe Hunter 2	Wesley Willis Records	2000

Syd Barrett

The Piper at the Gates of Dawn (Pink Floyd)	Columbia	1967
A Saucerful of Secrets (Pink Floyd)	Columbia	1968
The Madcap Laughs	Harvest (UK)	1970
Barrett	Harvest (UK)	1970
Relics (reissue comp., Pink Floyd)	Starline	1971
Syd Barrett (repackage of two Barrett solo LPs)	Harvest (UK)	1974
Masters of Rock (reissue comp., Pink Floyd)	Harvest (UK)	1974
The Peel Sessions	Strange Fruit	1983

Opel	Harvest (UK)	1988
Crazy Diamond (3-album boxed set)	Harvest (UK)	1993

Eilert Pilarm

Elvis I	private cassette	1992
Eilert Pilarm sjunger Elvis II	private cassette	1993
Elvis III	private cassette	1994
Eilert Pilarm's Greatest Hits	Green Pig Prods.	1996
Eilert Is Back	Green Pig Prods.	1998

Lucia Pamela

Into Outer Space with Lucia Pamela (LP)	Gulfstream	1969
Into Outer Space . . . (LP reissue)	L'Peg	1978
Into Outer Space . . . (CD)	Arf Arf	1991

Captain Beefheart

Safe As Milk	Kama Sutra/Buddah	1967/1970
Strictly Personal	Blue Thumb	1968
Trout Mask Replica	Straight/Reprise	1969/1970
Lick My Decals Off, Baby	Straight/Reprise	1970/1970
Mirror Man	Buddah	1970
Clear Spot	Reprise	1972
The Spotlight Kid	Reprise	1972
Unconditionally Guaranteed	Mercury	1974
Bluejeans and Moonbeams	Mercury	1975
Bongo Fury (with Frank Zappa)	Discreet	1975
Shiny Beast (Bat Chain Puller)	WB	1978
Doc at the Radar Station	Virgin	1980
Ice Cream for Crow	Virgin	1982
Legendary A&M Sessions	A&M	1984
Grow Fins: Rarities (1965–1982)	Revenant	1999
The Dust Blows Forward	Rhino	1999

Shooby Taylor   no commercial releases

Florence Foster Jenkins

The Glory (????) of the Human Voice	RCA Red Seal	1962

The Legendary Stardust Cowboy

"Paralyzed" c/w "Who's Knocking on My Door"	Psycho-Suavé; Mercury (45)	1968
"I Took a Trip (On a Gemini Spaceship)" c/w "Down in the Wrecking Yard"	Mercury (45)	1969
"Kiss & Run" c/w "Everything's Gettin' Bigger But Our Love"	Mercury (45)	1969
Rock-It to Stardom (LP)	Luna/Amazing	1984
"Standing in a Trashcan" c/w "My Underwear Froze to the Clothesline"	Spider (45)	1987

Retro Rocket Back to Earth (LP)	Spider/New Rose	1986/1987
The Legendary Stardust Cowboy		
Rides Again (CD)	New Rose	1990
"Relaxation" c/w "I Ride a Tractor"	Norton (45)	1991
"I Hate CDs" c/w "Linda"	Norton (45)	1992
Retro Rocket Back to Earth/Rides Again	Last Call	1996
Live in Chicago	Pravda	1999

Robert Graettinger
All by Stan Kenton Orchestra except
   where noted

"Thermopylae"	Capitol 78 rpm	1947
"Everything Happens to Me"	Capitol 78 rpm	1949
A Concert in Progressive Jazz		
(includes "Thermopylae")	Capitol	
Innovations in Modern Music		
(includes "Incident in Jazz")	Capitol	1950
Kenton Presents		
(includes "House of Strings")	Capitol	1950
City of Glass	Capitol (10")	1951
The Kenton Era (includes "Modern Opus"		
and "You Go To My Head")	Capitol	1952
City of Glass/This Modern World	Capitol	1953

The Ebony Big Band

City of Glass: Robert Graettinger	Channel Crossings (Holland)	1994
The Ebony Big Band: Live at the		
Paradiso—Robert Graettinger	Channel Crossings (Holland)	1998

B. J. Snowden

Life in the USA and Canada	DeMilo	1996

Wild Man Fischer

An Evening with Wild Man Fischer	Bizarre/Straight	1969
Wildmania	Rhino	1977
Pronounced Normal	Rhino	1981
Nothing Scary	Rhino	1984
Sings Popular Songs		
(rec. 1974, with Smegma)	Birdman	1997
The Fischer King	Rhino Handmade	1999

SNAPSHOTS IN SOUND

Hasil Adkins

Out to Hunch	Norton	1986
The Wild Man	Norton	1987
Peanut Butter Rock and Roll	Norton	1990
Moon Over Madison	Norton	1990
Look at That Caveman Go!	Norton (LP/CD)	1993
Live in Chicago	Bughouse	1993

Achy Breaky Ha Ha	Norton	1994
What the Hell Was I Thinking	Fat Possum	1997

Alvaro

Drinkin My Own Sperm (rec. 1977)	Squeaky Shoes (LP/CD)	1977/1997
Mums Milk Not Powder	Squeaky Shoes	1978
The Working Class	Squeaky Shoes	1979
Four Sad Songs	Squeaky Shoes (cassette only)	1981
Repetition Kills	Squeaky Shoes	1982

Leona Anderson

Music to Suffer By	RKO-Unique	ca. 1953

Arcesia

Reachin'	Alpha	ca. 1970

Tom Arico

Born and Raised on Rock 'n' Roll	Northwind	1989
The Preacher	Northwind	1998

David Arvedon

The Best of David Arvedon	no label	1971
The Most Unforgettable Tree We Ever Met (rec. 1968–74)	Arf Arf	1996

Frances Baskerville (aka Francis Cannon), The Singing Psychic

Songs from Cannonville	Cannon Productions	1985
The Singing Psychic	Cannon Productions	1987
Songs from Beyond	no label	1999

Patricia Brady-Danzig

A Woman's Life in Love	PBD	1999

Stewart Brodian

Self Made Man	Mountain Records	1983

Brute Force

Confections of Love	Columbia	1968
The Extemporaneous Brute Force	B.T. Puppy	1971

George Coleman/Bongo Joe

Bongo Joe (rec. 1968)	Arhoolie (LP/CD)	1969/1991

Cosmic Lightning

Music for Fans, Vol. 1	Destruction	1987

Del Rubio Triplets

Whip It	no label	1991
Three Gals, Three Guitars	Del Rubio	1994
Jingle Belles	Del Rubio	1996
Anthology	Duve	1999

Roky Erickson

The Magic of the Pyramids	Collectables	1975
Roky Erickson & The Aliens	CBS	1980
The Evil One	Restless	1981
Don't Slander Me	Restless	1986
Gremlins Have Pictures	Pink Dust	1986
Casting the Runes	Five Hours Bac	1987
Holiday Inn Tapes	Fan Club	1987
I Think of Demons	Edsel	1987
Openers	Five Hours Bac	1988
Live at the Ritz 1987	Fan Club	1988
Reverend of Karmic Youth	Skyclad	1990
You're Gonna Miss Me	Restless	1991
1966–1967 Unreleased Masters Collection	Collectables	1994
All That May Do My Rhyme	Trance Syndicate	1995
Roky Erickson & Evilhook Wildlife	Sympathy for the Record Ind.	1995
Demon Angel: A Day & Night With Roky	Triple X	1995
Never Say Goodbye	Emperor Jones	1999
Live at the Ritz	New Rose	1999
Beauty & the Beast	Sympathy for the Record Ind.	1999

Howard Finster

The Night Howard Finster Got Saved	Global Village	1997

Bingo Gazingo

Bingo Gazingo	WFMU	1997

Giggling Psychopaths

Dance with Giggling Psychopaths	Caramel	1967

Ed & Alice Gorin

Street Is Neat	Cruisin' Music	1982

Roy Henry Alexander Gover (aka RHAG)

Life Goes On	Tractor Beam	1997

Sri Darwin Gross

It Just Is	Eckankar	1972
Golden Thread	Sounds of Soul	1986

Peter Grudzien

The Unicorn	P.G./Parallel World	1974/1995

Kenneth Higney

Attic Demonstration	Kebrutney	1977

Charles Ives

Ives Plays Ives	CRI	1999

Abner Jay

The True Story of Dixie	Brandie	late 1960s
Terrible Comedy Blues	Poison Apple	ca. 1970
Swaunee Water and Cocaine Blues	Brandie	ca. 1970
The Backbone of America Is a		
Mule and Cotton: American Classics	Brandie	1976

Jon

Smoke	Tzadik	1996

Jr. & His Soulettes

Psychodelic Sounds	HMM	1971

Jessica Kane

Varicose Days	Mekkatone	1996

Kaplan Brothers

Universal Sounds	Kap	1968
Nightbird	Quinton	1978

Kids of Widney High

Special Music From Special Kids	Rounder	1989
Let's Get Busy	Ipecac	1999

David Koresh

Voice of Fire	Junior's Motel	1994

Ray Korona Band

$5 Working People's Music Tape	Hobo Star	1998

Anton Szandor LaVey

Strange Music	(10" vinyl)	

Luie Luie

El Touchy	Penstar	ca. 1980

Fergus macRoy

Fergus macRoy at the Homestead Upright	Kilmarnock	
Almost an Hour With . . .	Kilmarnock	1979
Fergus macRoy (Mystic)	Kilmarnock	

Charles Manson

Lie: The Love and Terror Cult	Awareness	1970
Commemoration (rec. 1982–85)	White Devil	1995
Unplugged 9/11/67 Vol. 1	Archer Prods.	
The Family Jams (members of Manson		
family singing CM songs, rec. 1970)	Aoroa	1997
Manson Speaks	White Devil	
The Way of the Wolf	Pale Horse	

Jim Noste

Songs for You, Vols. 1 & 2 (&3?)	Island Home Center	1980s

**Congress-Woman [sic] Malinda
  Jackson Parker**
Tubman Goodtype Songs of Liberia   no label   ca. 1971

Washington Phillips
I Am Born to Preach the Gospel   Yazoo   1991

Pneumershonic
Frequencies of the Beast   Tray Full of Lab Mice   1996

Palmer Rockey
Palmer Rockey's Scarlet Love   A-B Rock Music   1980

"Dusty Roads" Rowe
*Always Raring to Go Hope You Will
  Enjoy This Album As He Travels
  to and Fro*   no label

San Lucas Band
Music of Guatemala   ABC Command   ca. 1975

Alexander "Skip" Spence
Oar   Columbia / Sundazed   1969/1999
*More Oar: A Tribute to the Skip
  Spence Album*   Birdman   1999

Joseph Spence
Happy All the Time (rec. 1964)   Hannibal
The Complete Folkways Recordings (1958)   Smithsonian/Folkways   1992
The Spring of Sixty-Five   Rounder/DNA   1992
Glory   Rounder/DNA   1992
Living on the Hallelujah Side   Rounder/DNA   1992
Good Morning, Mr. Walker   Arhoolie   1993

Supie T.
*Getdown Airwaves . . . Coming to
  a Radio Near You*   Spazz Action   1996

Jan Terri
Baby Blues   JT Records   1993
High Risk   JT Records   1994
The Wild One   JT Records   1998

Gordon Thomas
Brown Baby   Samhot   1984
Gordon   Samhot   1984
Gordon Thomas   Samhot   1987

Bobb Trimble
Iron Curtain Innocence   no label   1980
Harvest of Dreams   Bobb   1982
Jupiter Transmission   Parallel World   1995

Wayne
Wayne—At Last!	no label	1999

Gary Wilson
You Think You Really Know Me	no label	1977

Les Wilson
Take Me Home	Folk You	1995

Tom Wilson
All-American Boy	Aboveground	1982

Ya Ho Wah 13
(nine albums and three singles)	various labels	1973–78 (?)
God and Hair (13-CD boxed set)	Captain Trip (Japan)	1999

Various Artists
God Less America	CW	1995
Hollerin' (rural Festival from North Carolina)	Rounder	1976
Kenny Everett Presents the World's Worst Record Show	Yuk (UK)	1978
Lyrics By Ernest Noyes Brookings V. 1	Shimmy-Disc (LP)	1989
Lyrics By Ernest Noyes Brookings V. 2: Place Of General Happiness	ESD	1991
Lyrics By Ernest Noyes Brookings V. 3: Delicacy & Nourishment	ESD	1992
Lyrics By Ernest Noyes Brookings V. 4: Outstandingly Ignited	ESD	1995
Only In America	Arf Arf	1995
The Talent Show	Arf Arf	1996

AN INCOMPREHENSIVE BIBLIOGRAPHY

there is a dearth of available literature for many outsider artists. Most entries below are book references. Some academic journals have been included.

Web sites often contain bibliographies of articles originally published in popular and obscure journals. Keep in mind that Web site URLs change occasionally. Search engines can locate additional sites and Web pages about these artists, and many on-line CD retailers may have profiles on particular artists.

Album liner notes have not been included but are excellent sources of information about particular artists. See accompanying discography.

For updated Web links and the latest in the world of Outsider Music, check in at www.keyofz.com.

General—Outsider Music
Moore, Ron. *Underground Sounds*, 2nd ed. Self-published, 1998. (Available from P.O. Box 90635, Austin, TX 78709.)
Unterberger, Richie. *Unknown Legends of Rock 'n' Roll: Psychedelic Unknowns, Mad Geniuses, Punk Pioneers, Lo-Fi Mavericks & More*. Miller Freeman, 1998.
Vale, V., and Andrea Juno. *Incredibly Strange Music*. RE/Search Publications, 1993.
Vale, V., and Andrea Juno. *Incredibly Strange Music, Vol. II*. RE/Search Publications, 1994.
Weisbard, Eric, and Craig Marks. *The SPIN Alternative Record Guide*. Vintage/Random House, 1995.
Outsider Music Mailing List
wlt4.home.mindspring.com/outsider.htm

General—Outsider Art and Visionaries
A World of Their Own: Twentieth Century American Folk Art. The Newark Museum, 1995.

Beardsley, John. *Gardens of Revelation: Environments by Visionary Artists.* Abbeville Press, 1995.

Dinsmoor, S. P. *Pictorial History of the Cabin Home in the Garden of Eden, Lucas, Kansas.* Self-published, 1927. (Still available at landmark site.)

Finster, Howard. *Man of Visions.* Peachtree Publishers, 1989.

Finster, Howard. *Stranger from Another World—Man of Visions Now on This Earth.* Abbeville Press, 1989.

Horwitz, Elinor Lander. *Contemporary American Folk Artists.* J. B. Lippincott, 1975.

Kossey, Donna. *Kooks: A Guide to the Outer Limits of Belief.* Feral House, 1994.

Maizels, John. *Raw Creation: Outsider Art and Beyond.* Phaidon Press, 1996.

Maresca, Frank and Roger Ricco. *American Self-Taught: Paintings and Drawings by Outsider Artists.* Knopf, 1993.

Morgenthaler, Walter. *Madness and Art: The Life and Works of Adolf Wölfli.* Translated by Aaron Esman. University of Nebraska Press, 1992.

Oakes, John G. H. *In the Realm of the Unreal: "Insane" Writings.* Four Walls Eight Windows Press, 1991.

Shaw, Jim. *Thrift Store Paintings.* Heavy Industry Publications, 1990.

Tuchman, Maurice, and Carol S. Eliel. *Parallel Visions: Modern Artists and Outsider Art.* Los Angeles County Museum of Art/Princeton University Press, 1992.

Vertikoff, Alexander, and Mal Sharpe and Sandra Sharpe. *Weird Rooms.* Pomegranate Artbooks, 1996.

Wang, Harvey. *Holding on: Dreamers, Visionaries, Eccentrics, and Other American Heroes.* W. W. Norton and Co., 1995.

Weeks, David, and Jamie James. *Eccentrics: A Study of Sanity and Strangeness.* Villard Books, 1995.

Yelen, Alice Rae. *Passionate Visions of the American South: Self-Taught Artists from 1940 to the Present.* New Orleans Museum of Art/University Press of Mississippi, 1993.

The Shaggs

Helen Wiggin, interview by Lisa Carver, in *Roller Derby*, #20, 1997.

Schinder, Scott and the Editors of Rolling Stone Press. *Alt-Rock-A-Rama.* Delta, 1996.

www.cgocable.net/~focus23/shaggs/index.html

www.shaggs.com

Tiny Tim

Olmack, Heidi. "Death of a Soul Man." *Hermenaut*, No. 11/12, 1998.

Stein, Harry. *Tiny Tim: An Unauthorized Biography.* Playboy Press, 1976.

www.tinytim.org/

www.ponk.com/tinytim.htm

Jack Mudurian
Greenberger, David. *The Duplex Planet* (periodical). (Available from P.O. Box 1230, Saratoga Springs, NY 12866.)

Joe Meek
Chusid, Irwin. *The Big Book of Losers.* Paradox Press, 1997.
Repsch, John. *The Legendary Joe Meek.* Woodford House, 1989.
Joe Meek Appreciation Society, (U.K.) c/o 89 Hardy Crescent, Wimborne, Dorset, BH 21 2AR, England; (U.S.) 171 Lakeshore Court, Richmond, CA 94804
www.concentric.net/~meekweb/telstar.htm
www.geocities.com/SunsetStrip/Studio/4085/

MSR/Song Poems
www.aspma.com
www.wfmu.org/LCD/LCD_Articles/LCD_18/rodd.html

The Cherry Sisters
Acton, Lord Richard, and Patricia Nassif Acton. "The Cherry Sisters: A Case of Libel," *To Go Free: A Treasury of Iowa's Legal Heritage.* Iowa University Press/Ames, 1995.
Cherry, Effie Isabell. *The Blacksmith's Daughter (A Novel)* and *The Autobiography of the Cherry Sisters.* Unpublished, early 1920s.
Fuller, Steven J. "The Cherry Sisters," *The Palimpsest.* Vol. 60, No. 4, July/August 1979.
Gartner, Michael. "Fair Comment," *American Heritage.* Oct/Nov. 1982.
Rennie (Orville and Jane) Collection, Archives of the State Historical Society of Iowa, Iowa City, IA.
Slide, Anthony. *The Vaudevillians: A Dictionary of Vaudeville Performers.* Arlington House, 1981.

Jandek
www.cs.nwu.edu/~tisue/jandek/

Daniel Johnston
Yazdani, Tarssa, *Hi, How Are You?: The Definitive Daniel Johnston Handbook,* Soft Skull Press, 2000.
www.neosoft.com/~rockme/DJ/
www.hihowareyou.com/

Harry Partch
Blackburn, Philip. *Enclosure 3: Harry Partch.* American Composers Forum, 1997.

Dunn, David. *Harry Partch: An Anthology of Critical Perspectives.* Warren and
   Gooch, 1998.
Gilmore, Bob. *Harry Partch: The Early Vocal Works, 1930–33.* British Harry
   Partch Society, 1996.
Gilmore, Bob. *Harry Partch: A Biography.* Yale University Press, 1998.
Harry Partch Archives, Music Library, University of Illinois at Champaign-
   Urbana, Champaign-Urbana, IL.
McGeary, Thomas. *Harry Partch: A Descriptive Catalog.* I.S.A.M., 1991.
McGeary, Thomas, ed. *Harry Partch—Bitter Music: Collected Journals, Essays,
   Introductions, and Librettos.* University of Illinois Press, 1991.
Partch, Harry. *Genesis of a Music.* Da Capo Press, 1997 (orig. 1949; rev.
   1974).
www.spyral.net/newband/
www.corporeal.com/

Syd Barrett
Palacios, Julian. *Lost in the Woods.* Boxtree/MacMillan, 1998.
www.inkyfingers.com/TERRAPINS/Terrapins.html
rosolini.net/musica/syd/index4.html
members.aol.com/pgrsel/barrett/index.htm
www.geocities.com/SunsetStrip/Stage/2607/
www.geocities.com/Vienna/Strasse/2724/
www.pink-floyd.org/barrett/
www.fuzzlogic.com/argus/b/Barrett%2CSyd.shtml

Eilert Pilarm
www.algonet.se/~pergunne/eilert.html

Lucia Pamela
www.pandemic.com/lucia/

Captain Beefheart
Barnes, Mike. *Captain Beefheart: Alias Don Van Vliet.* Quartet Books, 2000.
Charlesworth, Chris, ed. *Frank Zappa: In His Own Words.* Omnibus Press,
   1993.
Cruikshank, Ben. *Fast And Bulbous: The Captain Beefheart Story.* Agenda,
   1996.
Ferrari, Luca. *Pearls Before Swine—Ice Cream for Crows.* Sonic Books, 1996.
French, John. *Beefheart: Through the Eyes of Magic,* self-published, 2000.
Harkleroad, Bill. *Lunar Notes: Zoot Horn Rollo's Captain Beefheart Experience.*
   SAF Publishing, 1998.

Slaven, Neil. *Zappa: Electric Don Quixote.* Omnibus Press, 1996.

Van Vliet, Don. *Captain Beefheart: Skeleton Breath, Scorpion Blush.* Gachnang and Springer, 1987.

Van Vliet, Don. *Stand Up and Be Discontinued.* Cantz, 1993.

Watson, Ben. *Frank Zappa: The Negative Dialectics of Poodle Play.* Quartet Books Ltd., 1995.

www.shiningsilence.com/hpr/

www.beefheart.com/index.html

Florence Foster Jenkins

Limansky, Nicholas. *The Incomparable Diva: Florence Foster Jenkins and Her Disputed Rivals, Dame Olive Middleton & Madame Mari Lyn* (LP liner notes). Legendary Recordings, circa 1985.

Robinson, Francis. *The Glory [????] of the Human Voice* (LP liner notes). RCA Victor Records, 1962.

Weeks, David, and Jamie James. *Eccentrics: A Study of Sanity and Strangeness.* Villard Books, 1995.

Legendary Stardust Cowboy

www.hear.com/paralyzed/

Robert Graettinger

Easton, Carol. *Straight Ahead: The Story of Stan Kenton.* William Morrow and Co., 1973.

Morgan, Robert Badgett. "The Music and Life of Robert Graettinger." Dissertation, University of Illinois, 1974.

Stan Kenton Collection, Music Library, University of North Texas, Denton, TX.

Wild Man Fischer

Eichhorn, Dennis, and J. R. Williams. *Real Stuff.* Fantagraphics Books, 1993.

www.erie.net/~bbelovar/wildman/

darkwing.uoregon.edu/~splat/Wild_Man_Fischer.html

Other Artist Links

Hasil Adkins

members.tripod.com/~Hasil_Adkins/

www.iserv.net/~jakeb/hazemain.html

Stewart Brodian

abbeyrd.com/brodian/

Frances (Cannon) Baskerville, The Singing Psychic
www.singingpsychic.com/

Del Rubio Triplets
www.geocities.com/WestHollywood/3331/

Roky Erickson
highrise.freeservers.com/rerickson.htm

Heino
www.geocities.com/Hollywood/5991/

J and H Productions
www.geocities.com/Athens/1885/jhhome.html

Rod McKuen
www.cyberhost4.com/vitalinf/link.htm
fairyweb.com/mckuen.htm

Erik Satie
www.af.lu.se/~fogwall/intro.html

South Bay Surfers
www.andyland.com/surf.htm

Les Wilson
www.teleport.com/~beater/leswilson.shtml

PERMISSIONS

Prologue "The Little Black Egg" by Chuck Conlon/ASCAP. Copyright control c/o Sylvan Wells. All rights reserved.

The Shaggs "Philosophy of the World" and "Who Are Parents" by Dorothy Mae Wiggin © 1969 by Music Sales Corp. (ASCAP) and Hi Varieties Music (ASCAP). All rights administered worldwide by Music Sales Corp. International copyright secured. All rights reserved. Reprinted by permission.

Tiny Tim "Jessica Hahn" by Tiny Tim © 1995. Copyright control.

Joe Meek "Doopy Darling" by Robert Duke/aka Joe Meek © 1960 by Ivy Music Ltd. International copyright secured. All rights reserved. Reprinted by permission of Music Sales Corp.

Jandek "Naked in the Afternoon," "Don't Know If I Care," and "Look at It" by Jandek © Corwood Industries.

Daniel Johnston "Never Relaxed" and "Cold Hard World" by Daniel Johnston © Eternal Yip Eye Music (BMI). All rights reserved.

Syd Barrett "Bike," words and music by Syd Barrett, © 1971 (Renewed) and 1980 Westminster Music International Ltd., London, England; TRO-Essex Music, Inc., New York, controls all publication rights for the USA and Canada. Used by permission. "Jugband Blues," words and music by Syd Barrett, © 1968 (Renewed) and 1980 Westminster Music Ltd., London, England; TRO-Essex Music International, Inc., New York, controls all publication rights for the USA and Canada. Used by permission. "Lucifer Sam," words and music

ACKNOWLEDGMENTS

Some sections of this book originally appeared in different form in the *New York Press* and *Tower Pulse*.

"Transistor Under My Pillow" was adapted from a monologue delivered at the St. Mark's Poetry Project in NYC as part of the series *Epiphany Albums: The Record That Changed My Life*. Thanks to Gillian McCain for the inspiration.

The Shaggs chapter appeared in very condensed form as the liner notes to *Philosophy of the World* (RCA Victor 09026-63371-2).

The Joe Meek chapter appeared in different form in *DISCoveries*.

The Jandek chapter appeared in condensed form in WFMU's program guide *Lowest Common Denominator #22*.

The Lucia Pamela chapter originally appeared in condensed form as the liner notes to *Into Outer Space with Lucia Pamela* (Arf Arf Records AA-037).

Thanks to: Jean and Morris Chusid; WFMU; John Strausbaugh/*NY Press;* Jackson Brian Griffith/*Pulse;* Erik Lindgren; Ken Swezey & Laura Lindgren; Celia Fuller; Ken Freedman; Brian Turner; David Greenberger; Phil Milstein; Richie Unterberger; R. Stevie Moore; Rosemary Chinnock; Shelley and Larry Orchier; Jeff Winner; Jim Shaw; Scott Lindgren; Dawn Eden; David Newgarden; Lou Smith; Kirk Biglione; Chip Rosenbloom; Terry Adams; Citizen Kafka; Michael Arlt; Peter Pickow; Piet Schreuders; Carolyn Dorsey; Danielle LeMaire; Jeff Roth; Ron English; Steve Liesch; Terry Sneed; Steve Shelley; Ellery Eskelin; Dionne Eskelin; Robin Edgerton; Katy Vine; Amy Anderson; Dan Anderson; Rich Hazelton; J. R. Williams; Mark Martin; Josh Tanzer; Tony Philputt; Marlies Dwyer; Evelyn Sasko; Paul Major; George Petros; Ron Moore; and Sylvan Wells.

For above-and-beyond editorial wisdom: PETER KEEPNEWS, XTINE, HEATHER OGILVIE, and RITA BALADAD.

Many of this book's subjects express thanks to God.

Special thanks to DON BROCKWAY for advice, editing, leads, insights, mentoring, swiped punchlines, and occasional counseling over the years.

To MICHELLE BOULÉ for codeveloping the Incorrect Music Archives.

And to YUVAL TAYLOR for casually asking if I felt like writing a book.

Thanks to the following artists for original illustrations:

Steve Bissette (Captain Beefheart); Greg Carter (cover); Walt Holcombe (Tiny Tim); Daniel Johnston; Mark Martin (Wesley Willis; Song Poems); Patrick Moriarity (Wild Man Fischer); Lucia Pamela; Sean Taggart (Syd Barrett); Wayno (Shooby Taylor); J. R. Williams (Legendary Stardust Cowboy); and Curtis Woodbridge (Florence Foster Jenkins).

INDEX

Page numbers in *italic* refer to illustrations.

A

ABC Command, 223
ABC Records, 7
Abdabs, 103
Adams, Dave, 28, 31–32, 33, 35
Adams, Terry, 2, 5, 9
"Adele's Laughing Song," 151, 152
Adkins, Hasil, 155, 199
"After My Buddies Got Killed in 'Nam," 226
"Ain't No Woman Gonna Make a George Jones Outta Me," 69
Air, 39
Albam, Manny, 167
Alexander the Grape, 225
Alice in Chains, 94
Allen, Daevid, 102
"All Shook Up," 115
All the Hits, Vol. 2, 31
Alpha Records, 125, 200
Alternative Tentacles, 94, 96
Always Raring to Go Hope You Will Enjoy This Album as He Travels to and Fro, 222, 223
Amazing Grace, 142
Amazing Records, 162, 163
American, 96
Anderson, Leona, 199–200
And on the 7th Day Petals Fell in Petaluma, 86
Angel Sound Studios, 142
Animals, The, 27
"Apology at Bedtime," 203

"Apples and Oranges," 106
A.R.C., 199
Arcesia, 200–1
Arcessi, Johnny, 200–1
Ardolino, Tom, 38, 39–40
Arf Arf Records, 22, 24, 125, 227
Arhoolie, 224
"Arnold Layne," 102, 104
Art Bears, 130
"Artistry in Rhythm," 166
Arvedon, David, 201
Ashley Hutchings Big Beat Combo, 31
"Astronomy Domine," 103
"Astrouniverse," 43
Atlantic Records, 76
"At the Time," 41–42
Attic Demonstration, 209, 209–10
Ayers, Kevin, 102

B

"Baby Lemonade," 109
"Bad Penny Blues," 28
Baker, Ken, 169
Balin, Marty, 224
"Ballad of MacLeod, Best, and Banting, The," 41
Barnes and Barnes, 195, 196
Bar/None, 70
Barrett, 108–9, 112
Barrett, Syd, *100,* 101–13, *108*
Barstow, 87, 90
"Basic Fischer, The," 191
Baskerville, Frances, 201–2

Beach Boys, 215
Bear Family, 19
Beat Happening, 11
Beatles, 14, 20, 104
Beat of the Traps, 38
Beattie, Brian, 76
Beckley, Gerry, 195
"Bell Song," 151
Berry, Mike, 30
Between the Buttons, 103
Bewitched, The, 86
"Biassy," 151
"Bike," 104–5
Billy, 3
Birdman Records, 225
Bizarre, 135, 191
Blake, Bobbi, 39
Blast First, 75
Bloch, Ernst, 84
Blom, Gert-Jan, 176
Blue Cat, 16
Blue Corpse, 57, 62
"Blue Hawaii," 115
Bluejeans and Moonbeams, 138
"Blue Moon," 229
Bolan, Marc, 102
Bongo Fury, 138
Bon Jovi, 94
Book of Life, The, 219
"Boola Boola," 22
"Bosom Friend," 24
Bowie, David, 32, 102, 155, 164
Bradley, Craig, 142, 144–46
Brave Combo, 19, 20
Brother Cleve, 19
Brubeck, Dave, 167
Brute Force, 203
Buck, Mike, 162
Buckley, Tim, 191
Bunnell, Dewey, 195
Burke, Solomon, 190
Burnett, James "Big Bucks," 20
Burnett, T-Bone, 159–60
Burns, Norm, 39
Burt, Heinz, 30, 32
Butler, Chris, 129, 205
"Butterfly Mind," 200
Butthole Surfers, 70, 155, 205
Byrne, David, 197

C

Cage, John, 84, 85
Cameo, 31
"Candy-Ass Lover," 208
Cannon, Frances, 201–2
"Can't Love That Woman," 209–10
Capitol Records, 175
Captain Beefheart, 10, *128*, 129–40, *136*, 190, 191, 197
Captain Howdy, 24
Caravan, 102
Cargo, 95
Carnage Press, 38, 42
Carpenters, 8
Carter, Benny, 169
"Casper," 70
"Catie," 76
Cats and Jammers, 95
Cattini, Clem, 30, 31
"Cease to Exist," 215
"Cello, A," 176
Chadbourne, Eugene, 19
Chair Beside a Window, 57
Charalambides, 62
"Charmant Oiseau," 151
Cherry, Addie, 46–55, *47, 53*
Cherry, Effie, 46–55, *47, 52, 53*
Cherry, Elizabeth, 46–55
Cherry, Ella, 46–55
Cherry, Jessie, 46–55, *47*
Cherry Sisters, 46–55
"Chicago (That Toddlin' Town)," 24
"Chicken Is Nice with Palm Butter," 220
Chiffons, 203
"Children of Sound," 209
Children of the World, 229
Chipmunks, 203
Christian Con Man, 203
Christian Con Man Goes Hawaiian, 203
Christy, June, 170
"Church Needs Good Deacons, The," 221
"Circle," 192
"Cities' Hospital Patients," 38
City of Glass, 42, 169, 170–71, 175–76
Clapton, Eric, 191
Clash, 130
"Clavelitos," 152
Clear Spot, 134, 137

"Click Your Fingers Applauding the Play,"
  204
Clooney, Rosemary, 190, 196
Cobain, Kurt, 58, 70, 101–2
Cochran, Eddie, 32
"Cognoscenti Are Plunged into a Demonic
  Descent While at Cocktails, The," 82
"Cold Hard World," 73–74
Coleman, Ornette, 2, 134
Collins, Glenda, 30
Columbia, 203, 225
Columbia Masterworks, 87
Columbine, 39, 45
Commemoration, 215
Complete Oar Sessions, The, 226
Composers Recordings, Inc., 86
Confections of Love, 203
Conrad, Jess, 160
Cooder, Ry, 135
Cooper, Alice, 191
Copland, Aaron, 84, 85
"Corporal Clegg," 107
Corwood Industries, 57, 59–60
"Cousin Mosquito," 220
Cowboy Junction, 216
Cowell, Henry, 84
Cramps, 155, 199
Cream, 27
Crenshaw, Marshall, 144
Crimson, King, 210
Crosby, Bing, 14, 18
Crow, Rob, 95, 97
"Cry of the Unborn Child," 224
Curtis, Ian, 101–2
Cyrkle, 203

D
Dahlberg, Nils Roland Eilert, 114–18, *115*
Dangerfield, Tony, 32
Daphne of the Dunes, 86
Darin, Bobby, 202
"Dark Globe," 102
Dark Side of the Moon, 131
Dave Clark Five, 27
Davis, Mike, 96–97
Dead Dog's Eyeball, 70
Dead Milkmen, 70
Decca, 223
DeFeudis, Ken, 203–4

Dell, Rollie, 16
Del Rubio, Eadie, 204
Del Rubio, Elena, 204
Del Rubio, Milly, 204
Del Rubio Triplets, 204
Delusion of the Fury, 87, 91
DeMilo, 180
"Depression Medley," 19
Desi, 3
Devo, 130
Dewan, Brian, 215
Diddley, Bo, 134
Die Fledermaus, 151
Diken, Dennis, 30, 205
Dino, 3
Division Bell, The, 113
Doc at the Radar Station, 137, 138, 140
"Dominoes," 109
Donovan, 27
"Don't Be Cruel," 115
Don't Be Scared, 73–74
"Don't Come Feelin' Up My Doorknob
  Anymore," 208
"Don't Know If I Care," 64–65
"Don't Make Me Over," 226
"Doopy Darling," 34
"Do the Clam," 117
"Do the Pig," 38
Dover, Darry, 16
Downloading the Repertoire, 22, 24, 25
Drake, Nick, 102
Dreyer, Charlie, 4–9
Drilling the Curve, 62
Duke, Robert, 34
Dump, 62
Dust Brothers, 96
"Dusty Sings Folks and Spiritual Songs,"
  222
"Dusty Sings Pop and Ragtime," 222
Dylan, Bob, 14, 207

E
"Eager Beaver," 166
Edlee, 45
Edwards, Lee, 203
18 Wheeler Records, 62
"Eight Hitchhiker Inscriptions from a
  Highway Railing at Barstow,
  California," 82

Eilert Is Back, 115, *116*
Eilert Pilarm's Greatest Hits, 115, 116
Elektra, 125
Ellington, Duke, 169
"Elmer 21 Century Hop," 38
El Touchy, 212, *212*
Elvis I, 115
Elvis II, 115
Elvis III, 115
EMI Records, 107
EMI Studios, 30
Emperor Norton, 204
Enclosures, 86–87
Encounter, 228
Endless Discussion, 20
Epic, 229
"Epitaph," 210
Erickson, Roky, 101–2, 204–5
Eskelin, Ellery, 38, 42, 45
Eskelin, Rodd Keith, 38, 42, *43*, 45
Esquivel, Juan Garcia, 166
Estrada, Roy, 135
"European Jewel (Incomplete)," 59
Evening with Wild Man Fischer, An, 190,
    191–93, *193*
"Everything Happens to Me," 170, 171–72

F

Fabian Road Warrior, 96
Fair, Jad, 24, 70
"Fair Columbia," 50
Fairport Convention, 31, 102
Fall, 130
Family Jams, The, 215
Feel the Power, 96
Feinstein, Michael, 18
Feldman, Eric Drew, 135
Fergus macRoy at the Homestead Upright,
    213
Ferguson, Maynard, 167, 172
Ferino, Vince, 125
"Fill Your Heart," 17
Film City, 39
Finley, Chester T., 37
fIREHOSE, 70
"First You Think Your Fortune's Lovely,"
    59
Fischer, Larry "Wild Man," *188*, 189–98
Fischer King, The, 196–97

$5 Working People's Music Tape, 211
"Flaming," 104
Flaming Lips, 94
Fleece Records, 62
Fleetwood Records, 5
Fleetwood Studios, 4, 6–7
"Flip, Flop, Fly," 120, 125–26
Folkways, 224
Ford, Mary, 29
Ford Theatre, 6–7
Fountain, Judson, 205
415, 204
"Fourteen," 20
Fowler, Bruce Lambourne, 135
Frances Cannon, the Singing Psychic, 201
French, John, 135, 136, 139–40
"(Friday Is My Day for) Fish," 199
Friedland, Steven, 203
Frisbie, 95
Frith, Fred, 105
"From the Chapel (to the Courtroom),"
    183
Fun, 76
Fun House, 10
Fuse, 96

G

Gane, Tim, 125
Gang of Four, 130
Garcia, Russell, 169
"Garden of Eden or The Original Sin,
    The: A Drama," 214
Gate 5, 86
Gazingo, Bingo, 205, 205–6
*Getdown Airwaves: Coming to a Radio
    Near You*, 226, 227
Ghetto Love, 96
"Gigolo Aunt," 103, 109
Gillard, Doug, 227
Gillespie, Dizzy, 228
Gillette, Lee, 175–76
Gilmour, David, 102, 106, 107–8
"Gimme Dat Ding," 8
"Gipsy's Warning, The," 50
Girl, 20
"Girl," 20
Giuffre, Jimmy, 167
Glad to Get Away, 63, 64
"Glass Eye," 74

Globe, 39
Glory (????) of the Human Voice, The, 151
"Gnome, The," 104
God Bless Tiny Tim, 17, 17, 18
Goddard, Geoff, 30
"Golden Hair," 102, 112
Golden Thread, 206–7
"Go to Rhino Records," 189
Graettinger, Robert Frederick, 42, 167–77, 168, 173
"Grandsons Pat and Lee," 203
Greek Studies, 87, 90
Greenberger, David, 22–25, 137, 227
Green Pig Records, 115
Gregory, Ian, 32, 34–35
Gross, Sri Darwin, 206–7
Grudzien, Peter, 207, 207–8
"Guadalajara," 229
Guilt Trip, The, 24
Gulfstream Records, 119, 125, 126
Guygax, Thomas J., Sr., 41–42

H
Haimer, Robert, 195
Hall, Dora, 208–9
Hammerstein, Oscar, 46, 49, 50–51
Hardin, Louis "Moondog," 16
Harkleroad, Bill, 135
Harmonicats, 141
Harper, Roy, 102
Harry Partch Collection, 86
Harvest Records, 107, 111
"Have I the Right," 27
Hazlewood, Lee, 44
Heavy Vegetable, 95
Hefti, Neal, 167
Henry, Joe, 142, 144
Henry Cow, 130
Herbers, Werner, 177
Herman's Hermits, 2, 3
Herne, Bobby, 4–6, 8–9
"He's the Santa I Love," 178
"Hey! Baby," 224
"Hey, Jude," 20
"Hey Paula," 224
Hi, How Are You, 71, 72, 75
Higney, Kenneth, 209–10
HillTop, 45

"His Eyes," 212–13
Hitchcock, Robyn, 102, 225
Holly, Buddy, 32
Hollywood Artists Record Company, 41
Hollywood Hills Orchestra, 230
Holman, Bill, 173
Homestead, 73
Honeycombs, 27, 34
"Honeysuckle Rose," 22
Hooker, John Lee, 134
Hopkins, Doug, 101–2
Hopper, Hugh, 108
"Hound Dog," 115
"House of Strings," 171
"House of the Rising Sun," 8
Howard, Gene, 172
Human Breakdown of Absurdity, The, 38
"Human Canary, The," 15
"Human Horn, The," 141
Hunch, 199
"Hunky Honky," 208
Hunter, Brad, 96
"Huskie Team," 30

I
I Am Born to Preach the Gospel, 221
IBC Studios, 28
Ice Cream for Crow, 138, 140
I Died Today, 38, 42
"If I Ruled the World," 228
"(If There's Sexual Harassment, I'm) Calling the Law," 211
"I Got You, Babe," 17
"I Hate CDs," 163
I Hear a New World, 32–33
"I'll Never Fall in Love Again," 215
I Love Me, 19
"I Love Trash," 193
"I Love You So Fucking Much I Can't Shit," 206
"I'm Glad," 134
I'm Just the Other Woman, 38, 40
"I'm Sorry That I Got Fat," 96
"I'm the Meany," 196
"I'm Working for the Federal Bureau of Narcotics," 191
"In Canada," 180, 181, 185–86
"In Conclusion," 192
Incredibly Strange Music Vol. 2, 125

"Indian Alphabet Chant," 120
Ingber, Elliot, 135
Ink Spots, 141
"In Love, In Love," 125
"In My Father's House," 115
Innovations Orchestra, 166–67, 176
In Search Of The Most Unforgettable Tree We Ever Met, 201
"International Colouring Contest," 125
"Interstellar Overdrive," 103
Into Outer Space with Lucia Pamela, 119–27, *126*
"I Ride A Tractor," 164
"I Save Cigarette Butts," 71
"I Saw Mr. Presley Tip-toeing through the Tulips," 19
"Isotopic Spatial Series," 43
"I Take It That We're Through," 34
"It Is Obvious," 109
It Just Is, 206, *206*
"It's a Hard Business," 196, 197
It's Hard to Believe It, 30
"It's No Good Tryin," 109
"It's Now or Never," 116
"I Whupped Batman's Ass," 94
"I Write the Songs," 218

J

"Jailhouse Rock," 115
"Jambalaya," 229
Jandek, 56–66
"Janitor's Dead," 57
Jefferson Airplane, 224
Jenkins, Florence Foster, 147–53, *148*
Jennings, Waylon, 209–10
Jesus and Mary Chain, 102, 107
Jet Lady, 229
"JFK—I Was Their," 202
Jimi Hendrix Experience, 31
"Jimmy Carter Says 'Yes'," 37
"Jobs for All," 211
Joe Meek Story: The Pye Years, 33–34
"John F. Kennedy Was Called Away," 38
"Johnny Remember Me," 29
Johnston, Daniel, *67*, 67–78, 195
Jolson, Al, 215
Jones, Glenn, 132
Jones, Malcolm, 107
Jones, Tom, 32

Jordan, Tommy, 213–15
Joy and David, 34
"Joy Spoken in Rhumba," 43
"Jugband Blues," 106–7
Junior's Motel, 211
"Just a Closer Walk with Thee," 142
Justice, Willie, III, 37

K

Kaiser, Henry, 134, 139–40
Kane, Jessica, 210
Kaplan Brothers, 210–11
Karlstr m, Tobbe, 116
Kaufman, Irving, 18
Kebrutney Records, 209
Keith, Rodd, 38, 42, *43*, 45
Kelly, John, 40
Kent, Dick, 39
Kenton, Stan, 166–77
Kerr, W. R., 41
Khaury, Herbert, *12*, 13–21
Kick Out the Jams, 10
Kids of Widney High, 211
"King Kong," 70
King Oedipus, 86, 87
"King of Fuh, The," 203
Koresh, David, 211
Kramer, Mark, 24, 70
Kronos Quartet, 87, 90
Kunkel, Charles, 121, 122, 123

L

"Lady Is a Tramp, The," 218
Lakmé, 151
La Livre de Vie, 219
Lane, Cristy, 142
"Larry's Songs, Unaccompanied," 191
"Larry Under Pressure," 192
"Last Kiss," 224
"Late Night," 103
Later On, 64–65
"Laurie," 160
Laurie Records, 228
Leary, Paul, 76
Le Cam, 224
Ledge, 154–65, *157*, *161*
Led Zeppelin, 20
Lee, Arthur, 101–2
Lee, Dickie, 160

Legendary Stardust Cowboy, 154–65, 157, 161
Legendary Stardust Cowboy Rides Again, 163
"Legend of Killer Whale," 202
Lennon, John, 71
LeRoi Brothers, 162
Let a Frown Be Your Umbrella, 193
"Let Us Pray," 209
Lewis, John, 167
Lewis, Peter, 225, 226
Leyton, John, 29, 32
Liberace, George, 125
"Liblanders Cahoot," 43
"License to Kill," 62
Lick My Decals Off, Baby, 137
Lie: The Love and Terror Cult, 215
Life in the USA and Canada, 180–81, 182
"Lift Every Voice and Sing," 142
Lightning Seeds, The, 102
"Like a Bird," 151
"Limburger Lover," 199
"Little Betsy and Her Goat," 37
Little Marcy, 211
Little Marcy Talks with the Animals, 211
Living End, The, 62
"Living in a Cavity," 201
"Lo, Here the Gentle Lark," 150
Long, Johnny, 18
"Look at It," 65
Los Angeles, Alex, 214
Love, 103
Love, Larry, 15
"Love, Love, Love, the Angel of Love," 183
Love and Rockets, 103
"Love Me Tender," 115
"Love Shack," 182
"Love You," 109
Lowe, Ralph, 39
L'Peg, 125, 126
Lucas, Gary, 131–32, 133, 135, 139
"Lucifer Sam," 102, 103
Luie Luie, 212
"Lulla-Lulla-Lullabye," 214
Lunceford, Jimmie, 169
Lyttleton, Humphrey, 28–29

M

MacArthur, Edwin, 150
macRoy, Angus, 213

macRoy, Fergus, 212–13
Madcap Laughs, The, 108–9, 112
Madden, Gale, 175
Magic Band, 129–40
Magic Flute, The, 151
Magic Key, 45
Maiden, Willie, 172
Makers of Smooth Music, The, 38, 41–42
Mallis, Constance, 213–15
Manne, Shelly, 167, 173
Manson, Charles, 215
Marks, Franklyn, 167
Mars Audiac Quintet, 125
Marshall, A. J., 215, 215–16
Marshall, Gene, 39
Mason, Nick, 103, 113
"Matilda Mother," 104
Max, Buddy, 216
"May Your Heart Stay Young Forever," 34
MC5, 10
McCarty, Kathy, 70
McKuen, Rod, 216
McMoon, Cosme, 150, 151
McNew, James, 62
Meat Puppets, 155
"Mechanical Doll," 200
Meek, Joe, 26–35, 27, 28, 31, 105
Mekkatone, 210
Mekons, 11
Melba, Dame Nellie, 151
Mercury Records, 137, 138, 154, 160, 161
"Merry-Go-Round," 192
"Misty," 218, 228
Mitchell, Mitch, 31
Moby Grape, 224–25
Monkees, 3
"Monkeys Versus Donkeys," 191
Moore, R. Stevie, 205
More Oar: A Tribute to the Skip Spence Album, 225
More Songs of Pain, 71
Morton, Rockette, 131
Most, Mickie, 27, 30
Mothersbaugh, Mark, 190
"Mother's Last Word to Her Son," 221
Mothers of Invention, 190, 191, 193
Movie Album, 222

"Mr. Decay Germ," 201
MSR Records, 37–39, 42, 45
MSR Singers, 41–42
Mudhoney, 225
Mudurian, Jack, 22–25
Mumy, Bill, 195, 196, 197, 198
Musical Pirates, 123
"Musical Snuff-Box, The," 151
Music Machine, 138
Music of America, 41
Music of Guatemala, The, 223
Music to Suffer By, 199, 200
"My Baby Doll," 33
"My Dreams Are Getting Better All the Time," 18
Myers, Ray R., 216–18, 217
"My First Cigar," 54
"My Little Red Book," 103
"My Pal Foot Foot," 4, 5, 7
Mystic, 212, 212
"My Way," 218

N

"Naked in the Afternoon," 59
"Nancy Sings," 61
"Nearer My God to Thee," 142
Nelson, Ricky, 3
Nelson, Sandy, 33
"Neutron Dance," 204
"Never Learn Not to Love," 215
"Never Relaxed," 71–72
Newband, 87
Newimproved Music, 76
New Rose, 163
New Town, 64, 65
"New York, New York," 203
Nice, 102
Nicol, Simon, 31
Nightbird, 210
"Night You Told a Lie, The," 34
"98," 180
"No Break," 61
"No Heavy Truckin'," 209
Norton Records, 163, 199
Noste, Jim, 218
Nothing Scary, 195
Novicki, Frank, 165
NRBQ, 2
Nugent, Ted, 94

O

Oar, 225, 226
Oberon, Rex, 214
Obukhov, Nicolas, 218–20
"Octopus," 108
Odam, Norman Carl, 154–65, 157, 161
"Ode to Billie Joe," 202
"Ode to Lesley," 179, 184
Oglio, 96
"Oh, How I Love the Blessed Sugmad," 206
"Oh God, Please Send Me A Kid," 195, 196
"Oh Madonna (You Stole My Pants)," 206
"Oh Youth, Where Is Your Destiny?," 214
Oldfield, Mike, 102
Oldham, Andrew Loog, 27
Olivia Tremor Control, 130
"Omaha," 225
"Once You Understand," 228
$^1/_2$ Japanese, 11, 24, 70, 130
"On the Old Front Porch," 17
Opel, 112
"Orchestra, An," 170
Oscar the Grouch, 193
Ostin, Mo, 16–17
"Outside the Hospital," 195
"Over the Rainbow," 20, 142
"Owed T'Alex," 134

P

P. J. Harvey, 130
"Painted My Teeth," 57
Palmer, Harry, 6–8
Pamela, Georgia, 123
Pamela, Lucia, 119–27, 120, 122
Pamela Sisters, 123
"Paper Roses," 8
Parallel World, 208
"Paralyzed," 154–62, 165
Parker, Malinda Jackson, 220
Partch, Harry, 79–91, 80, 82, 88, 177
Pascarella Chamber Music Society, 149
Pastels, The, 70
Paul, Les, 29
"Peanut Vendor, The," 166
Pearl Jam, 70, 76
Pearl of Brazil, The, 151
"Peg O' My Heart," 142

Penstar, 212
Pepper, Art, 167, 172–73, 175
Pere Ubu, 130
Perry, Richard, 17
Personal, 199
Phair, Liz, 94
Phillips, Gretchen, 74, 77–78
Phillips, Washington, 221, *221*
Philosophy of the World, xxviii, 1–11
Pilarm, Eilert, 114–18, *115*
Pink Dust, 204
Pink Floyd, 19, 101–13
Piper at the Gates of Dawn, The, 101,
    104, *104*
Pipkins, 8
"Pistol Packin' Mama," 22
Plant, Robert, 155, 225
"Please Tell Me What Color," 226
Plymouth, 208
Poison 13, 70
Ponk/Seeland, 19
Postell, Carrie and Bonnie, 40
Presley, Elvis, 114–18
Preview, 39
Prisoner of Love: A Tribute to Russ Columbo,
    19
Pronounced Normal, 195
"Psychic Cigarette," 43
Psychopaths, 201
Psycho's Psychopaths, 201
Psycho-Suavé, 160
Puck, Guy, 214
Pussy Galore, 10
"Put a Ring on Her Finger," 29
"Put a Ring on My Finger," 29

Q
"Queenie Wahine's Papaya," 117
"Queen of the Night Aria," 151

R
Ra, Sun, 135
Rainbow, 45
Raincoats, 11
Raitt, Bonnie, 2
Ramsey Kearney Song Service, 45
Ratledge, Mike, 108
"Rats," 109
"Rats in My Room," 199

Raunch Hands, 155
Ray Korona Band, 211
Razor and Tie, 30
RCA Victor, 9, 151
Reachin', 200–1
Reader, Pat, 34
Ready for the House, 57–58, *59*–60
Red Hot Chili Peppers, 130
Red Rooster/Rounder, 9
Red Seal, 151
Reed, Jimmy, 134
Rejected Unknown, 76
"Relaxation," *164*
"Release Me," 116
R.E.M., 102, 205
"Remember a Day," 107
Ren, Dap, 206–7
Reprise Records, 16–17
RE/Search, 125
Residents, 130
Restless, 204
Retro Rocket Back to Earth, 163
Revelation in the Courthouse Park, 87
Rey, Alvino, 169
Rhino Handmade, 197
Rhino Records, 145, 189, 194–95,
    196–97
Rigby, Will, 163
Riot Squad, 34
*Rise and Fall of Ziggy Stardust and the
    Spiders from Mars, The*, 155
RKO Unique, 199
"Rock and Roll at McDonald's," 94
"Rock and Roll Santa," 228
"Rocket Ship," 70
Rockey, Palmer, 221–22
Rock-It to Stardom, 155, 162
"Rock Lobster," 183
Rogers, Rod, 42
Rogers, Shorty, 167
Rolling Stones, 27
Rose, Biff, 17
Rosen, Maury S., 39
Rounder, 2, 9, 20, 211, 224
Rowe, "Dusty Roads," 222–23
Rubinson, David, 225
Rugolo, Pete, 167, 174
"Run for Cover Lover," 203, *204*
Russell, George, 167

Russo, Bill, 175
Rydell, Bobby, 31
Ryko, 224

S

"Saddest Story, The," 40
Sadier, Laetitia, 125
Safe As Milk, 134, 136
Saints, 30
Samhot, 228
Sanders, 205
"Sandy Craws is Comin' to Town," 224
"San Francisco: A Setting of the Cries of Two Newsboys on a Foggy Night in the Twenties," 86
San Lucas Band, 223
Saucerful of Secrets, A, 101, 106–7
Savitt, Jan, 169
Scarlet Love, 221
Schillinger, Joseph, 174
Schneider, Fred, 178, 180, 182–83
"School Teacher," 181
Schuller, Gunther, 176
Scott, Raymond, 135
Scroggins, Mrs. D. J., 37
"See Emily Play," 102, 104
Sequel, 33–34
"Serenata Mexicana," 151
Sessions, Roger, 84
Sex Pistols, 130
Sgt. Pepper's Lonely Heart Clubs Band, 104
Shaggs, 1–11, 62
Shaggs' Own Thing, 9
"Shake Hands with Mother Again," 217
Shank, Bud, 167
Shatner, William, 223–24
Shell, Scott Anthony, 95
Shelley, Steve, 44, 75, 78
Shimmy Disc Records, 24
"Shine on You Crazy Diamond," 112
Shiny Beast, 134, 137, 138
Shonen Knife, 11
"Silent Night," 115
Silver, Eddie, 29
Simon, John, 203
Six and Six, 57
Slapp Happy, 130
"Sleepy Lagoon," 230
Slowdive, 102

Smashing Pumpkins, 102
Smith, Major Bill, 160, 161–62, 224, *224*
Smith, Sterling R., 56–66
Snowden, B. J., 178–87, *179*
"So Fly, Max," 63
Soft Boys, 103, 107
"Softly and Tenderly," 142
Soft Machine, 102
"Some Historical Notes," 192
"Some Saxophones," 170
Something Good, Something Sad, 46, 49–50
"Something I've Got to Tell You," 30
"Some Velvet Morning," 44
"Song for Wesley," 95
"Song of the Burmese Land," 44
Songs for You, Vols. 1–3, 218
Songs from Beyond, 201
Songs from Cannonville, 201
Songs of an Impotent Troubadour, 19
Songs of Pain, 71–72
Sonic Youth, 70
"Soul Tormented by Contemporary Music Finds a Humanizing Element, A," 82
Sounds of Soul, 207
Spa Studios, 178
Special Music by Special Kids, 211
"Speeding Motorcycle," 70
Spence, Joseph, 224
Spence, Skip, 101–2, 224–26, *225*
Spider Records, 163
"Splish Splash," 202
Spooky Disharmonious Conflict, 96
Spotlight Kid, The, 137
"Stairway to Heaven," 20
"Standing in a Trashcan (Thinking of You)," 162
"Stardust," 20
Staring at the Cellophane, 57, 62
Stars, 111
"Star's Ghost," 202
"Star-Spangled Banner Waving Some-where," 208
Sterling, 39
Stewart, Cara, 44
Stewart, Rod, 32
Stigwood, Robert, 27
"Stinky Poodle," 229

Stooges, 10
Straight, 135, 137, 191
Stress, 73
Strictly Personal, 134–35
Strivant, Gary, 144
Suite for String Trio and Wind Quartet, 176
Sundazed, 226
Sunrise, 39
Supie T., 226–27
"Swan Lee," 112
Swordfishtrombones, 90

T
Take Me Home, 229–30, 230
Talent Show, The, 24, 227, 227
"Talk Talk," 138
Talmy, Shel, 27
"Tampico," 166
"Tapeworm of Love," 203
Tartakov, Jeff, 73, 74
"Taster, The," 192
Tattoo of Blood, 24
Taylor, Cecil, 134
Taylor, William "Shooby," 141–46, 143
Tea Set, 103
Teenage Fan Club, 103
"Teen Beat," 33
Telegraph Melts, 57
"Telstar," 27, 30–31, 33
Ten Little Indians, 201
Tepper, Jeff Morris, 135
Tepper, Jeremy, 163
"Terrapin," 102, 109
Terri, Jan, 227–28
Texas Instruments, 70
"That Little Sports Car," 4
Theman, Dan, 226–27
"There's No Room to Rhumba in a Sports Car," 117
"Thermopylae," 169
"These Boots Are Made for Walking," 44
Think, 228
Third World, 1, 5, 6
13th Floor Elevators, 204
"This Guy's in Love with You," 215
This Modern World, 172, 176
This Mortal Coil, 103
Thomas, Gordon, 228

Thompson, Richard, 31
"Thought, A," 170
Three Peas in a Podd, 228
304 Holloway Road—Joe Meek: The Pye Years, Vol. 2, 34
Thumm, Francis, 85
Thunders, Johnny, 101–2
"Tico Tico," 142
"Time Will Tell," 34–35
Tiny Tim, 12, 13–21, 159
Tiny Tim's Second Album, 18
Tiptoe Through the Tulips/Resurrection, 19
"Tip-Toe Thru' the Tulips," 17
"Tonight We Love," 230
"Too Much Time," 134
Tornadoes, 27, 30–31
"To Sit on a Sandwich," 203
"Train Your Child," 221
Trance, 204
Transformed Man, The, 223–24
"Tribute to Buddy Holly," 30
"Tribute to the Challenger," 216
Tricoli, Tangela, 228–29
Trilogy for the Masses, 7
Tripp, Art, 135, 191
"Tropical Hot Dog Night," 139
Trout Mask Replica, 10, 129–40, 132, 190, 197
"Trumpet, A," 172
Tubman Goodtype Songs of Liberia by Congress-Woman Malinda Jackson Parker, 220, 220
Turner, Big Joe, 120
TV Personalities, 102
"Twelve Minutes Since February 32'nd," 57
20/20, 215
Twink, 111
"Two Pack Shaker," 206
Typhoid Mary, 96
Tzadik Records, 38

U
Ulysses Departs from the Edge of the World, 87
Ummagumma, 108
Unconditionally Guaranteed, 138
Unicorn, The, 208
"Units, The," 57–58
Unplugged: 9/11/67, 215

"Up Your Jurassic Park," 206
Urge Overkill, 94
Urrutia, Mary, 37
U.S. Highball, 86
"U.S. Navy Song," 180, 183

V

Vallee, Rudy, 18
Van Vliet, Don, *128*, 129–40, *136*
"Variant," 62
Varicose Days, 210
"Vegetable Man," 102, 107
Velvet Underground, 10
Ventures, 31
Villachaize, Herve, 229
Vinyl Retentive, 19
Virgin, 138
"Virgin Child of the Universe," 40
Voice of Fire, 211
Volt, Son, 225

W

Waits, Tom, 90, 225
"Walking on the Moon," 123–24, 125
Walking Seeds, 103
"Walk Like An Egyptian," 204
Walls, Waskey Elwood, Jr., 37
Warner Bros., 16–17, 132, 138
Waters, Muddy, 134
Waters, Roger, 103, 107–8, 111
Water! Water!, 86
Watts, Dave, 31
Wayne, 229
Wayne—At Last!, 229, *229*
Weaver, Kay, 39
Wesley Willis' Greatest Hits Vols. 1 and 2, 96
"We Will Have Dignity (Sweatshops, Globalization, Child Labor)," 211
"Wheels," 3
Whittinghill, Dick, 203
Who, The, 27
"Who Are Parents," 4–5
"Who's Knocking On My Door?," 161

"Why Am I Living?," 160
Wiggin, Austin, Jr., 1, 3–9, *5*
Wiggin, Betty, 1–11
Wiggin, Dorothy, 1–11
Wiggin, Helen, 1–11
Wiggin, Rachel, 2–11
"Wild Man Fischer Story, The," 192
Wildmania, 194–95, *196*
Williams, Hank, 207
Williams, Paul, 17
Willis, Wesley, *92*, 93–99, *96*, 195
Wilson, Brian, 33
Wilson, Dennis, 215
Wilson, James, Jr., 43
Wilson, Les, 229–30
Windsong, 86
Wish You Were Here, 112
Wood, Andrew, 101–2
Word Records, 211
Work in Progress: The Triumph Sessions, 33
Workman, Greg, 94, 97
World's Worst Record Show, 160
Wright, Rick, 103, 107, 111
Wyatt, Robert, 102, 108

Y

Yanaway, James, 162, 163
Yazoo, 221
"Yesterday Once More," 8
Yip/Jump Music, 72
Yo La Tengo, 70, 228
"You and Your Big Ideas," 125
"You Are My Destiny," 203
"You Go to My Head," 171–72
"Young Girl," 144
Your Turn to Fall, 62

Z

Zappa, Frank, 1, 2, 91, 132, 135, 137, 138, 139, 190, 191, 193, 196
Zoot Horn Rollo, 131, 133–37
Zorn, John, 38, 42
ZZ Top, 205

ABOUT THE AUTHOR

IRWIN CHUSID is an apostate Boomer suffering from chronic short attention span following a youth wasted on Top 40 radio and idiotic sitcoms. In his putative adulthood, he ignored commercial radio and TV and became a societal castaway, preoccupied with cultural marginalia and out of touch with mainstream America.

This hapless misfit has nonetheless made noteworthy contributions to the planet by helping preserve the legacies of such neglected geniuses as Raymond Scott, Esquivel, the Shaggs, Lucia Pamela, Jim Flora, R. Stevie Moore, Ladislaw Starewicz, and the Cherry Sisters. As a chronicler of music arcana, Chusid is living proof that seemingly frivolous pursuits can be parlayed into gainful employment.

The author's goal in life is to watch the director's first cut of Erich von Stroheim's 1924 film *Greed*.

Chusid has hosted a radio program at WFMU since 1975. This is his first—and last—book. He lives in Hoboken, New Jersey, but not for long.

"too strange for radio...."

Wondering what for-real musical outsiders sound like?

GET THE CD!

SONGS IN THE KEY OF Z
The Curious Universe of Outsider Music
Produced by Irwin Chusid
(Which? Records WHI2367)

Outsider musicians may lack conventional tunefulness and self-awareness, but they display an abundance of earnestness and passion. And they're worth listening to, often surpassing all contenders for inventiveness and originality.

The CD features songs by many artists profiled in this book.

Hear:
- the uninhibited coyote howls of the Legendary Stardust Cowboy
- the arrested-adolescent passion of Daniel Johnston
- a romantic duet between Tiny Tim and his wife Miss Sue
- the LSD-cabaret crooning of Arcesia
- Joe Meek's ultra-rare, wobbly "Telstar" vocal demo
- the Shaggs aboriginal backwoods rock
- Lucia Pamela's vertigo-bent outer space lunacy

Also includes tracks by Wesley Willis, Captain Beefheart, Jandek, "Dusty Roads" Rowe, B. J. Snowden, Shooby Taylor the Human Horn, Eilert Pilarm, Jack Mudurian, and others, including a genuine Song-Poem!

The album **SONGS IN THE KEY OF Z** promises an unforgettable romp through music too strange for radio, but too fascinating to ignore.

SONGS IN THE KEY OF Z: *The Curious Universe of Outsider Music*
A measly $10 (shipping included) send check/MO, or purchase through website:

Which? Records
PO Box 659 Village Station
New York NY 10014
<http://www.whichsight.com>